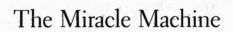

The Miracle Machine

The Miracle Machine

Doug Gilbert

Coward, McCann & Geoghegan, Inc.
New York

Copyright © 1980 by P. T. L. Consultants Ltd.

Library of Congress Cataloging in Publication Data

Gilbert, Doug, date.
  The miracle machine.

  1. Sports—Germany, East. 2. Sports and state—
Germany, East. 3. Physical education and training—
Germany, East. 4. Olympic Games, Montréal, Québec,
1976. I. Title.
GV612.6.G54   796. 4'8'09431   79-13603
ISBN 0-698-10952-X

Printed in the United States of America

To Artur Takac and Klaus Ullrich-Huhn

Contents

6

Introduction

Early in May, 1945, the Allied armies were bringing down the final curtain on World War II in Europe. At that time you would have received incredible odds against the suggestion that, in a little more than a generation, sons and daughters of the defeated, destitute residents of the soon-to-be Soviet Occupied Zone of Germany would create a sporting machine capable of out-pointing the United States in the Olympic Games. And in 1949, when the Marshall Plan crushed Communist hopes of a unified, socialist German nation and led to the unilateral declaration of independence for the German Democratic Republic as a Soviet satellite state, those odds might have grown even longer. Even in 1961, when Nikita Khrushchev and Walter Ulbricht opted to build the Berlin Wall to check the annual flow of hundreds of thousands of East Zone Germans to the higher paying jobs of the West, few had any hint of the depth of the athletic blitzkrieg that was already being planned in the halls of the Leipzig Sports Institute and in the Berlin offices of the German Gymnastics and Sports Union (DTSB). And yet, in the last two weeks of July, 1976, it came to pass in the stadiums, pools, and sports halls of Montreal in the Games of the XXI Olympiad.

In the space of those fourteen days and nights the athletes in the blue sweatsuits with the small worker-and-farmer symbol and the letters DDR *(Deutsche Demokratische Republik)* on the heart piled up 40 gold medals, just seven fewer than the Soviet Union's 47 and six more than the U.S. total of 34. When you add on the 24 silver, 25 bronze, 25 fourths, 22 fifths, and 14 sixth place finishes you come up with 638 points in the "unofficial" wire service point standings based on a 7-5-4-3-2-1 point allocation for the first six places. That's a comfortable 31 more than the U.S. total of 607 points off final total placements of 34-35-25-13-18-19. (These standings, though, are frowned upon by the International Olympic Committee as an unseemly exercise in nationalism.) Some American statisticians have taken comfort in the U.S. medal total of 94, against 89 for the GDR, but that would give equal value to gold, silver and bronze medals and create a new scoring system as yet unknown to any prior Games or wire service.

But nitpicking about medals and points isn't what it's all about anyway. Until the 1950s there was one great Olympic power—the United States. The Soviets came along to make it a twosome in Melbourne in 1956 and the superpowers traded "unofficial" victories through the 1960s and into the 1970s. But now the GDR, with a population of only about seventeen million people—less than a third of the 62 million across the frontier in the Federal Republic—has come along to make it a threesome at the top.

Montreal, of course, was not a complete surprise. There were indications of things to come in Mexico in 1968, the first time the GDR was allowed to compete with its own team after twelve years of participation in a combined German team. In Munich in 1972 they became a full-fledged world power when, with their own flag and anthem for the first time, they swept up 66 medals including 20 gold—but without winning a gold medal in a single event in women's swimming. A year later, though, at the first-ever World Swimming Championships in Belgrade in 1973, they won 10 of 14 gold medals and, between that historic week and Montreal, went on to break every women's world swim record several times over.

Today the GDR is the dominant power in men's and women's rowing, women's track and field, the equal of the U.S. in men's track and field, and standing at or near the top in every other Olympic discipline with the exception of the equestrian events, modern pentathlon, basketball, and field hockey, which they do not attempt at the elite level. Although their ice hockey is halfhearted for lack of facilities, and they scrapped downhill and slalom skiing more than a decade ago for lack of suitable terrain, in winter sports the GDR is at or within a step of the top in luge, bobsled, ski jumping, and figure skating, with solid strength in Nordic skiing and speed skating.

How have they done it?

This is the question that has been fascinating the rest of the world's athletes, coaches, administrators and sports journalists throughout the 1970s. The answer, sad to say for those who would like to see a devious Communist plot behind every gold medal, and a series of Frankensteinian experiments and secret drugs behind every world record, is neither sensational nor miraculous.

It is simply the result of some very thorough planning by a government that (1) gives sport a higher priority than it is given anywhere else in the world; (2) seriously promotes the unified development of both mass sport for the total population and elite sport for the international-level performer; (3) has processed more than 8,000 professional coaches through the Leipzig Institute since its creation in 1951 and, beyond that, has found them jobs within the system to maximize use of their talents; (4) has certified more than 200,000 volunteer coaches at the Little League and mass sport levels; and (5) has placed the country's medical research system at the disposal of Sport.

This is the system, so envied by the West, that has produced computerized medical records of every individual elite athlete, right down to the state of every individual metabolism, every daily nutritional need. They have virtually taken the guesswork out of coaching at the international level.

They have created special sports boarding schools to make sure those selected for elite training keep up with the special educational needs for the jobs they will move into when the competitive days are finished.

At the mass level, the GDR constitution guarantees everyone's right to participate in sport. This might sound frivolous to Westerners as we fight our societal battles for equal rights for women, racial minorities and gays, but in East Europe it is important because it allows sports officialdom to take action against any community, factory, school district, or even collective farm that balks at providing facilities and opportunities. The United States has a law to enforce equal rights in employment, leaving every employer open to harassing court action if he operates with bias. But we haven't given sport anywhere near that much social importance. That's why stickball stars and sandlot basketball players will continue to come out of the urban ghettos to hit home runs and dunk baskets, while pitchers and football players will come from the better organized suburban middle classes, and the Olympic rowing team will come from those with upper-class university and elite social club backgrounds.

The DTSB, as governing body of GDR sport, is active everywhere, with committees in towns and districts from one border to the other, from Czechoslovakia in the south to the Baltic in the north, from Poland in the east to the Federal Republic in the west. If there's an adult or child who wants to partake of sport for fitness and recreation, he has the chance at their mass sport and factory-based clubs. But if there's a youngster with the ability and desire to make it to the top internationally, they'll find him out just as surely as any American university can find a halfback in high school.

That's how they do it, and by itself it's a subject that could be and has been covered in newspaper and magazine pieces. Although this basic background is essential to an understanding of GDR sport, it's not my central purpose here. Some five years in the making, this book is more an attempt to get closer to the system's human elements in hopes of finding out what sport at this level of intensity does to people. What are the athletes like? The coaches? The officials? The doctors and researchers? The people on the street? What becomes of an athlete once he's done with sport? And what's it like to be a young, promising hopeful on the way up?

This approach is automatic in the American style of journalism where such stories are put together every day by people-oriented media, but it's not so common outside North America where reporters are more inclined to review from a distance and offer personal praise or criticism more in the way the New York *Times* might cover a Rudolf Nureyev ballet. As a result, most of the coverage of GDR sport has had a distanced, political emphasis: American reporters at an Olympic or dual meet find themselves blocked from intimate personal interviews by the language barrier and security-conscious coaches and officials. When East European athletes come to compete they come to do just that, not to give philosophical interviews to Western media personalities.

But whatever impression they make abroad, the athletes do lead full personal lives at home. Wolfgang Nordwig is no longer the tense pole vaulter who battled Bob Seagren in the committee rooms and on the field in the great pole vault controversy of Munich. He's now a physicist, just another businessman in his thirties trying to keep fit while working long hours and occasionally pole vaulting "about the fourteen-foot level" on the weekends for fun. Christine Errath is sharpening her German in hopes of becoming a TV commentator. Others are working on careers in sports medicine, coaching, and politics.

We cannot forget the politics. The story of sport in the GDR is both ·a history of 300 years of German sports and exercise tradition, and the more immediate story of a thirty-year postwar struggle for international acceptance both in sport and world politics. This is the touchiest piece of ground of all, since every political anecdote has both a GDR version and an opposite Western one as well. There is no question that both the GDR and the Federal Republic have occasionally given sport a thoroughly political cast in their battles for and against German reunification. Neither likes to admit it. Athletes have often been the pawns caught in the middle, just as the unfortunate Taiwan and African athletes were politically caught in the middle at the Montreal Olympics. This book will not attempt to adjudicate the rights and wrongs in these disputes. Just as there is a Northern and a Southern version of the U.S. Civil War, so must there be a Western and an Eastern version of the politics of sport in the two Germanies. The anecdotes in this book deal directly with the way those in GDR sport perceive themselves and their system.

Which brings us to one final ground rule, the very name of the country itself.

To the Western world, this patch of about 41,802 square miles situated smack in the middle of Europe has been and still is referred to as East Germany. We, for the sake of geographical convenience rather than deliberate political insult, have divided much national real estate along east–west and north–south delineations. We have our East Germany and our West Germany; our North Korea and our South Korea. I myself refer to the GDR as East Germany in newspaper and magazine writings, at least when it comes to first mention of the place, both as a simple matter of recognition for the reader and because it is demanded by the style books of most newspapers and magazines. What's more, when I send mail I underline *East*

Germany on the bottom of the envelope in the knowledge most North American post offices won't be sure where it's going when you put GDR, and will almost invariably send it to West Germany if you put German Democratic Republic. I do this with a shudder, though, knowing that people in the GDR consider it a diplomatic insult ever to be referred to as East Germany.

The correct name is the *Deutsche Demokratische Republik,* or DDR, which translates to GDR in English and RDA in French when it's the République Démocratique Allemande. West Germany comes off as the BRD in German, FRG in English, and RFA in French, which is more than enough to keep anyone on his toes when running a multilingual Olympic scoreboard.

In the Cold War of the 1950s when the West, and particularly the West Germans, spent most of their time dreaming of German reunification under a Western-style capitalist democracy, our diplomatic insistence on such terms as East Germany, or even Soviet Occupied Zone, made political sense. But that was more than twenty years ago. Today the GDR has formal diplomatic relations with most of the countries in the world, including the United States and the Federal Republic. At official levels, whether it be the UN, the Olympics, or any other international gathering, they are always properly referred to as the GDR. And yet, when it comes to sport and our media they are the East Germans to millions of fans who have no intention of being insulting at all.

I can remember starting off as a sports writer in Chicago at the time when Cassius Clay first changed his name to Muhammed Ali for personal religious reasons. A lot of people didn't like that. My paper, the *American,* used to call him "What's His Name?" Ali survived. The paper died.

Although Quebec is still a part of Canadian confederation, many francophones do not like to be referred to as French Canadians. They want to be known throughout the world as Quebécois. And so it is with the German Democratic Republic. For simple good manners, if no other reason will suffice, this book will refer to the country as the GDR. I hope the story of its sporting development is as much fun to read as it was to research and write.

1

Buchenwald

Buchenwald. Sunday, July 24, 1977, 10 A.M. The place and time will be forever etched in my mind. Imagine yourself, if you can, standing at the top of a knoll overlooking what was once a horrendous Nazi concentration camp, to witness the lighting of the symbolic torch that would in turn light another flame, this one to burn for a week, in the tower atop the Leipzig Stadium, as beacon of both the Sixth National Sports and Gymnastics Festival of the German Democratic Republic, and the Sixth Children and Youth Spartakiad Games. Here, surely, was a solemn occasion in sport.

I have been to the openings of three sets of Olympic Games. I have furtively wiped my eyes when the Olympic torch completed its journey from historic Greece and entered the stadium. I have thrilled as teams of all nations marched past. And to the Olympic cantata. Pan-American Games. The Commonwealth Games. The same. An Olympic Congress with a full symphony playing music composed just for the occasion in honor of sport. These are considered, the International Olympic Committee insists, "solemn" occasions. But after standing atop that knoll at Buchenwald on a clear and sunny Sunday morning, I will never again describe them in such terms.

The Sports Festival in the GDR is not an annual event, or, like the Olympics, even a quadrennial one. There have been just six of them since the GDR declared itself an independent country in 1949. There is nothing in North America that can even remotely match it—an entire nation turned inward in a week-long dedication to sport. Mass sport: recreational Workers' Sports Club finals, jogging, the Spartakiad (which is actually a nationwide junior Olympics set to a Grecian precedent with all events, involving three different age groups), and elite international competition as well. An American might well try to imagine the Super Bowl, the World Series, the Mardi Gras, and New Year's Eve in Times Square thrown together with all of the NCAA championships in all sports being held in one city at one time. But only in the GDR would the opening ceremony to all of that take place in an erstwhile concentration camp—lest anyone forget the memory of the Communist sports officials who lost their lives there in the world's struggle against Fascism.

To me, just standing there, the feeling was overwhelming, too much to contemplate all at one time. After a few minutes it's as if a protective shield comes across the mind to blank out the horror and revulsion and once again allow the instincts of reportorial observation to take command.

I had always pictured German concentration camps as remote and barren places, located in wastelands well away from towns (how else could so many people say "we never knew"?), linked to the outside world by rail lines to allow for the transportation of the victims by cattle car. Buchenwald's reality is not that at all. Nestled on a beautiful hilltop, eight winding kilometers uphill from Weimar, it is one of Germany's more historic tourist attractions in its own right.

Now it is surrounded by a Soviet Army base, and on that particular morning, hundreds of inquisitive Russian soldiers came to line the fence along the rise outside the gates. From this vantage they could peer directly down on a small building a hundred yards distant on the right, a completely inoffensive-looking structure standing alone amidst the foundations of what must have been dozens of bunk-houses. The building, with tiled roof, stucco walls, and a small courtyard, could have been an officers' quarters, or perhaps a small storehouse. In fact, it was the crematorium where an estimated 56,000 human bodies were reduced to ashes between 1937 and 1945. If that number seems small, keep in mind that Buchenwald was not an extermination camp like Auschwitz or Treblinka, but a detention camp for political prisoners of the Nazis. It was that until the final months of the War, when the camp population more than doubled with the influx of prisoners shipped from other camps before they could be liberated by the advancing Allied armies.

In the final days, there were at least 18,000 Jews in Buchenwald, but in the beginning, Buchenwald's prisoners were mostly Germans, particularly Communists and other left-wing activists, including many of the leaders of the prewar Workers Sports Clubs, sponsored by the trade unions. Later the camp was home to political prisoners shipped to Germany from captured foreign territory.

Even though it wasn't a death camp, Buchenwald still came to be one of the most, if not the most, dreaded camp of all, as the headquarters of some of the most revolting medical "experiments" ever inflicted by man upon fellow man. Ilse Koch, the infamous camp commandant's wife who had a fetish for collecting lampshades made of human skin, with a special affinity for the tatooed variety, did her work here and will be remembered throughout history as the "Bitch of Buchenwald." Dietrich Bonhoeffer, the Christian martyr who first left Germany and then felt the inner command to return and practice his ministry at the very gates of hell, spent some time here. And Ernst Thälmann, a prewar founder and leader of the German Communist Party, the man who polled more than ten million votes while finishing in third place in the election that brought Hitler to power in 1933, was murdered here shortly before the end of the War. Thälmann's ashes—and government officials say they are sure they are his because he was the only victim cremated that day with his clothes on—are buried in a small plot in the crematorium courtyard marked with an eternal flame burning in the memory of all who met their deaths at the hands of the Nazis.

Although the crematorium courtyard could adequately hold about fifty people, an apparent two hundred were jammed in shoulder to shoulder that July twenty-fourth, each in silent contemplation. There were old men, veterans of the struggle of the Thirties, holding the old Workers' Sports Club flags from the prewar era. Many of them had been in the concentration camps themselves. There were young children, members of the Communist Party's Ernst Thälmann Young Pioneer Clubs, who have the duty of lining the route from the crematorium to the main gate. (In technical terms, the GDR ruling party is the SED, or *Sozialistischen Einheitspartei Deutschland*, which translates to Socialist Unity Party.) And then there is the official

party made up of Johannes Rech, a vice-president of the DTSB
(German Gymnastics and Sports Union), the ruling body of all sports
in the country; Siegrun Siegl, the world-record holder in the long
jump and Olympic gold medalist in the women's Pentathlon in 1976,
dressed in her national track team warm-up suit; and Erich Rochler—
there because he was once a friend of the legendary Werner
Seelenbinder.

Seelenbinder, moving from near total obscurity thirty years ago to a
central place as *the* great historic sports figure in the GDR, is now the
symbol around which all political aspects of the national sports policy
revolve. When the torch reached the Leipzig Stadium in a day's time,
it would be the Werner Seelenbinder memorial bell that would toll
mournfully prior to the formal lighting, and again prior to the
extinguishing of the flame a week later. The Seelenbinder Hall in
Berlin is the main indoor sports facility of the capital, and his features
dominate the sports museums that are just now beginning to open
around the country. And yet, outside the GDR he is a total unknown.
Seelenbinder was a wrestler on the 1936 German Olympic team,
who—had he not lost his opening match—would have done what
John Carlos and Tommie Smith did to the United States Government
in the 1968 Olympic Games in Mexico City in receiving their medals
with a black-power salute. As a Communist, Seelenbinder initially felt
he could not compete for Hitler's Reich in the 1936 Games, in spite
of the fact he was quite possibly the best wrestler in his weight class in
the world. But that sacrifice, his Party friends felt, would have no
symbolic value whatever. No one would ever know the reasoning
behind it. Their idea was to have Seelenbinder compete and then
mount the victory podium and refuse to give the Nazi salute that all
the German winners were snapping off. Seelenbinder, instead, would
offer the solitary second finger on his right hand. Then, his friends
imagined, Werner could head for the international press conference
and tell the world exactly what he thought of his country's present
government. Imagine their chagrin when, after several years of
undefeated wrestling, he went into the ring and lost the first match of
the Games!

"How," his friends reportedly demanded later that night, "could
you let us down this way?"

"Perhaps," Seelenbinder is said to have replied, "because what you are asking of me is no small thing. I can probably expect to live about one day after the close of the Games." Seelenbinder finished fourth, one discouraging spot short of the Olympic medal dais.

In 1944, just before the end of the War, the Nazis tried and executed Seelenbinder in Brandenberg concentration camp. His capital offense? They said he had harbored known Communists in his apartment. His death was typical of many in the final stages of the War as the Nazis, even though they knew defeat was upon them, couldn't resist evening the score with hundreds of their old tormenters. Just as the Christian Church has its Dietrich Bonhoeffer, so the GDR sports movement has its Werner Seelenbinder.

After about thirty minutes of the appropriate speeches on this sunny Sunday morning, Seelenbinder's old friend Erich Rochler took the torch and strained on tiptoe to get it lit. It sputtered and smoked like a giant Fourth of July sparkler. He then handed it over to Olympic champion Siegl. Finally, with cameras flashing and television crews careening backwards through their own cables, Siegrun began to walk respectfully forward out of the small courtyard. It might be well and good to run with the Olympic torch during the quadrennial world festival, but not in the midst of the memories of Buchenwald. A film helicopter hovered overhead as Siegl, torch raised to shoulder height, strode through the line of Young Pioneers, followed by the flags of the Sports Clubs, the bearers looking like a squad of American Legionnaires on Memorial Day. And all of this beneath the eyes of the silent Soviet soldiers beyond the fence. What must they have been thinking?

On the political level there is no alliance stronger than the one between the GDR and the Soviet Union. Friendship slogans abound. The quiet speech at the crematorium had, of course, carried mention of the glorious celebration coming up in November of the sixtieth anniversary of the Bolshevik Revolution of 1917. But at the level of the man on the street, the War is still much too personal and too recent a thing. Almost everyone in both countries lost relatives in the War, and no matter what the Party leaders wish, the average Russian and the average German don't care to share many embraces. For those Russian soldiers, Buchenwald's grim past may well have more meaning than the present festivities.

The idea of turning Buchenwald into a national German memorial seems to leave many GDR citizens cold, too. One of my interpreters

on this project shuddered when the visit popped up on both the
January and the July itineraries. "Would you be upset if you went in
there alone?" one asked. "I have taken people to Sachsenhausen, and
to Ravensbrück, and to Buchenwald, and honestly, the scene makes
me ill. I can't stand to even think about these reminders of what really
did happen."

The Federal Republic's Germans over on the other side of the
Berlin Wall also get upset when they hear of these GDR sports
commemoratives at Buchenwald. They view it as a GDR political
attempt to make the capitalist West seem solely responsible for Hitler.

"I reject that completely," one Frankfurt journalist was to say in
Leipzig in a few days time. "There were many opportunists in
Germany during the Hitler era, and I think there are a lot of them
getting along quite well in the GDR today. The GDR government
can't wash its hands of everything that happened under Hitler and say
it was all our fault."

In his eyes, Siegrun Siegl walking along with her torch was evoking
a sentiment similar to that which would be created in the United
States if thousands of Vietnam draft dodgers and deserters were to
gather at Kent State University to tell the entire United States
population "we told you so, and don't blame us."

When she reached the gate, Siegrun passed the torch to a young
Spartakiad runner, who immediately loped off in the direction of the
Avenue of Sorrows on a symbolic lap of the grounds. The Avenue of
Sorrows is an ever-narrowing street through a series of narrowing
arches, getting tighter and tighter until finally you have a feeling of
squeezing through the far end. Then the course turns left past
eighteen mass graves, one for each of the countries represented by the
56,000 who died on this site. Finally, the torch comes back to the
memorial tower, which dominates the whole region much as the
Washington Monument dominates the U.S. capital.

While the Spartakiad runners were carrying the torch along this
route, I was standing on the back edge of the monument with Horst
Schiefelbein, the Erfurt County reporter for *Neues Deutschland*, the
GDR's national newspaper.

Horst is one of those delightful types who has found satisfaction
within his profession. He has a solid grasp of German history, a track-
and-field-nut's devotion to the statistical ins and outs of the sport, and
the good fortune to have escaped the intrigue of bustling Berlin for an

outpost in the Thuringian Forest, where there is a world of time for quiet contemplation.

"Why," I had asked him as we were scrambling around, he to cover this story, I hoping to snag a ride back to Leipzig, "is it necessary to put everyone through the agony of Buchenwald in order to open a Sports Festival?"

"I will tell you," he puffed, "when we get to the tower."

The view from the back of the memorial tower might be one of the prettiest in the GDR. If Weimar were an American city, this would be the most expensive piece of suburban property in the entire area. As I marveled at the view, Horst smiled. "That city down there at our feet is Weimar, the historical home of Goethe, Liszt, and Schiller. You can go far beyond the fact that this was the home of the pre-Hitler Weimar Republic and claim Weimar as the home of an entire tradition of German humanism, of all the things we hold dear in the development of the German people. The Nazis could have built Buchenwald anywhere they pleased. They could have built it at Oberhof, or hidden it off at any one of dozens of remote locations in Thuringia. But they didn't. They built it right here on the highest point of land overlooking Weimar, and they did it to show people exactly what they thought of the traditions of German humanism. That's the reason we are here today, and why this memorial is here today. To show the world what we think of Nazi Fascism."

By this time European champion Dieter Fromm was carrying the torch past us, holding it high in a cloud of smoke, with four young runners in close pursuit, heading up the Avenue to Freedom, an ever-widening street that brings one, and one's memories, out of the spiritual nightmare that is Buchenwald. At the end of the Avenue to Freedom, the torch was placed in a pylon on an open truck and sent off with police escort, their lights flashing, to Leipzig, where it would get a twenty-four-hour rest at the Sports Institute before the opening ceremony of the Festival.

And right behind it, I took off, bundled into the front seat of a sporty green GDR Wartburg car, a late model with a sun roof, driven by *Neues Deutschland* photographer Werner Eckstein. When we got back, a DTSB interpreter wondered if we had ridden home on bicycles. Werner Eckstein, you see, was the 1961 world road race cycling champion!

2

"Waldi"

If the GDR sports system is indeed a miracle machine, then the miracle man within the machine has to be Waldemar Cierpinski, the amazing marathon runner who emerged from obscurity on a rainy afternoon in Montreal to take the Olympic title away from Frank Shorter on a day when the American defending olympic champion was running as well as he ever ran in his life.

It was a miracle even to the GDR athletes, reporters, television commentators, and coaches. In the final mile approaching the Montreal Olympic Stadium they were all awaiting Shorter's final burst, along with millions of viewers sitting up at home in spite of the fact that it was already past one o'clock in the morning, German time. It wasn't until Waldemar was rocketing out of the ramp and into the stadium for his final lap that the television commentators claimed the triumph.

"He's done it! He's done it!" came the cry through every GDR television set. "Our young man from Halle has done it! He has defeated the Olympic champion. Toot a horn if you live in Halle. Shout to your neighbors. Tip your caps to everyone in the streets. We have won the classical Olympic race! We have won the marathon!"

Across the street in the Olympic Village, the GDR soccer team was getting prepared for the gold medal final against Poland, knowing the country would sit up all night back home to watch that, too. Their toughest game of the Games. But they too were caught up in the television drama of the incredible marathon. "We just sat there staring at each other," goaltender Jurgen Croy would later admit, "thinking that if this living example of mediocrity can lift himself up and win the marathon, and we don't beat Poland, we are never going to hear the end of it from football fans. No team has ever gone into an Olympic final more determined than we were that night. The lift he gave us was absolutely tremendous."

And so was the lift he gave to the mass sports movement back home at the sports clubs in Berlin, Halle, Leipzig, Rostock, Thuringia, Dresden and the rest. All week there had been a media push to have sportsmen come out in the final day of the Olympics, a Sunday, with no TV planned other than the closing ceremonies, to run the 1,977-meter Festival Mile in honor of the big 1977 show and the performance of the Olympic team. The thinking was that perhaps 200,000 would do so all over the country. In the wake of Cierpinski, that figure swelled to 510,000 runners, all of whom seemingly could talk of nothing else than the Montreal marathon. On returning home, "Waldi," as he was now affectionately known to all, became the poster model for the "Start with Bronze" mass sport fitness medal project. He was voted the GDR's Athlete of the Year for 1976, far outpolling athletes who went into the 1976 Games with far more fame than he had. This book would have been more than incomplete without his story. And yet it almost didn't happen.

"Cierpinski will be a problem," I was told when first arriving in the GDR for on-the-scene research in January 1977. He's out of the country, probably somewhere in North Africa, and won't be back until after you leave."

No problem, I thought, we'll pick him up in July at the Festival. Still the interview seemed to be a problem. The DTSB was having a terrible time tracking down Cierpinski when I showed up at the Festival in July, and for several days no one was sure whether he was injured, sick, ducking publicity, or out of the country training once again. I had all but given up hope three days from the end of the research phase of the project, when lo and behold, he showed up at the Festival track meet as a last-minute entry in the 10,000 meters. Since Waldi competes for the Chemie Halle Sports Club, I rushed to the Halle bus with an interpreter after the meet to arrange an interview, only to find that he hadn't come on that bus at all and had once again disappeared, seemingly into thin air. Two days later, on my final morning in Leipzig, I met him in a temporary radio booth in the middle of all the downtown Festival exhibits, signing autographs. A couple of hundred signatures later we worked our way back up to the press center and settled down to talk about the intricacies of Olympic long-distance running.

Why, I wondered, had he never given an interview to a Western journalist in all the time that had passed since the conclusion of the Games in Montreal? Cierpinski looked startled by the question.

"As far as I know," he said, "you are the first one to ever ask for one."

"And where," I asked, "have you been?"

"Right here," he said, still amazed, "finishing my studies in Leipzig. Since the Montreal Games I have been concentrating heavily on studies to try to get ahead in my program so I can return to running in the fall of 1978 and start the preparations for Moscow anew. I was only on low maintenance training in the last part of 1976 until now. Right now the important thing is school. In a year's time it will be running again."

Suddenly the whole scenario came into focus. The DTSB head office in Berlin phones the Chemie Halle Sports Club and asks for Cierpinski. Haven't seen him in weeks, they say. A message is left. And nothing comes of it.

Nothing comes of it because Waldemar Cierpinski is the antithesis of everything the GDR sports science system stands for. In a system that prides itself on planning and balanced preparation, he's forever getting overlooked and then popping up as if by accident.

To start with, he lives in a city where Canada's preeminent sports medical specialist Dr. Don Johnson, creator of the Carleton University Sports Medical Clinic, insists no marathoner could possibly live. Dr. Johnson stayed in Halle in July 1977, since that was the closest available hotel space to Leipzig for a Canadian group visiting the Festival, and all who joined him for early-morning and late-evening jogs came back gasping from the pollution.

It's no accident the sponsor of the Halle elite Sports Club is called Chemie. The city's rustic Saxon beauty is all but enveloped by the fumes from the chemical industries. The city was surely magnificent in the early days of the Reformation—famed Wittenberg is just up the road a piece, and Martin Luther University is there today—but on a quiet, still afternoon, it can be a lot like Gary, Indiana. That's nothing against Gary, Indiana, mind you, it's just that Frank Shorter wouldn't think of training there.

"It's true," says Cierpinski with a laugh. "Halle doesn't have the greatest air in the world, but I guess it's good enough to produce an Olympic winner. Actually, I try to get away from it by running down along the edge of the Saale River in an area called the Marshes. It's really a very beautiful area. There's even a song about it."

But the truth of the matter is that Chemie Halle's plans for Cierpinski did not initially call for a career in marathoning at all. Starting with Chemie Halle as a sixteen year old, ten years prior to his Olympic performance, Cierpinski was singled out by the coaches and sports scientists as one who might make a great 10,000-meter runner and steeplechaser.,

In a sense they were right. By 1975, Waldemar was running the 10,000 in 28:28 and the 3,000 steeplechase in 8:36.6, both excellent anywhere in the world, but both almost a half a lap back of a medal-winning Olympic performance. Just slow enough to keep him completely anonymous with the entire GDR population, with the exception of the true track fans, who lap up statistics in all countries. Waldemar Cierpinski seemed destined to be a footnote in GDR track and field history, an athlete who would race with minor distinction, get his diploma and fade into the ranks of club-level coaching.

And then he and his young wife, Maritta Politz, herself a GDR 800-meter record holder with 1:59.9 back in 1973, went to Prague for a 1974 vacation. "When we got there," he says, "we found they were having a marathon and I decided to enter to see how it would go. I thought I would run as far as I could."

Cierpinski ran the entire 26 miles 385 yards in 2:20.28, finished in seventh place, and enjoyed himself immensely. So much so that a year later in 1975 he went back and tried it again and improved his mark up to 2:17.30, his placing to fourth, finally convincing his coaches to make a permanent switch away from the steeplechase. "I had always found long distances easy and relaxing," he says now. "Much easier than training for the steeplechase."

Also, the national track coaches had by this time come across Frank Baumgartl, an astounding nineteen year old from Karl-Marx-Stadt, who had just dropped his 3,000-meter steeplechase time from 8:44.2

to 8:17.6 in the pre-Olympic year. If Baumgartl hadn't tripped going over the last hurdle in the Olympic final in Montreal, he'd have possibly won the gold medal and set a new world record to boot. As it was, he still picked himself up and finished third.

The door was open for Cierpinski to turn his full attention to the marathon, and he did it, training much as he pleased from his home in Halle. "My home is not far from the club," he says, "and my technique, particularly in winter months, was just to go out the front door and run until I felt I had had enough of it. Often I would run fifteen to twenty kilometers (nine to twelve miles) but occasionally, when I really felt in the mood, I would run up to sixty kilometers (thirty-seven miles)!"

Perhaps the most important thing, when it came to the Montreal marathon, was the fact Cierpinski did this, day after day, week after week, and month after month, without incurring a single major injury. No hamstring problems, no groin problems, no knee problems, and no ankle or foot problems. "That," Frank Shorter was to observe months later, "is a very important factor."

In his first marathon run under serious training, Cierpinski carved out his first win in 2:13 early in 1976, and then he came right back in the GDR trials and won again, bettering that time with a 2:12.21.

"That was the fifth fastest time in the world in 1976," says Waldemar, "but when I arrived in Montreal I knew there were at least twenty people in the field who at one time or another had run faster than I. My own expectations were to finish in the top ten—I would have been disappointed if I hadn't done that—and I will admit that at times I allowed myself to dream of a bronze medal. But as far as the race itself went, I didn't have a personal strategy. I was just going to run with the leaders until something happened.

"Before we even started I was emotionally impressed by the way we were received by the 70,000 spectators. As we jogged around in the stadium before the start, the feeling was overwhelming."

Frank Shorter was overwhelmed by a different sort of emotion. "I was wearing a prototype shoe for a certain manufacturer who shall remain nameless," says the 1972 Munich champion, a man recognized throughout the world as the Jack Nicklaus of marathoning in the 1970s. "But a few minutes before the race, when it started to get wet, the sole started to peel right away from the boot.

"I had to have a friend rush back to the Olympic Village and get my old pair of shoes, and he didn't get back until about five minutes before the start of the race." While Waldemar Cierpinski jogged around, enjoying baptism in the emotion of 70,000, Frank Shorter sat down on the edge of the track and tied his shoes.

And then they were off and running. First, north along Viau for the opening few miles, and then west on Gouin Boulevard following the natural contours of the back river into the face of the gentle midsummer rain. "I hate the rain," says Shorter, "it puts me off completely." Cierpinski loves it.

"I don't like running in the heat," he counters. "I find the rain both refreshing and relaxing. Particularly in Montreal when it didn't seem to affect the crowd at all. I had never before run in a race with so many enthusiastic people all along the route. It stimulated me very much even though they didn't know who I was at first. As we would be running along in the lead group they would be shouting for Shorter and Bill Rodgers and the other faces who were familiar—such as Canada's own Jerome Drayton and Finland's double gold medal winner, Lasse Viren—but they never mentioned my name. I felt like an unknown runner, as if I were dreaming."

He was even an unknown runner in his own country at that stage of the race. In the first half of the marathon the worldwide television hookup was having an awful time with identifications since the numbers, black on a red background, proved indecipherable once the cloth got wet in the rain. What's more, Cierpinski was not wearing the GDR colors of blue top and white shorts, but was dressed in plain white instead, with no identifying team mark on the top.

"That had been done because of the risk of hot weather," he said. "When they had the pre-Olympic marathon in Montreal exactly a year before the Games, it was more than 100 degrees of heat. It's a known fact that white deflects heat on that kind of a day and color absorbs it. Since you had to register your uniform two days before the race, we felt there was no choice but to go with the white. Then, when it came up rain the day of the race, there was just nothing that could be done about it."

Waldemar's anonymity came to an end just past the 23-kilometer mark, nearly halfway through the race, when Shorter made his first serious attempt to pull away from the pack and race on the lead by himself.

"If it hadn't been raining," says Shorter, "I'd have broken a lot sooner than that."

Cierpinski thought it was a very early move.

"He broke away with great strength and broke the field right apart," says Cierpinski, "and it forced me to make a very important decision. Would I go after him and break my own pace, or just stay at the present speed and wait for later?"

If Cierpinski hadn't been a steeplechaser and 10,000-meter man, he would certainly have let Shorter go. Most of the marathoners in the world consider the race to be a battle of one man against the mental torture inflicted by the distance itself, and not a straight footrace. Most marathoners run all but oblivious of their opponents, totally drawn within their own personal individual battle against the 26 miles.

"For me," says Cierpinski, "it is never a battle against nature or time, it is a race against others. I would rather win in a slow time than finish second in a very fast time."

"For me," says Shorter, "it's a little of both."

"It was a hard decision," says Cierpinski, "because in my own mind I was only the twentieth fastest in the race. I would have felt happier if some others had gone after him, but I was almost sure if we all let him go right then he would win, just as in Munich.

"The question was whether I could finish if I set out after him. The key fact for me was that I had enjoyed such good training with no injuries. I knew I was well prepared for this race. So, as soon as he slowed his pace and I could see he was running at the same speed as the rest of us, I took off and caught up with him.

"It was a wonderful feeling when I came alongside. I glanced at Shorter as I did so, and looked right into the eyes of the man who was my idol as a marathon runner. I knew all about him. And yet I could tell by the return glance that he didn't know much, if anything, about me. The psychological advantage was mine."

"It didn't really matter at that stage," says Shorter. "Anyone who is still with you at that stage of the race has to be considered a major challenger. I knew of Cierpinski mostly as a steeplechase runner in Europe, but I also knew he had run his 2:12 and that was enough to make anyone into a contender."

"Shorter made many small surges in quick succession," says Cierpinski in describing the events of the next five miles, "and sometimes he broke contact with me. The first time, though, he only opened half as much distance as he did on the initial 23-kilometer break, and it wasn't too hard to catch up. The last time he didn't get more than twenty-five yards ahead of me, and when I came up this time I looked again, and knew he didn't have any surges left.

"I did not really favor those surges for my strategy, but they had served to drop all other runners a considerable distance behind us. And now, just past 30 kilometers, I suddenly felt that I had the necessary reserves needed to win the race."

By now the whole sports world knew who Waldemar Cierpinski was, particularly the amazed millions watching on home television in the GDR. All afternoon and evening in Europe they sat watching their gold medal total creep toward the 40 mark in the battle to edge past the United States into second place in team standings. The relay teams had come through, the soccer team was favored in the final with Poland set to come right after the track meet. And here they were head to head with the U.S. in the marathon, the one event everyone had all but conceded to Frank Shorter, a man who just happened to be running the race of his life. Shorter's Munich gold medal had been achieved in 2:12:19.8 under perfect conditions. On this day in the rain he would run 2:10:45.8 and still be denied the gold.

For the GDR officials it was a dream. Their television cameras, which could have been giving flashes of the marathon while concentrating on the high jump and relays, instead gave flashes of high jump and relays and concentrated on the marathon.

"Looking back on it," says Cierpinski, "one can only commend the Canadian television crews, who had developed the capability for mobile cameras to bring this kind of continuous close-up action. No one in Europe had ever seen the drama of a marathon quite so closely before. When I left for Montreal, I was an almost anonymous member of our track team. When I returned I was a national figure. Indeed, a great deal of my spare time since has been spent answering letters from all strata of our society."

One place the cameras missed was the McGill University campus. The path through this stage of the course was too narrow to permit camera-and-press vehicles. The two runners went into this phase— just a few hundred yards in duration—even. When they came out, the race was all but over.

"The campus was deserted," says Shorter, "and psychologically it was a perfect place for him to break contact and take the lead."

"It was a very emotional moment," says Cierpinski. "Until then, everything had been in Frank Shorter's favor. Now, knowing I had the reserves, I knew they were in mine, and yet I wanted to break away just in case some of the others back in the pack were making a move on both of us."

When the pair turned onto Sherbrooke Street they were just under five miles from the finish, and they must have been the toughest five miles of all. In fact, only Belgium's bronze medal winner, Karel Lismont, and American Don Kardong, who finished fourth, came those last five miles faster than Cierpinski and Shorter, and they didn't come it much faster.

"Once again," says Cierpinski, "the lift of the crowd was fantastic. The cheering and the encouragement were constant all the way to the stadium. I don't think there was an empty space of ground all along the route. There was just no chance to get lonely and feel sorry for yourself."

Shorter felt much the same way. At one point, perhaps three miles from the finish, Frank pulled to within thirty yards, but could get no closer.

"I never gave up on it," he says, "not until we were in the stadium at the end, because you never know what can happen to the guy in front of you. But all I can say now is that Cierpinski was marvelously prepared for that race. Any time you get under 2:10 in a marathon, you are having your kind of a day. I myself have actually run about fifteen seconds faster than I did that day, but considering the rain and all, the Olympic race was certainly by far the greatest effort of my life."

Cierpinski will never forget the feelings he had when he swept down the ramp and into the stadium as first man home, and even a year after the event he couldn't express them. "There are no adequate words for that feeling," he admits. "I was literally overcome. It made me dizzy."

His early arrival had the organizing committee's competition director, Larry Eldridge, feeling faint as well. Eldridge was the man responsible for getting the track meet finished and the soccer game started, both with capacity crowds of 70,000, and less than an hour's turnaround time between events. Less than fifteen minutes before Cierpinski's arrival in the stadium, Eldridge had realized the marathoners were going to arrive in the middle of the medal presentation ceremony for the women's 4 x 400 meters relay. Once the first marathoner arrived, the infield would be cut off from the track.

What followed was perhaps the most hastily organized Olympic medal presentation in history and only a few insiders will ever know how close it was. As the winning GDR relay team marched back across the track, Cierpinski hit the homestretch. They missed each other by exactly five seconds.

But for Waldemar the confusion was just beginning. Everyone, including Waldi, knows that the marathoners have to come into the stadium and run 1 lap of the track before the finish. The infield lap counter had been left at "1" to mark it for all runners.

But Cierpinski, feeling overcome and dizzy as he was, missed the "1" the first time around and didn't pick it up until he hit the homestretch heading to the finish line.

"I kept waiting for it to go down to '0' just like it does in the regular track races," he says, "but it didn't. Then I waited for someone to indicate the race was over. But they didn't. So I ran another lap just to make sure. I felt really foolish about this later, because I had saved my strength to sprint home, the last 100 meters, which would have given me a faster time, enough to move up one more place to 4th on the all-time list."

The organizing committee felt a little foolish, too. Next time there will be a bell to warn all runners they are heading into the last lap.

And yet in a way it all seems fitting. Why not an extra 400 meters for the only marathon runner in Olympic history who ran so fast that when he made his final approach lap of the outside of the stadium complex, he almost arrived in the stadium in the middle of the playing of his own national anthem, an anthem that was in fact being played for the women's relay team. "I never heard a note of it," he says, "the crowd around the outside of the stadium was making too much noise." And so were the people back home:

The idea of "Run a Mile for Your Health" had first been introduced in the GDR back in 1973 as a promotional gimmick for mass sports participation. That year they had turned it into a lottery where the only way to get a ticket was to run a supervised mile at a sports club, or do the equivalent in another sport, perhaps swimming 400 meters. Those who did it had their times compared to age-and-weight charts to give them some indication of the state of their physical fitness. The obvious hint was that if you weren't up to snuff, you should consider joining a DTSB mass sports club. They wound up with more than thirteen million tickets in that 1973 lottery, not bad for a population of over seventeen million, even if many people did take the opportunity to do it over and over again to increase their lottery chances. But, by 1977 it was the "Festival Mile" run at the distance of 1,977 meters in honor of the calendar year. And, Waldemar Cierpinski had 510,000 out running it the day after his marathon.

Overnight he had become Waldi. They shout it and chant it wherever he runs, even when is far back in the pack, as he was in the Festival '77 meet, just another marathoner trying a 10,000 to develop a little leg speed.

And they also emulate him in the Start Mit Bronze program, successor to the first GDR sports-badge program first launched away back in 1948. Anyone who wishes to win one of the new sports badges—and 6.2 million of the previous badges were given out between 1970 and 1976—has to survive a tough test of all-around ability on speed, strength, endurance, and accuracy.

Cierpinski, as the first man in the country to attempt the new program, tried long-distance running (he had the option of hiking), chin-ups (with the option having been push-ups), the standing triple jump (he could have done a standing long jump), shooting (with the option having been throwing a ball at a target), and slalom racing on foot through a series of poles. Waldi barely qualified for the bronze, his skill at shooting and his natural talent at distance running overcoming his weakness in chinning and jumping.

The papers loved it. If the athlete of the year has a tough time winning his way into the basic bronze class, then no one need feel bad about trying and failing, and everyone who qualifies for the little lapel pin can wear it with pride.

"It was tough," says Cierpinski, "and I had to struggle to get the bronze. I think if I trained on some of the events I wouldn't have much trouble getting the silver, but the gold would likely always be beyond my reach. It would take a decathlon specialist. But it is a good scientifically designed test measuring not only speed and strength and endurance, but also hand-to-eye coordination and balance."

Waldi will never be accused of being a great specialist. At the Olympics he was embarrassed to have to admit he had never even heard of the carbohydrate overload diet that a lot of marathoners, from Boston joggers right on up to superstars, swear by. That's the one where you eat nothing but protein for three days, and then nothing but carbohydrates for the final three before competition. The carbohydrate overload is supposed to make it easier for the body to carry the distance.

"I had never heard of that," says Waldi, "until the matter was brought up in the international press conference following the race in Montreal. But I don't believe in those things. They may be good for some people, but they are certainly not good for all people. I have a controlled diet all year round of 60 percent carbohydrate, 20 to 25 percent protein, and the rest fat, and I find this gives me my best results."

Frank Shorter subscribes to this opinion as well.

"If you have done the training and done the preparation," he says, "you don't need any special last-minute carbohydrate diets. Those things are only an attempt to shortcut and disguise a lack of training. When you are really fit, you don't need any of that stuff."

If Frank and Waldi are both still at it and fit come Moscow and 1980 it could be quite a rematch.

3

The Boss: Manfred Ewald and the DTSB

The astonishing Sportfest and Spartakiad represent a climactic coming together of every facet of the GDR sports system, a system involving millions of East Germans, but ultimately operating under the guiding influence of one man: Manfred Ewald.

The president of the *Deutscher Turn und Sports Bund* (or German Gymnastics and Sports Union), and the National Olympic Committee of the GDR, would be quick to disagree with that Western observation, since he operates in a country that credits the collective decision-making process over the individual contribution, and, indeed, it does slight dozens of extremely talented DTSB bureaucrats. But, no outside observer of GDR sport can be on the scene for any length of time without coming under the spell of the Ewald charisma, and noticing its far-reaching effect.

Throughout the entire '77 Festival, he seemed to be constantly at the side of Erich Honecker, General Secretary of the Party and Chairman of the Council of State. They were together at the opening ceremonies when Ewald introduced Honecker to a roaring crowd estimated at 160,000. They were side by side at sports events, at the

30,000-strong mass gymnastics sport show, at the 45,000-strong parade past the entire Central Committee of the Party, and together at the closing ceremonies.

An hour and a half before the start of the parade there had been a state-sponsored cocktail party for the entire Central Committee and all foreign guests of the Festival. The room was carefully arranged, through the use of table settings, to allow important politicians to circulate at one end of the hall in private huddles with the important VIPs.

But always it was Ewald and Honecker, first having chats with half-a-dozen gold medal winners from the Montreal Olympics, then a word or two with Spain's Juan Samaranch, the vice-president of the International Olympic Committee. Presidents of important world sports federations were ushered up to the front. Mike Wallace, on hand to do a documentary for CBS television's "60 Minutes," chatted with Artur Takac, an IOC technical adviser.

"Tell me," Wallace asked, with the disarming half-friendly, half-sinister tone of voice he can bring to bear on anyone to cut to the heart of a matter, "does Manfred Ewald have any political ambitions?" Takac, the diplomatic Yugoslav to the end, looked a little startled. Then he laughed.

And yet, in the Western context, it was an apt question. In our political system, the supposed supreme dream is to become the President of the United States, or a Prime Minister, or some other political power figure. Not to be Pete Rozelle, or Bowie Kuhn, or any other of the sports czars of our time. Isn't it the same in theirs? Not from the guffaws the Mike Wallace question brought from every GDR official I put it to in the following weeks.

"Now that he's used sport to create the great success story of our country," said one, "do you think maybe he'd like economy? or the mines? or the pollution? or foreign trade? Although it may have seemed to you that Ewald was sticking close to Honecker's side for the entire week of the Festival, let me tell you there are many people in the GDR who look on it the other way around. Honecker was sticking close to Ewald. Manfred Ewald already has the best job in the GDR."

But the above, although it may be widely believed, isn't completely true. Erich Honecker has been the patron saint of Manfred Ewald's sports career from its beginning on October 1, 1948. What's more, the special friendship and alliance between these two men is the single

most important organizational factor in lifting GDR sports development above some very similar systems in other Eastern European
countries.

Back in 1973, Takac, then the special technical adviser to the
Montreal Games, told me Ewald was "without a doubt the best sports
general manager in the world," a statement I took with a grain of salt
based on the fact there are a lot of U.S. pro sport general managers
that Europeans have never heard of. Three years would pass before I
finally managed to meet Manfred Ewald face to face, but in the
meantime I heard a lot of stories.

One of the best relates to the soccer World Cup of 1974. The two
Germanys had never met in a football game, thanks to political
barriers, but by the luck of the draw among the sixteen countries
reaching the 1974 final round, they both drew into Group One. They
would now have to meet. There were four teams in each of four
groups, with two teams from each group to qualify for the final eight
spots after a single round robin. In no time at all it became obvious
that the 1974 Federal Republic team of Western Germany was one of
the great football teams of all time. They powered their way to two
quick impressive wins while the internationally inexperienced GDR
team struggled to a win and a tie. Expert opinion had the Federal
Republic winning the first-ever soccer showdown—between East and
West—and winning it by at least five goals. Instead, the GDR won
1-0.

The upset caused absolute chaos in the '74 World Cup. With two
wins and a tie, the GDR had won Division One, while every soccer
fan in West Germany had bought his final round tickets based on the
premise his team would win Division One. Now, instead of tickets for
West Germany's final round games, they all had tickets for the GDR's
final round games. Although the West Germans eventually went on
to win the World Cup, it gave the GDR team a delightful sensation to
play before half-empty stadiums in the finals and know that every
ticket had been purchased at absolute top dollar.

But the story behind the story took place in the dressing room prior
to the game. As occasionally happens in North American sport, the
GDR players got together on their own, without the coaching staff,
and had a heart-to-heart talk about their shameful performance in the
first two games. They asked each other how they could possibly go
back home and face Manfred Ewald after the support and funding the

DTSB had poured into this team throughout the Seventies. And then they went out on the field and played a perfectly mistake-free football game built totally on defense, which continually thwarted the Western attack. When they got one scoring chance in the second half, they made the most of it, and that was that. One to zip. Two years later there was an Olympic gold medal.

Who is this man who can evoke the old Notre Dame win-one-for-the-Gipper spirit in a Communist setting? What is the secret? Like most things in GDR sport, there isn't one. The talents of Ewald are things that some people have and others do not. Basically, he is himself. I see him as a little bit of several people I have come across in North American sport.

I can remember my first interview with Vince Lombardi; he would glance at his watch when he didn't care for the line of questioning. And I remember wandering through the Green Bay dressing room over a period of weekends just drinking in the respect the Bart Starrs, Fuzzy Thurstons, Willie Davises and Gerry Kramers felt for a man with whom they all conducted a strange love–hate relationship.

I can remember sitting in the Northwestern dressing room as a college sophomore, putting on a track suit with my back to the wall of the football film room while Ara Parseghian went through slow-motion replays of Saturday's performance. Oh, the shouting and screaming and negativeness of it all. Good moves weren't singled out for praise, they were expected. A few years later as a reporter, I could stop by a coffee shop not far from the stadium and find Ara waking up over an early morning cup, not long after sunup. The level of dedication was incredible. You wonder how they live through it.

There's a little George Allen in Ewald, too. Washington Redskin reporters would never believe it, but back in the mid-Sixties, when George was an assistant with the Bears, he used to sneak the inside tips to the reporters, who could never get the time of day from George "Papa Bear" Halas; he never even announced his cuts during training camp. At least one enterprising Chicago reporter used to get them by phoning the St. Louis Cardinal training camp up the road in suburban Lake Forest. The Cards were kept informed by the League teletype machine, and some of their people loved to rat on the Bears. But by the time he got to Washington, George Allen ran the most secretive football operation in the history of the National Football League. More secretive, I think, than anything I found in the entire

GDR project with the possible exception of the medical facilities of the Leipzig Research Center.

And finally, there's a lot of Sam Pollock in Manfred Ewald. Pollock's the front-office wizard who put together the modern Montreal Canadien hockey dynasty, before retiring in 1978, a man with an astonishing ability to play one side against the other, both sides against the middle, and always end up on top, usually without ruffling a single feather on the guy whose pockets he had just picked.

And there's a little bit of Bill Veeck in Ewald, too: the ability to look beyond the questions of the moment to assess the overall long-range picture, a calm pragmatism when discussing the business of sport.

The first time I ever saw Manfred Ewald, I had the advantage on him, because he didn't see me. It was almost a week before the opening of the 1976 Olympics and I had wandered down to the athletes' reception area to see how well the organizing committee was handling check-in functions.

A couple of days earlier the press had been barred from the area when four Israelis with large parcels had shown up as the advance guard of the full team, which wasn't expected until the next day. When the security guards on duty asked them to open their parcels they refused, and a bit of a scene ensued while the chiefs of Olympic security were tracked down. Once they arrived, the Israelis were ushered off to a private tent, but one photographer was able to sneak up and snap a picture. What he got was pretty strong evidence that the bulky package contained machine guns, Israel's final insurance policy against a repeat of Munich no matter what the Olympic Village rules might say. The picture and story caused a considerable behind-the-scenes flap.

But with press restrictions now lifted, I arrived at the check-in area at the same time as the incoming GDR women's handball team and was able to follow them right through to the front door of their Village quarters. Who should be awaiting the arrival but the boss himself, dressed in slacks and shirtsleeves. He quickly and properly made the rounds, shaking hands and greeting everyone involved—athletes, coaches, trainers and officials—on a first-name basis. Then, when the baggage showed up on a tram he ushered all the girls into the lobby and, with the aid of a couple of staff assistants, lugged in the bags himself.

While this was going on, you can be sure the presidents of most other National Olympic Committees were living it up in posh quarters in downtown Montreal hotels. Not Ewald. The GDR chief personally headed an entire Olympic command post from a suite of rooms on the seventeenth floor of the Olympic Village. They were equipped with tallying systems and analysts to break down incoming results into fine detail. There were people working on translations of virtually everything said and written about the GDR at the Games, all brought to Ewald for his perusal. There were strategy rooms, meeting rooms and reception rooms. A complete battle plan. Just the way Al Davis of the Oakland Raiders would probably run the U.S. Olympic team if he were placed in charge. And much the way George Allen and Sam Pollock would run it, too.

For three weeks, this book idea had been under discussion with several of Ewald's lieutenants, including DTSB vice-president Johannes Rech. On the closing morning of the Games, I was invited into this seventeenth-floor command post to share some German beer, vodka, and sausages, and talk about the whole idea. To my amazement, considering what a busy fourteen days it had been, Ewald seemed totally familiar with everything I had written before and during the Olympics. He asked some pointed questions about what I had in mind, and then smiled broadly.

"Maybe," he said, "it's time we did something like this to get a Western viewpoint of our system." With Ewald's support, the full cooperation of the GDR and DTSB officials was assured, but it wasn't until seven months later, at the midpoint of all the research, that I finally got to sit down with him in Berlin for a deeper personal chat. Even then, and after a fair bit of give-and-take, I had been told thirty minutes would be tops. He was just too busy.

But, as it turned out, we spent two hours together and, finally, it was I who broke it off in order to make it to a dinner engagement, now delayed an hour and a half. I left with the feeling he was willing to go on all night, and we easily could have.

"What was it like for you personally," I had asked Ewald for openers, "in the beginning?" Ewald's eyes narrowed, for what seemed like a very long minute, and he cocked his head to one side, making me wonder if raking up these wartime and postwar memories was something that just isn't done in German society.

"I suppose you have heard," he finally said with resignation, "stories about how I was a member of the Hitler Youth." As a matter of fact, I hadn't, but I just sat there noncommittally.

"Just as well," he finally continued. "It's something that ought to be on the record directly from me anyway. The charge is basically true. I was involved with a Hitler Youth group, but the matter needs explaining.

"I was born in 1926, which made me thirteen years of age when the War started in 1939, and eighteen going on nineteen when it ended in 1945. But my involvement really started in 1922, well before I was born, when my father became a member of the German Communist Party. He never left it, remaining a loyal anti-Fascist all through the Nazi period and the War. Being my father's son, I was drawn in, too. From the age of sixteen on, I had some duties in the Nazi Youth, but really as a secret agent for the Communist underground. There was a group of us and we were all betrayed in 1944, with the result that seven were executed. It would have been my fate but for the intervention of well-placed friends within the Nazis, who prevented my being named, even though they knew, or must have strongly suspected, I was indeed involved.

"That was absolutely all there was to it. Do you really suppose, with the kind of screening there was on everyone's activities at the end of the War, I would have received an administrative job in the Soviet Occupied Zone of Germany if I had really been an active leader in the Hitler Youth?"

Probably not, but on the other hand it's hard to tell. Everything Ewald says is believable, because to know him is to like him. Whether or not the story is true, he would probably have naturally gravitated to a leadership role no matter what the political system was. And certainly true is that he did move up the ladder with remarkable agility in the Soviet Zone in the immediate months and years after the War.

"At the end I was fighting on the western front," he continued, ruefully looking at a right hand with the first two fingers missing. "I lost these in an air attack. It's hard now to even think back to then. It's such a bitter memory. I know outsiders can look at pictures of devastation, see the piles of rubble, and hear the stories of how hard it was to get food and keep warm in the first winters. But, really, it's more than that. There was more rubble in the German mind than on the German streets. For two generations we had been told we were supermen, the master race. For five years we were told we would have victory, or we would have death, but no more German humiliation. Well, here we were in the spring of 1945. The War was over. And those of us that were left were not dead. Reconstructing cities is one thing. How do you reconstruct minds?

"That's what the leadership of this country has been trying to do ever since the War ended. It's one of the things we have been trying to do with our sports program. The fact is, we are no better than anyone else in the world; we are just people. Sports is a forum where you can teach that message through sportsmanship.

"At the end of the War, everything came to a stop. All federations and all institutions simply ceased to exist. There was nothing. You had to get permission from the military command for everything, even to gather and play a football game, if you could find a place. Nothing without a permit.

"I was working in Mecklenburg, first with a small university anti-Fascist committee, and then with the first formation of the Free German Youth (FDJ) organization. I was the first chairman of our local committee in 1946. Our prime job in the FDJ was the reeducation of the youth into anti-Fascist thinking through youth committees, so naturally we got involved in offering leisure-time activities as well. At first it was football, angling, chess, and track and field. It was a very big task."

While all this was going on between 1946 and 1948, Erich Honecker had come out of a twelve-year stay in concentration camps to take over the leadership of the Free German Youth at the national level.

On October 1, 1948, after permission had been granted to set up a central sports organization, Honecker sat down for a weekend with Hans Jendretzki, the head of the trade unions, which in the case of a Communist society are not adversary unions battling capitalist managements in the Western sense, but the collective groups controlling industrial output. Honecker and Jendretzki, with their aides, were the architects of the first all-inclusive sports system in the Soviet Zone. Once the idea was down on paper, the next problem was to find the right people to run the bureaucracy.

Honecker had someone in mind—his twenty-two-year-old district FDJ manager from Mecklenburg—Manfred Ewald. He thus immediately became one of the six vice-chairmen of the initial sports committee.

"In the beginning it was a huge task," says Ewald. "Our first steps were toward a mass program. Competitive sport didn't seriously begin until 1952. Our first chore was to stop the privileges held by certain strata of the population and give every chance to the working-class people and the young people to live an equitable life."

Asked if he was initially prepared for the task, Ewald smiles. "No one was prepared for the task," he says. "Look at me. I was just past my twenty-second birthday. We didn't have anything. No stadiums, no universities, everything was destroyed and finished. We were a people completely down. But we had to get on with it. I didn't have a particularly strong sports background—a little track and field and a little skiing was all—but it was obvious sport was going to play a very strong role in the overall development of our national political reconstruction program. Right from the start the large FDJ youth meetings always had a place for sports. Even in 1947, at the meeting of the second parliament in Meissen, we had a big sports show.

"The Soviet Union, of course, was the example for all of us. Most of our first leaders studied there. But although both we and they were faced with similar problems, each country had to develop its own possibilities. Thus, the U.S.S.R. has built sports organizations on the foundation of large national trade unions. They have their state committee and their union clubs. We, on the other hand, have a municipally based system built around local enterprises and town and village communities. Theirs was the best for them, ours has proven best for us."

Ewald's rise through the bureaucracy was meteoric. By the time he was twenty-eight years old, he was the nation's sports minister, right on top of the State Committee for Physical Culture and Sport. With that title, and membership in the Comintern, he was a young man of considerable political power and influence. But it wasn't satisfying. Ewald, one gets the impression, didn't care for the lofty ministerial limousines and high government trappings. If he was going to make the new system really work, he wanted to be back in the pit where the fur was flying.

What the GDR was faced with at the time, which by now was 1957, was the same problem that has come along to frustrate every government-controlled sports system in the world. With political jobs frequently changing hands and politicians, by the precarious nature of their profession, concerned more with self than with public interest, t's difficult to set up and perpetuate effective government organiza- ions. Politicians, it has been said, do as much harm as they can and is much good as they must.

In 1957, Ewald and the GDR managed to circumvent that problem. They created the Deutscher Turn und Sports Bund (DTSB), or the German Gymnastics and Sports Union, a union of all existing sports federations in the country, and gave it not only full control of a budget, but full authority for the major decisions in running the sports system. It was an act of central significance for East German sport. As soon as the DTSB was in place, Ewald backed right down the ladder from his ministerial post, and took over its presidency. Since it was not technically a government agency, he was able to draw the National DTSB Committee in under its umbrella and declare himself president of that as well. In a masterful political move, the day-to-day operation of mass sport, elite sport, workers' sport clubs, and the whole recreational sports system was made independent of direct day-to-day political decision-making.

The Sports Minister's office, on the other hand, is still responsible for sports science, the College of Physical Culture in Leipzig, and, in conjunction with other ministries, all educational aspects and matters relating to the production of sports equipment.

In every other country of the world, East or West, the man in Ewald's job would be a civil servant reporting to a Minister of Sport and, quite possibly, a host of other political authorities. In the GDR, it is the other way around. The sports ministry's political function is to work towards solving the political needs of the DTSB. The situation is unique in the world of sport, and because of it, Manfred Ewald indeed does not have any of our Western-style "political ambitions."

Other countries are moving toward an arrangement similar to the DTSB. Canada has one virtually in place in the form of its Ottawa-based Sports Administration Center, but all the power and budget control have been retained by politically minded government ministries. The United States could be heading in this direction, if it follows the suggestions of the President's Commission on Olympic Sports and sets up an "umbrella organization" to coordinate the nation's sports federations, a move designed to end once and for all the feud between the National Collegiate Athletic Association and the Amateur Athletic Union. But there is still no consensus on what role the government will play, or who will finally wind up calling the important shots.

Everyone in the West, caught in the British tradition of sport as a hobby, is in a muddle. France has a government Sports Ministry. Britain has its Sports Council, Australia its new Confederation of Australian Sports, and Western Germany, trying desperately to close the gap with the East, has an impressive consortium of private business supporters. Italy has put the power into the National Olympic Committee and funded it with seventy million dollars a year from football-lottery profits.

In the beginning there is a spirit of great hope as these new groups set out to saddle up an army of public information in the cause of justice in sport. But then, often as not, the "army" immediately rides off into the swamp of divisiveness and jurisdictional jealousies.

But what else can result when sport is so diversely controlled with professional promoters, college and university administrators, national sports federations and confederations, federal, state, and local funding agencies, all independent of one another, and further influenced by the independent broadcast and print media?

While all this goes on, the GDR has moved from 9 gold medals in Mexico City, to 20 in Munich, and 40 in Montreal. Their achievements in elite development speak for themselves.

In the GDR, almost by definition, nothing is really independent of governmental control in the Western sense of the definition, but all politics aside, a straight analysis of the bureaucratic system reveals that, thanks to some very special circumstances, not the least of which is the close relationship between Manfred Ewald and Erich Honecker, the DTSB is in a position to run a totally unified sports system without a lot of interference from within or without.

They have already accomplished what every other sports system in the world still dreams of accomplishing, starting with the proper foundation through the development of the mass base.

In 1948, their mass sports movement had 220,000 members. In 1955, it had 1,163,256. Today, the DTSB rules over 8,000 sports clubs, 2.7 million members (which is 16 percent of the total population), 191,000 trained and certified volunteer coaches, 93,000 judges and referees (also graduates of training clinics), and 300,000 elected officeholders at all levels of management from the national level right on down to the villages and the collective farms.

That's a pretty impressive base. Watched over by a pretty impressive boss.

4

Organized Excellence: The German Gymnastics and Sports Union

Many Western countries currently are centralizing, or trying to centralize, their amateur sports organizations much in the manner of the GDR. But in the immediate postwar years in what was then called the Soviet Zone of Germany, sport planners were coping with problems of organization created by a lot of old habits and decidedly capitalistic tendencies.

Profit-making professional sports clubs were banned in the immediate postwar period, but theater was permitted, a loophole that was very soon taken advantage of. Professional wrestling—and who can forget the way that "sport" dominated the early days of North American television—was considered theater and was almost as big an attraction in the Soviet Zone of Germany as it was in the United States. The wrestlers barnstormed around the country battling for the "Golden Girdle" and as many as three European "champions" were being crowned in a single week.

"It was an awful business," recalls *Neues Deutschland* Sports Editor

Klaus Huhn, "but it had a degree of popularity and the managers of the German Sports Council spent some time wondering whether this sort of thing should be permitted at a time when we were trying to build a new sports system. Finally, distinct and restrictive orders were enacted and published. At first the managers of the wrestling circuses just laughed, figuring their popularity would win the day. Then they became enraged when they finally realized the new orders meant more than the paper they were written on. One of them commanded his fighters to 'go and show them.'

"At his bidding, several wrestlers came to the offices of the German Sports Council, entered it by force, and almost reached the very room of the man responsible for curbing their 'theater.' But then, just as they were about to do some 'showing,' they themselves were confronted by a troop of very athletic young people who seemed to be really angry. An alarm had called out all the football players, track and field men, and swimmers. Faced with the prospect of this unpaid-for confrontation, the wrestlers turned tail and left in some haste. Within weeks, most of the wrestlers who were in any way interested in continuing in sport came forward to apply for their amateur cards." So much for the short history of commercial, private-profit sport in the GDR. Next came the question of outside sponsorships. One of the first of the successful sports in the young GDR of the late Forties and early Fifties was cycling. Gustav (Tave) Shur, a man that Dr. Tittel of the Leipzig Institute credits with the highest oxygen-uptake capability he has ever tested—that's the ability to transfer oxygen into energy, by the way—was the first great sports hero of the land, and twice world road-racing champion.

Back when Tave was a youngster, a leading brandy producer came forward and offered to grant a full sponsorship for the leading national cycling road race. It was a well-meaning offer, and only the permission of the German Sports Council was missing.

"We were loath to let amateur cycling roll under the sponsorship of a brandy flag," says Huhn, who in addition to his sportswriting duties served a term as president of the GDR cycling federation and helped instigate the internationally known Tour-de-France-style Peace Race through the cities and countryside of Poland, Czechoslovakia and the GDR.

"But the early question was how to do things on our own without accepting such tempting sponsorship? A lot of people were fainthearted and nervous at the prospect of refusing sponsorship, but they were not a force in our organizational meeting. By the time we were done, we had added a lot of our own ideas to those of the brandy producer and our new adventure started with boundless optimism—and no brandy flags.

"Everyone set about to scavenge up what they could find with whatever means were at hand. Every prize had to come from the volunteer efforts of the members of the sports movement. Even today some of the participants of that first race are apt to ask me for the secret behind the meat that was supplied for the goulash served at the end of each racing session. There was no meat available at the time in our shops.

"We had special prizes for special bonuses. A mountain-time bonus for the fastest cyclist between Magdeburg and Wittenberg: a jar of canned fruit for the winner. A sprint bonus for the fastest cyclist around the square of Stadtroda: a half pound of butter. Another sprint bonus for the fastest time through the market square of Malchin: an edition of Goethe in three volumes. Prizes that would scarcely excite anyone today caused a tremendous sensation at that time. As far as anyone knew, there was not butter in Stadtroda."

Sport was beginning to show what it can do on its own.

If it can do it on a small scale, why not on a grand scale?

In the West, sport or any other field of endeavor must be subservient to its source of funding. If the government pays for sport, sport must live with the bureaucrat. If private sponsors pay the bill, then sport has to mold its efforts to accommodate corporate sales interest. If television comes along to pay the way, then television executives will decide when the events will be held, how they will be conducted, and what rules, if any, will be adjusted to suit the purposes of television.

In the GDR, now that the DTSB has control of funding, decision-making, and planning, these problems that plague much of the rest of the world have been eliminated domestically. What's more, since sport has acquired such command over its own destiny it automatically picks up power within the political system vis a vis other ministries. Contrary to the Western image of GDR sport as government-controlled, the reality at times seems almost the reverse with sport imposing its will on governmental priority systems, just as, say, the Defense Department seems to do at budget time within the U.S. political system.

Most governments, no matter what their social and political

origins, tend to react only when the pressure is consistent and unified. And so, when faced with a multitude of conflicting appeals on a single subject, most governments tend to do nothing until the disputes are resolved and a single consensus opinion is presented. In the United States today, one could sit down with the leaders of the National Collegiate Athletic Association (NCAA), the Amateur Athletic Union (AAU), the United States Olympic Committee (USOC), the independent sports federations, major league baseball, the National Football League (NFL), or any of the other pro sports, plus federal, state and municipal recreation officials and find continual agreement on every basic issue concerning the overall purposes and aims of sport.

And yet, whenever a government attempts to get them all together—as with the U.S. President's Commission—self-interest and fragmentation rule supreme. Need it be so? Is there anything to be learned from the DTSB example?

The DTSB came into being in April of 1957 as a replacement for the German Sports Council, which had started the socialist re-work of German sports traditions in October of 1948. In effect, sport was no longer controlled by a government department, but had a measure of independence within the system. This independence now permitted Ewald to bring the National Olympic Committee under his personal control, since NOCs, by Olympic rules, must be chartered as independent sports bodies apart from government. Ewald is thus able to serve as president of the DTSB and president of the GDR National Olympic Committee. Gunther Heinze is able to serve as DTSB vice-president for international affairs, and vice-president of the NOC as well, while Dr. Horst Rörder can serve as DTSB vice-president for the development of elite sport and chef de mission of the Olympic team in residence in the Olympic Village. In one stroke the GDR thus solved the natural strife that bedevils relations between NOCs, government sports officials and sports federation officials in too many countries.

The U.S. President's Commission recognized the need for a unification of this sort in its 1976 study of Olympic sport in the United States, proposing that the U.S. Olympic Committee assume the role of cover agency for the management of Olympic sports. Until the AAU and the NCAA come to terms with this, however, political agreement on the question will prove elusive.

In the DTSB it is no problem at all. When the German Sports Committee was first created in 1948, it had 220,000 members, authorization to work on the first Youth and Sports Promotion Act, a mandate to organize construction of the German College of Physical Culture (DHfK) in Leipzig, and a desire to increase the membership in the mass sports clubs. By 1957, when the decision to create the DTSB was reached, the mass movement was already up to more than 1,250,000 members, physical education had become compulsory for all pupils in all schools, and a handful of GDR athletes had reached the Olympic level with boxer Wolfgang Behrend winning the first gold medal in Melbourne.

"But," as Ewald says of the German Sports Committee, "we were becoming an awkward government department."

Interestingly enough, in the Canada of 1978, exactly the same feeling has developed sixteen years after the Canadian Government first created its Fitness and Amateur Sports Branch with an annual grant then of "up to five million dollars" directed toward the upgrading of the competitive level of Canadian amateur sport. By 1978, Canadian Government spending was up to thirty-two million dollars a year, with twenty-two million dollars of that going to the elite development program. Government sports officials in charge of funding these programs were, however, tending to control all the major decisions to the irritation of sports federation volunteers in the ranks below.

Back in the GDR of 1957 when Ewald gave up his position as Sports Minister to take command of the DTSB—ostensibly a step down in the power structure—his great coup lay in the fact that he was able to bring the real power of his ministerial office right along with him. Today the State Secretary for Sport, though controlling an immense support budget quite apart from DTSB funding, tends to take orders from the DTSB rather than issue them. And, if arms ever have to be twisted in intra-governmental relations over matters of support for elite sport, Ewald would not hesitate for a minute to climb right back up the ladder and personally do the twisting, largely thanks to the fact that Chief of State Erich Honecker, the man who gave Ewald his first job in the system back in 1948, is still one of his closest friends.

But it takes more than friendship to consolidate an entire sports system under one roof. It takes the mastering of administration and organization, plus a thorough understanding of one's own political system. The DTSB, which boasted 2,951,352 members in January

1977, a membership roll that was increasing at a rate of between 200,000 and 300,000 a year with a fairly stable population of seventeen million, scores top marks on all counts.

One of the first, and certainly the most important, of GDR sports political moves was to get the so-called "right to sport" written directly into the constitution. Anyone who has been party to a lobby battling for an amendment to the United States Constitution knows the importance of this. Once something is in the Constitution as a right, then legal action can be taken to enforce it. The various civil rights movements in the United States have all fought this battle. The sports community has never even thought of it.

Article 18, paragraph 3 of the GDR Constitution says:

"Physical culture, sport, and tourism as elements of socialist culture serve the all-round physical and intellectual development of the citizen."

But the real crunch comes a little further along in *Article 25* when it says:

"For the full and distinctive development of the socialist personality and the growing satisfaction of cultural interests and requirements, the participation of citizens in cultural life, physical culture and sport is guaranteed by state and society."

Article 44 delineates the trade union role in promoting the cultural and sports activities of the working people.

Critics of GDR sports, both Eastern- and Western-based, have expressed the opinion the DTSB could have a hard time maintaining its budgetary levels now that so many of the political objectives of the nation, such as normalization of relations with other countries, trade agreements, and recognition within the United Nations, have been achieved.

"Sport has done wondrous things for the GDR," says Yugoslavia's Takac. "Their willingness to share Leipzig's technical developments with the Third World has opened many doors. The international successes of their top athletes have opened more. But now that the diplomatic successes have been registered, one wonders if they will maintain the levels of sports spending of the 1960s and 1970s on into the future."

My own personal experiences indicate there should be no problem whatever. Ewald has covered his political flanks beautifully.

Under the GDR political system, seats in the parliament are slated through percentages with the ruling Socialist Unity Party (SED), getting 41 percent and varied interest groups getting smaller fixed percentages. Representatives of labor get so many seats, representatives of women get a set number, and so on, including the Free German Youth organization, which gets the right to slate fifteen members of the national assembly. Five of those fifteen are active athletes at the elite level. Other athletes sit in the Women's Party, and several are within the SED itself. More than half of the members of the GDR Parliament are active members of the DTSB as well. It's a lobby that any interest group in the world would be envious of, with reason.

All of this intense political activity resulted in some interesting paragraphs within the Youth Act of the GDR, passed into law on January 28, 1974. Such as:

Article 34: "Physical culture and sport are a part of life for young people in socialist society. Regular sports activity is desired by young people and necessary for the development of their personalities. The socialist government guarantees physical education and sport for young people in all walks of life, and promotes the activity of the German Gymnastics and Sports Union as the initiator and organizer of sport."

Article 35: "Teachers shall encourage initiative and a readiness on the part of pupils and students to engage in sports in the German Gymnastics and Sports Union, the Free German Youth, the Society for Sports and Technology, the Confederation of Free German Trade Unions, in school sports clubs, and in workers' teams. Specific plans to stimulate sports activities shall be included in the annual enterprise plans as well as the enterprise collective agreements. The German Gymnastics and Sports Union has the right to make suggestions for the encouragement of regular sports activities. Managers and executive bodies shall recognize the value of and encourage sports."

Article 38: "The Council of Ministers, in agreement with the national executive of the German Gymnastics and Sports Union, determines the responsibilities of the state in regard to physical education and sport, and guarantees that the main aims will be accomplished and the material base for these plans is taken into account in the national economic plan. The State Secretariat for Physical Culture and Sport of the Council of Ministers is responsible for the implementation and control of these plans. The National Executive of the German Gymnastics and Sports Union has the right to make suggestions to the Council of Ministers as to who shall be a member of the State Secretariat."

No sports organization anywhere in the world has its role so entrenched within the law of any land as the DTSB in the GDR.

However, in spite of all the political power, there is still the massive job of creating a cohesive and functional organization within the DTSB, an organization capable of operating a sports system without the rancor and ill will that always seems so typical of the volunteer and professional levels of sports management.

The basic unit of the DTSB is the mass recreation sports clubs, which are found literally everywhere you turn within the borders of the country. Everyone has the right to join the DTSB, and any collection of seven people within any enterprise or living unit have the right to form a DTSB sports club.

When they do form a club, they are assessed monthly fees of 1.30 marks (approximately 71 cents) for workers; 0.80 marks (approximately 44 cents) for students, housewives, old-age pensioners, and apprentices; and 0.20 marks (about 11 cents) for children.

In return for this fee the members get free use of DTSB facilities and equipment for all sports, including such costly ones as Olympic class sailing and equestrian sports, a schedule for team games if they form a team in volleyball, handball, tennis, soccer, bowling, or whatever, the provision of trained officials for their games, and small compensation for their coach if he or she has passed DTSB coaching certification programs.

DTSB sports clubs can be found in factories, agricultural collective farms, craft cooperatives, administrative units, universities and colleges, technical schools, urban and rural residential areas, the Army, and the police stations.

And that's only within the mass program. The major financing for all this comes from the budgets of the industries throughout the country. Since most industry is state-owned, everyone comes in for a form of profit-sharing, unlike the free-enterprise system in the West where industrial profit goes to company shareholders. Thus, as a basic guideline, 7 percent of the profits of all industries within a municipal area is directed in the general direction of sports programming within that area. Decisions on how to spend that money come under the jurisdiction of county and district DTSB committees, who work out the local priorities within a general guideline set down by the national DTSB office.

The elite program is quite separate from this. Basically, the larger industries in the various cities and counties support the high-performance sport clubs within their areas. Thus, the Chemie Halle Sports Club is supported by the vast chemical industries of the city of Halle. The Motor Jena Club, home of such track and field greats as Wolfgang Nordwig, Renate Stecher, Bärbel Eckert, Rolf Bielschmidt, Ruth Fuchs, and Marlies Göhr, is supported by industrial giants like Carl Zeiss in Jena.

The military and police budgets are certainly not forgotten, with the Army clubs—Vorwärts, which translates to Forward—and the police clubs—Dynamo—among the biggest and best equipped in the country. There are twenty-seven elite sports clubs in all, nineteen of which are equipped with special sports schools to attend to the educational needs of their young stars, a project that brings yet another department, that of education, directly into the sports development process.

Sometime during 1977 the three millionth currently active member of the DTSB took out a card, and although the chances are that he or she was a beginning athlete in the mass program, member number 3,000,000 could just as easily have been a coach, instructor, referee, or sports judge. The DTSB is governed by some 300,000 elected officers, a ratio of one officer for every ten members; more than 180,000 volunteer coaches and instructors, all of whom have passed varying levels of certification tests; and 80,000 volunteer referees and judges, all of whom must also be equally well qualified.

And how, any Westerner will be quick to ask, do they get so may volunteers to act as coaches, referees and judges? Like almost everything else in the system, it's done through incentives, small perks, like time off from work at full pay.

The certification class I dropped in on in Berlin was the fifth session in a series for prospective Level I swim coaches, and the class included a construction worker, an engineer, several young gym teachers, a musician, an electrical mechanic, and a plumber. The level of teaching appeared to be excellent.

After completing ten sessions of study and lectures, these would-be coaches would have to pass a written exam before qualifying for their caps and whistles, and even then they could only work as assistant coaches at the youth level, perhaps the equivalent of Little League baseball in the United States.

After one year of these duties, they would become eligible for the second stage, which involves a forty-hour course taught at a university. It is usually done all in one week, including five eight-hour sessions with another exam at the end. All of the applicant's expenses, including room and board, are picked up by the DTSB. What's more, the time taken for the course must be honored by the employer and cannot be charged off as vacation time. By reaching Level II, the volunteer can be head coach at the Little League level, and then after another year or two has passed he can again move up the line and take a much more advanced forty-hour course leading to the Level III diploma.

With a Level III permit the volunteer coach becomes eligible for postgraduate courses at the university level to allow him or her to keep up with all the latest developments in the science of coaching. Level III coaches work closely with the professional graduates of the Leipzig Institute when it comes to administering the entire sports program. Statistics show that 55.1 percent of all GDR volunteer coaches hold Level I certification, 26.3 percent have reached Level II, and 17.8 percent have reached Level III.

As a result, anyone who goes out for sport at any level is guaranteed to receive instruction from people who have some idea of what they are supposed to be doing. And the volunteers, for their part, have some idea of what to look for in the way of promising youngsters to move along for further testing at the high-performance sports centers.

What is even more interesting is that when a top-qualified coach or official has a conflict between his work schedule and his DTSB assignments, the work schedule is adjusted and he is given time off to carry out his sports duties. If an employer decides to question any of this, Ewald and his friends just point back to the Constitution's Article 44, where it spells out the sport support responsibilities of the trade union movement.

One might suspect that productivity would fall, as a result of this policy, but in the GDR they say that has not been the result at all, but rather quite the reverse. They say trade union support of sport has increased their on-the-job productivity. The overall figures seem to back that up, too. In 1974 the GDR moved past Italy into eighth place among the world's most industrialized nations.

The DTSB is a government unto itself. It has four levels of management with national at the top, fifteen county organizations, two hundred and twenty district branches, and finally, the local management of every individual sports club.

The supreme organizational body of the DTSB is the Gymnastics and Sports Congress, which meets every four years and, among other duties, elects a national executive of a hundred and fifty members drawn from the lists of officials, coaches, instructors and active athletes. Within the National Executive stands the Presidium, formed by Ewald and his seven DTSB vice-presidents in charge of international relations, elite competition, major festivals, mass sport programming, and Olympic development.

Ewald and his vice-presidents meet once a week throughout the year, an easy matter since they all work together in the DTSB headquarters building in Berlin. They keep in close contact with the National Executive, and once every four years they hold a congress where new elections are held and fresh faces are introduced.

Each of the fifteen GDR districts has its own DTSB office with about sixty members, all of whom serve on a voluntary basis, while the two hundred and twenty local organizations each have approximately thirty volunteer officials.

There are a handful of full-time DTSB employees and professional coaches within each district and county operation directing the development of sport in their own areas and making sure that everything keeps heading in the general direction set by the National Executive. On an administrative chart it looks like this:

PRESIDIUM

CENTRAL AUDITING COMMISSION	NATIONAL EXECUTIVE	SPORTS FEDERATION PRESIDIUMS
COUNTY AUDITING COMMISSIONS	COUNTY COMMITTEE	COUNTY SPORTS COMMITTEES

DISTRICT AUDITING COMMISSIONS	DISTRICT COMMITTEE	DISTRICT SPORTS COMMITTEES
AUDITING COMMISSIONS OF THE SPORTS CLUBS	SPORTS CLUBS	SECTION LEADERS FOR EACH SPORT

On paper it works. The big difference between the GDR and the rest of the sporting world, however, is the fact that in the GDR it works in practice as well as it does on paper.

The fact that it does is the true miracle of GDR sport. Not the medals, not the world records, not even the world's most impressive mass participation statistics. The simple fact that the bureaucracy is functioning in practice as it was planned on paper.

Some will quickly, and with a degree of historical accuracy, point out that this has always been the case with Germans. As a people steeped in authoritarian upbringing they have always been able to organize things more efficiently than any other people on earth. That has to be a factor, and so does Germany's two-hundred-year-old tradition in the development of gymnastics and the modern concept of exercise. It's much easier to organize something that is traditional in a country than something that is novel.

But in the case of GDR sport it is more than that. I can think of no other governmental system in the world that has ever allowed a bureaucrat to go down the ladder from a ministerial position into the pit of the operational phase, and take much real authority down there with him. That happened because of Ewald's relationship with the highest levels of Party politics. Sport, to be effectively managed, must respond to someone with power at the top.

Baseball's greatest hours came when Judge Kenesaw Mountain Landis was given an authoritative hand after the Black Sox scandal in Chicago. No scandal, no Landis. Indeed the owners have, to their own detriment, made sure there has never been another Landis since.

The National Football League has flourished under Pete Rozelle's control with a lot of central-office authority in league matters. But those are examples from the private sector. Can a Judge Landis or a Pete Rozelle work in a major U.S. umbrella sports setting? My feeling is yes, but only if the need for such action were perceived as a major national political priority.

And things are not that bad yet, the opinions of many amateur athletes in the United States notwithstanding.

5

Leipzig's College of Physical Culture

No country in the world can progress far toward the creation of a top-flight competitive sports system without confronting immediate "chicken and egg" decisions. What comes first, the athletes, the facilities, or the coaches? The profit or the long-term investment? The government or the private sector? Many countries in the world have tried to fit these pieces together with a variety of results.

France has first-rate coaching and excellent facilities, but the lack of a strongly supportive school physical-education feeder system has left them with few top-notch athletes.

Britain, still bound to the nineteenth-century thought of sport as a noble hobby, leads the world in moralizing over the role of sport in society, while its athletes sink deeper and deeper in the world-class rankings. Australia and New Zealand, with the exception of herculean individual efforts, have been following Britain's path.

The United States has both the world's most extensive school sports system and, its first cousin complementing that, a professional-commercial sports system thanks to free enterprise. Although total expenditures have never been recorded, it's a safe bet that total spending of U.S. high school, college, and university sport today dwarfs the expenditure being made by any government-supported sport system in the world. There are literally millions of high school athletes in the United States, primarily in football and basketball, but also in the so-called "minor" sports, which do not create enough revenue to pay their way as spectator sports. These millions of young athletes, and thousands of accompanying paid coaches, form the base of an enormous elite sport pyramid where upward mobility is strictly related to performance on the field. Winning high school coaches become major college coaches. Winning college coaches become professional coaches, and their athletes follow the same progression, with high school stars winning college scholarships and the best of these moving on to the professional ranks, where they can realize the American dream by getting rich quick. The remainder, however, and this list includes those who toil in sports without redeeming commercial value, have been left to fend for themselves, with the predictable result of a comparative decline in U.S. performance in a wide range of international and Olympic sports.

Canada, with a population of twenty-two million (comparable to the GDR's 16.8 million), has a life-style parallel to the United States in most everything except university sports. Canadian institutions of higher learning have steadfastly refused to follow the U.S. example of college sports scholarships, a course of action that they readily defend by citing everything detrimental about commercial college sport and overlooking everything beneficial. They decry the fact that coaches wind up with reputations greater than professors, and cite the evils of high-pressured recruiting aimed at building winning teams, and the compromise of educational standards to help a star athlete stay eligible. They overlook the number of kids who otherwise could not receive an educaton at a good school, the alumni interest in sports and subsequent funding support, and the income from ticket sales that can be directed toward better programs. They also overlook the role of the universities in the national elite sports feeder system: the universities have not only the lion's share of the physical sports facilities, but also are the center for advanced research projects.

All three levels of Canadian Government—federal, provincial, and municipal—do their well-meaning best. But the federal government, though now charged with developing a national plan for sport, has no control over schools and school policy. Education is a provincial responsibility. And the provinces have no direct control over the municipalities, which in turn are burdened with an ice hockey program, which has brought artificial ice surfaces to every town in the country, but which costs more than one billion dollars a year.

Most countries are concerned about their amateur sports malaise today. The United States had the President's Commission on Olympic Sports with its voluminous study of the apparent ills of the system. Canada created its first government sports ministry in 1977. Britain is developing a system of increased private industry sponsorship of top athletes parallel to the Sporthilfe effort of West Germany. Italy has its lottery.

The GDR, meanwhile, keeps on setting world records and winning more Olympic and world championships. They answered their chicken-and-egg dilemma way back in October 1950. The answer was to opt for coaching: trained, professional coaching. Coaches who would go out and find the athletes while getting along with makeshift facilities and equipment until better facilities and equipment could be developed.

They did this by inventing the DHfK—pronounced Day-Hah-ef-Caw in case you are ever giving directions to a Leipzig taxi driver—the *Deutsche Hochschule für Körperkultur,* or the German College of Physical Culture. In less than thirty years it has become the leading sports university in the world, an institution virtually in a class by itself—with all apologies to the Soviet Central State Institute in Moscow—when it comes to the application of science to sport at the high-performance level.

This elevation of coaching to the level of a science has been an alien idea in America, something that goes against the grain of every suburban volunteer who ever donned a cap and a whistle and set out to impart his self-acquired wisdom to generations of Little Leaguers. It's hard for us to imagine people spending four years in a university, let alone three more in a Ph.D. program, with all their efforts directed toward an education in coaching.

But it was an alien idea in the just-born GDR of 1950, too. If the orders hadn't come directly from the Political Bureau of the Party at the national level, it could never have come to pass. And even then, with all the clout of the Political Bureau, the local citizenry still had to be convinced.

Dr. Fritz Jahn, director of the DHfK's department of foreign studies, gets glassy-eyed remembering the early 1950s.

"There was a lot of opposition," he says bluntly. "We went to neighborhood meeting after neighborhood meeting to explain our purposes and positions to people who could not understand the priority for a sports school at a time when our housing needs were so urgent. We kept talking about the future importance of the school vis-à-vis the entire development of the GDR as a country, and they kept talking about housing problems. Still, if we were going to make sports available to the masses, as our first Youth Law decreed, we simply had to have a place to train our coaches and teachers."

And, in addition to the lack of public support and funding in a country still coping with severe economic deprivation, talented teachers were crossing the frontier to western Germany in droves, following the lure of better working conditions and much higher salaries.

The beginnings, then, were modest indeed. The first classes, with two small buildings and one sports hall for a campus, had ninety-six students and a total full-time and part-time faculty of fourteen teachers. Even then the teacher–student ratio was a remarkable seven to one.

That ratio, even with the tremendous expansion of the DHfK in the Sixties, has not changed much. Today there are more than 2,000 students directly involved in Leipzig in a variety of programs under the direction of a faculty in excess of 300. There are eleven sports halls today, enough to take care of the practical side of the training of coaches for every Olympic discipline, plus outdoor 400-meter tartan tracks, an indoor 50-meter Olympic pool and Olympic-sized diving facility, and the magnificent 100,000-seat Leipzig Stadium, home of the Sports Festivals and major international soccer matches. A river, which winds its way directly behind the campus, is used for rowing and canoeing activities, while the legendary research facilities, which are under the budget of the Sports Minister, directly adjoin the DHfK property but are not considered a part of the campus. And all this within a mile of the absolute city center.

How does one explain the phenomenal development of the DHfK from such inauspicious beginnings? The fact is, despite the original public skepticism, it was a perfect time to start a new system—and perhaps the only time. When you are filling a void—very few sports teachers survived the War in any zone of Germany—you can do whatever you wish. Once people are already placed in positions within a system it is difficult, if not impossible, to uproot the system completely.

Those first ninety-six students of the DHfK became the vanguard of today's army of more than 7,000 Leipzig graduates, more than 300 of whom have gone on to pick up doctoral degrees as well. As their numbers grew, these professional coaches provided the framework for the developing new system.

Today it might be an easy matter for any Western country, or even a single U.S. state, to start a sports university with ninety-six students and fourteen teachers. But what would we do with the graduates four years later? Who would offer the jobs in the existing system? What of the threat they would create for job holdings in physical education already psychologically and philosophically tied to the present system? Starting from scratch in 1950, the GDR had none of these problems.

National swim coach Rudi Schramme was in that first graduating class, and so was Dr. Gunther Stiebler, today's rector of the Institute, and his deputy rector, Dr. Hans Georg Hermann. In 1957, after he had become the national sports chief, even Manfred Ewald enrolled as a student and spent four years taking the entire coaching certification course at home, at night, as a correspondence course.

"Without it," he says, "I couldn't function in the way I have functioned as president of the DTSB. How can I make decisions in sport if I don't know as much about it as the coaches, doctors, and researchers I am working with every day?" The answer is that he would have to do it the same way his fellow politicians do it in the West—through the use of batteries of advisers and professional consulting firms. He could call for Congressional hearings and spend half his waking hours in the company of lobbyists building a case for this point or that. He would totally lose personal control of his own bureaucracy and become dependent on others.

Dr. Kurt Tittel is another who was there from the very beginning, but as one of the fourteen teachers, not one of the ninety-six students. Kurt Tittel was a young man twenty-eight years ago, with a lot of "strange" ideas about the teaching of medicine, ideas that were not accepted even by his own colleagues at other schools within the country, ideas as novel and practical as the sports system that now gives them central importance.

Today you can immediately sense the feeling of pride when he gets up from his desk and strides to the bookshelf for a copy of his own text, *Functional Anatomy*, a forbidding and bulky affair of the sort that must fill every first-year premed student with a feeling of foreboding.

"When I first wrote this," he says with a twinkle, "there wasn't a single university outside of the DHfK that would accept it for use on their students. Today it is the accepted text in every anatomy course in the GDR and in Western Germany and in several other European countries as well. In addition, negotiations are underway for an English translation that could be available in the U.S. in a couple of years.

"Most anatomy courses at the university level begin with rote memorization of all the different parts of the body. You see these charts of the human body all marked out, and you spend weeks and weeks memorizing all the different structures. Personally I cannot imagine a more boring approach to the study of anatomy.

"Now," he said, flipping the pages to a diagram of a weightlifter poised with the bar halfway from the floor to a press with the lifter still in a semisquat position, "now tell me what's happening. I don't want my students simply to be able to name the muscle masses here, I want them to be able to tell me of their interactions at this particular moment in this particular exercise. I want them to tell me which muscles are under strain, which are not, which need to be developed, and which do not. Once you start to approach the matter this way, you are turning anatomy from a boring exercise in memorization into a very interesting study. And you are beginning to understand the basic essence of the science of sports medicine.

"Normal medicine is an involvement in the treatment of illness and injury, an attempt to return sick people to full health. Sports medicine is an attempt at reaching an analysis and understanding of the functions of the human body. At first, back in 1950, it was difficult. Even in the GDR such work was not completely understood and accepted. Of course, now all that has changed. Now sports medicine is completely accepted for its central role in our whole sports system."

Although Tittel is basically an anatomy professor and the department head of the Leipzig medical teaching faculty, he may well go down in history as the father of modern sports medicine. The nice thing is, he's still around to say "I told you so" to a lot of people.

The basic job of Tittel and his staff is to teach the elements of sports medicine to every one of the 300 new coaches-to-be who enters the Institute every fall, and to teach the elements of coaching to those who are there working toward careers as medical researchers. The overall idea is not to have coaches coming out of one side of the school and sports medical doctors out of another, but rather to have both coming together at the end in possession of the kind of applied knowledge that will allow them to work together as a team for the future development of elite athletes.

Canada's Dr. Don Johnson, a top orthopedic surgeon and sports doctor who founded the Carleton University Sports Medicine Clinic in Ottawa, just shook his head as he went over the detailed curriculum for the students of coaching when he was in Leipzig in 1977. Dr. Johnson is by no means enamored of all aspects of East European medicine. Walking down the streets of Leipzig, he would seldom manage a block without his trained eye seeing an orthopedic problem in an elderly person.

"It is obvious," he said, "that in this society the money and attention have gone to the youth rather than to the elderly, who are past productive work years. Where we would do a complete hip-joint replacement, they have obviously offered a cane and told their patients to make the best of it. And yet when it comes to sports medicine, the average coach coming out of the Leipzig Institute, and note I am saying coach, not doctor, has a better knowledge of soft tissue medicine and its applied techniques than any trained doctor coming out of a medical school in North America.

"I have tried to put this material into my own lectures at Carleton University, and, frankly, I have been disappointed in the reaction. To be blunt, most of our young medical students are not interested in it, and I suppose that's because there isn't the potential of a lot of money in the field. When it comes to sport, our knowledge of nutrition and soft tissue development is woeful. So much so, I am tempted to suggest we have to get sports medicine out of the hands of doctors."

The setup of the curriculum in Leipzig may be interesting to those wondering how one profitably makes a four-year study out of the art of coaching. The year is divided into eight semesters and the hours are long by North American standards. Except for the last semester at the end of the fourth year, students spend between thirty-seven and forty-four lessons a week in regular class activities, almost 50 percent in the form of applied practical work in gymnasiums or on outdoor sports fields. The curriculum for the direct study program is shown on the following page.

As one can readily see, a considerable amount of time is spent on indoctrination into the political system, a basic understanding of which seems paramount all through the country for major job promotion. But once that's done, little time is wasted getting down to the practicals. The theory would seem to be that if you don't know how to do it yourself you probably won't have much success teaching it. As a result, although a Leipzig coaching graduate might only be able to put a shot 20 feet, or high jump 4½ feet, he or she will be able to do it with Olympic-medal winning form.

I saw an example of this in practice in Dr. Jahn's foreign-student program when I first visited in 1973. This is a GDR foreign-aid program that has brought would-be coaches to Leipzig from all over the emerging Third World for eight months to two years of intensive training. Here the ratio is never higher than four students to a teacher and the GDR picks up the full tab for every student, including travel, meals and lodgings. Within the last year, the time spent in Leipzig has been increased from eight months to a more productive two years at a time. Lessons are taught in English, French, or German, depending on the natural abilities of the students. Currently, the program is only available to governments that make formal arrangements with the GDR Government.

First I watched a volleyball trainer hard at it with two Egyptians, a Guinean and a Congolese. And then we moved on to watch a wrestling coach lecture in Iraqi, a Yemeni and an Indian with the lesson being taught in English. After several minutes of blackboard work, the coach signaled two of the students to the mat to demonstrate the lesson. For ten seconds the two students slithered around the mat like a couple of crabs locked in combat.

"Impossible," said the coach quietly, talking to the man on top. "Look where you are letting him brace his elbow for balance. When he does that you must kick the elbow with your knee and force him to flip over underneath you." A fast knee and a grunt later the coach was proven correct. It had all been explained in the verbal part of the lesson, but the practical demonstration is what the coach-to-be will never forget.

This can be contrasted with North American schools of physical

TYPICAL CURRICULUM AT LEIPZIG INSTITUTE

Study Complexes	I	II	III	IV	V	VI	VII	VIII	Total	
	SEMESTER									
				(Lessons per week)						
1. Fundamentals of Marxism-Leninism	2	3	4	4	3	3	2	4	300	
2. Introduction to logics	3								66	
3. Sports Pedagogy	2	2	2			3	5		104	
4. Sports Psychology	4	4					2		120	
5. Theory and History of Physical Culture					3				57	
6. Sports Policy						2			34	
7. Leadership in Socialist Physical Culture						3	3	6	82	
8. Mathematical and Cybernetical Fundamentals	3	2		2	2				166	
9. Fundamentals of Natural Science	6	3	3						222	
10. Sports Medicine	1				3	3	2		130	
11. Biomechanics				3			2		48	
12. Theory and Methodology of Training in Specific Sports:										
Basic Training	13	15	9	16	7	6	2		1,032 Men 936 Women	
Special Training	2	2	2	2	4	6	8		270	
13. General Theory and Methodology of Training				4	4	3		10	181	
14. Practicals			6	6	6	6	6		324	
15. Training	5	5	5	5	5	5	5		585	
16. Foreign Languages—										
Russian,	2	2	1							
2nd Foreign Language,				2	2	1			85	88
Instruction in speaking (pronunciation, etc.)	1								22	

education where the emphasis is theoretical, a system that produces people with great knowledge, but an inability to impart their knowledge to athletes in the field. Some schools even seem to be developing a mental block with their students on this entire subject. Twice in the last two years I have had students in a university physical education class come up in the question period following a talk on GDR sport and say:

"From what you say the GDR has developed a very intensive coaching development program, but I can't see where that applies to our situation because we, after all, are training to be physical educators."

This is a puzzling attitude. Consider a man like Jim Counsilman of Indiana University, a man recognized as one of the great physical educators in the United States, but also as one of the half-dozen top swim coaches in the world. I am absolutely certain Counsilman has never thought he was demeaning himself when he stepped down from a lectern and onto a pool deck. And yet the concern of the students was real. They don't feel the title of "coach" has sufficient status in the North American context. If these feelings are widespread, the problems we are facing are greater than ever suspected. It brings to mind the oft-quoted saying of Pogo, the swamp-dwelling possum creation of the late cartoonist Walt Kelly: "I have seen the enemy and he is us!"

It is safe to say the students of the DHfK in Leipzig do not have any identity problems about the role they will play in GDR society. But one occasionally wonders what jobs are available for the 300 graduates coming out of the school every spring.

"So far it's not a problem at all," says deputy rector Dr. Hermann. "While it's true we now have more than 7,000 certified professional coaches, we have 10,000 schools and 8,000 workers' sports clubs in addition to our high-performance programs and foreign-aid needs. Right now I would say we have developed about half of the total number of coaches we could employ immediately, and it has taken almost thirty years to do that. I can't see the end of it really, with the likelihood of expansion in our population in the next couple of decades. By the time we have enough to fill our current needs, we will probably need a lot more."

This will be particularly true if they continue to be inundated with requests from foreign countries. Not too many people know, for instance, that Tanzania's great 1,500 meters World record holder Filbert Bayi was developed by a GDR track coach named Werner Kramer. Or that Cuba's Montreal Olympic 400 and 800 meters double gold medal winner, Alberto Juantorena, has a Polish coach.

Leipzig's Dr. Jahn has a few second thoughts on this trend, however. "Our experience has been that it is better to bring coaches from developing countries to Germany and train them here," he says, "rather than send our coaches out to work with them there. Our coaches tend to bring our culture and push it on the country where they are supposedly helping out. Sometimes it works well, but sometimes it does not. I feel it is better to bring their young coaches here for the training, and then send them back home to adapt whatever they can from our system into their own life-style."

The development of Canada's 1976 Olympic team would tend to prove Dr. Jahn correct in his assessment. A battalion of top-flight European coaches poured into Canada in the six years between Montreal's winning the right to stage the Olympic Games and the Games themselves, and many of the coaches left with bitter frustrations at the lack of programmed support for North American sport.

At least one, a Hungarian coach, said he had been admonished by a colleague who, on hearing of the new job in Canada, had said, only half humorously: "To seriously attempt the practice of sports science in North America is to risk death by laughter."

"But in the beginning," says Dr. Tittel, "the laughing was on the other side of the fence. Everybody thought we were humorous, sending young sports medicine doctors along with our teams to collect blood samples and medical data."

But the young Leipzig graduates were not in the least deterred by the laughter of others, any more than the Wright brothers were deterred by suggestions that flight was impossible. They were into something new and they were intrigued by the possibilities.

Journalist Klaus Huhn cites the story of the 1954 European Nordic ski championships in Sweden.

"It was the first time the GDR had ever competed in the world ski championships," he recalls, "and we had a terrible trip home with our ship locked in the ice and unable to get into the harbor at Sassnitz. There was a train car waiting on a siding, though, and thankfully the conductor had gone the rounds of the local factories to collect enough coal to keep the car warm for the skiers. They were some skiers. In the jumping competition our two athletes had finished in the 50th and 69th places.

"When everyone finally arrived and climbed into a thankfully warm car, the coaches gathered in the middle and one of them opened that day's copy of a Swedish newspaper from Falun. The paper had a cartoon of a group of finish-line judges sitting around a fire in the moonlight looking as if they were freezing to death. The cartoon caption said: 'Waiting for the East German women's relay!' "

"That is about what everyone thought of our efforts in those days," says Dr. Tittel. "There are no accusations of medical miracles when you are not winning, just cartoons and behind-the-back laughing."

"But," says Huhn, "there was one of our new coaches on that train home from Falun who was not deterred by the lack of success. His message to the other coaches was clear as regards ski jumping. 'What we have to do,' he said, 'is find a substitute for snow so that we can train better and longer.' Even his fellow coaches were laughing at this suggestion. What a fantasy!

"Still, when Hans Renner returned home he went to work on the problem. He and other experts in the field tried to find a substitute. They consulted ex-champion Erich Recknagel, who had jumped 22 meters on fir needles in Berlin in the 1930s. They were going nowhere.

"Finally Renner had reached the point where he was examining sheets of polyvinylchloride for possible use, and threw them out into the garden when they didn't work. In the morning he got up and found them wet with dew, a condition that had the sheets showing just the characteristics he had been looking for. To achieve best results the sheets were processed into strong PVC fibers, which, bundled into mats, turned out to be the ideal snow substitute. The world's first-ever competition on these mats took place on September 26, 1955.

"One year later in the Cortina Olympics of 1956 young Harry Glass surprised us all by winning the bronze medal in the Games. Afterwards a Finnish journalist came up to him and asked him why he hadn't been competing in Falun in the world championships of 1954.

" 'But I was,' Glass replied with some surprise, 'I finished in the 69th place.' "

This was the beginning of the era of Glass, Werner Lesser, and Helmut Recknagel, the first three musketeers of GDR ski jumping.

When Recknagel won the Olympic gold medal in Squaw Valley in 1960, a few people had to stop laughing. Suddenly GDR medical research teams in their little white smocks following athletes through training sessions didn't look quite so strange anymore. And nobody was waiting around at the finish line either.

At least not for the GDR.

6

A Man Called Smith

Although there were no serious attempts at high-level competition in the immediate postwar years in Germany, the training did go on, and when it became obvious in the course of 1949 that the GDR was on the verge of declaring itself an independent country, the first international sports invitation came by telegram. The Eastern Zone of Germany had been formally invited to send a team to compete in Hungary's Communist-sponsored Budapest World Youth Festival in August of '49. The news, according to those who can still remember it well, was electrifying. No one had expected such an early international invitation.

Football coaches came together to cooperate in the formation of their first "national" team. Runners increased laps in training. Boxers bashed each other all around the ring in an attempt to qualify. And the veterans who had competed in the Olympic Games before the War tried to tell the youngsters how tough the competition really was at the international level.

The first problem was logistical. How would they get the team to Budapest? There were so few intact railway coaches, even four years after the War, that they would have had to paralyze all rail traffic between Berlin and Dresden in order to have enough cars for one Festival Train to Budapest. Since that was unthinkable, a horde of

FDJ (Free German Youth) volunteers set to work repairing bombed-out cars that had been deteriorating on sidings since the end of the War. It took a lot of time, but finally the Festival Train rose like a phoenix from the ashes of World War II.

"For entertainment," Klaus Huhn recalls, "we hooked up a record player with a speaker system and piled stacks of records in the luggage compartment. That was not such a well-thought-out move. With the first lurch of the train as we pulled out of the Ostbahnhof station in Berlin, the records came tumbling down out of the racks and all but one were smashed. We spent the entire journey playing the Russian revolutionary song 'Sailors of Kronstadt' over and over again. The tune must still be imprinted on every mind."

Nor will they forget their arrival in Budapest, and the thrill of sitting down to breakfast and eating the first white bread any one of them had seen since the end of the War.

"Since before the War, really," says Huhn. "Rolls as big as your hand. I hadn't seen one for more than ten years."

Then the troubles began. Even though this was a Communist Youth Festival, the international sports federations had to give sanctions to the competitions. None of these federations recognized the East Zone Germans as members, and it was ruled that they were ineligible. For a couple of days the athletes wandered around the Peoples' Park aspect of the Festival, entering impromptu competitions for Festival fitness badges being offered to mass sport enthusiasts. Then, finally, a bit of good news. The Hungarians decided they would hold a Germany–Hungary dual meet behind closed doors, well away from the eyes of the International Amateur Athletic Federation, with all gates closed and no spectators permitted. It wouldn't be a meet in a formal sense, just a practice session.

The shame of it was that a young shot putter named Ernst Schmidt broke the national record in the meet with a toss of 13.35 meters. That was modest by today's standards, but electrifying news for the state of GDR athletics in 1949. Even though the result couldn't count officially, Schmidt, whose last name translates to Smith, picked up the nickname "Shotsmith" in the Berlin papers.

Two years later, during early preparations for the Helsinki Olympics of 1952, Schmidt had upped his performance beyond the 15-meter mark to rank as one of the top contenders in the world. The problem, once again, was that although West Germany would have a team in the Helsinki Games, the GDR still lacked a National Olympic Committee and would not have one.

The West Germans, at this point, made a special offer to all top GDR athletes saying that any who came over to the Western side would be eligible for places on their Helsinki team, a chance to put politics aside and bring glory to themselves and the German Olympic team. Schmidt's reply was that as a citizen of the GDR he could not possibly accept an invitation to compete for anyone else's team in the Olympic Games. The West Berlin newspapers immediately changed his nickname. Then, in the early McCarthy days in America and with an escalating Cold War atmosphere everywhere, he became known as "Redsmith."

Ernst Schmidt, from his lofty position as GDR national throwing events coach, can laugh at all this today, but at the time it must have cut him to the quick. There isn't an athlete in the world who doesn't dream of the possibility of competing in the Olympic Games.

One day in 1954, Schmidt, now a proud new father, was pushing a pram down a Berlin street when he crossed the path of Huhn, the sportswriter.

"He had accepted the fact," says Klaus, "that he would never compete in the Olympic Games because of the political situation. But he told me that without a shadow of a doubt, the passage of twenty years' time would solve the political problems in time for the little boy in the baby carriage to grow up and compete for the GDR in the Olympics."

Normally, that would be the end of this story. After all, what father, particularly one who is a top-flight athlete, doesn't dream of the possible prowess of his first-born son?

Well, in this case the baby won the silver medal in the discus throw in the Montreal Olympics! Thirteen months later, in track and field's first-ever World Cup in Düsseldorf, Wolfgang Schmidt reversed the defeat he suffered in Montreal at the hands of Portland, Oregon's world-record holder, Mac Wilkins, and won the gold.

The story behind the Wilkins–Schmidt Montreal medals had to be the most misunderstood human-interest story of the entire Games.

It had been an interesting year for the discus. Early on, it looked like John Powell, the hulking policeman from San Jose who held the world record of 69.08 meters, would be the morning line favorite to win the gold medal for the United States. And then, suddenly, it was

Mac Wilkins breaking the world record. Then doing it again and again, a bearded giant who had come from well down the list to astonish every track and field statistician in the world. Geoff Capes, Britain's huge shot put champion, had seen it coming in training sessions, but when he returned to Europe and told everyone about Wilkins, no one initially believed it possible.

By the Olympics, they were all believers. On the second throw of the competition, Big Mac lofted the discus out 67.50 meters, a hell of an effort considering Montreal's Olympic Stadium is totally roofed-in, without the natural breezes that can carry a discus those few precious record-setting feet farther. It was the gold medal throw. Powell, on his third attempt, got it out 65.70 meters and seemed to have wrapped up the silver. Schmidt, who was struggling right from the beginning, went into the last round in fourth place with a best throw of 65.16 meters.

Then, on the last throw, when the pressure couldn't have been greater, he finally got his spin together and hurled the implement exactly 66.22 meters from the front edge of the circle. It was a little like hitting a bases-loaded home run in the last of the ninth to claim the winning seventh game of the World Series.

Not surprisingly, Schmidt, who might be the most perfectly proportioned man in the history of throwing events, was excited. But before he could make more than a single bound of joy, here was Wilkins, up off the competitor's bench to scoop him up in a giant bearhug. A GDR athlete had just taken a silver medal away from an American, and here was another American waltzing him around the infield in a victory dance.

The U.S. press corps was speechless. The medal winners came off the field and into the interview room and then a flood of questions poured forth. Some were antagonistic, to put it mildly. As a result, Wilkins got his back up. Seven months later, during the indoor season, he sat down and told his side of the whole affair.

"It started earlier in a meet in Cologne," says Wilkins. "I have always respected Schmidt as an athlete, and, in fact, I consider him to be the one discus thrower in the world who is capable of beating me when I'm having a good day, particularly when we are in an enclosed stadium with no wind. He has the power needed to be the best in the world in a windless situation.

"We sat down to try to have a discussion over a beer, something that proved a little difficult because of the language barrier. He surprised me by asking how I could stand to live in a country like the United States. He spoke of crime in the streets, the labor problems, the unemployment, the social injustice, everything, I suppose, that people in his country hear about people in our country.

"From there we went on to talk sports and training, and the more we got into it, the more I realized that I really liked this guy. We had a lot in common, which is something that has always been a problem between myself and John Powell. Let's face it, I am a basic liberal young schoolteacher, and John Powell is a typical police officer. We don't hate each other, but we don't have very much in common either. Not much to talk about.

"Then, when our paths crossed in the Olympic Village in Montreal, Schmidt and I sat down to talk again, and he seemed to be having second thoughts about some of the things he had said the first time around. The GDR team had been training at Laurentian University of Sudbury, Ontario, for a week before coming on to the Olympic Village, and Schmidt had now decided North America wasn't half so bad as he first thought it was. He asked me what it was like in my town of Portland, and I told him I thought he'd prefer it to a mining town like Sudbury, Ontario. He then wondered if his sports federation would consider letting him come over for a few months to train with us in California, and I said the invitation would be open any time he could arrange it.

"And that's the frame of mind we were in at the time of the competition. Two friends struggling for one gold medal. I wasn't thinking about nationalities at all. My feeling is that the Olympic Games are something special. It's the one competition the public remembers. They remember Olympic gold medal winners long after they forget world-record holders. In the Olympics, I like to see people come up with their best.

"In my case, I knew I was the best in 1976. But Schmidt was the second best, as I said, the only guy I was afraid of and I was suffering right along with him when I could see he was having a difficult day. When he finally got off the big throw, I was happy for him, not because he is a German, but as a friend and fellow competitor.

"Since those really were my motives, I was surprised when I came off the field and faced the hate and hostility of the American reporters. Are these the same people who complain of excessive nationalism in the Olympics? Are these the people who keep writing stories about how politics and sport should be kept separate?

"I'll admit I did say I would be happy if I won my gold medal and the GDR won all the rest of the gold medals, but I said that for a purpose, too. I know, from Schmidt and the others, quite a bit about the way the sports system functions in that country. And I know even more about the way it functions in my country. I did not win an Olympic gold medal because of the sports system in effect in the United States; I won the gold medal in spite of it. Perhaps that's my nature, too.

"But how about my responsibility as a schoolteacher? I look at my young students coming up, and I look at our system, and I wonder how on earth they are ever going to be competitive in ten and fifteen and twenty years' time. As an American schoolteacher, nobody pays any attention at all when I speak out against the system. But during the Olympics, when I'm an Olympic gold medal winner and the media is all over the place, they have to listen to it.

"I'm just sorry so many Americans took the message the wrong way. I lost a lot of respect for the media in general the day I won my gold medal, but, in spite of that, not one individual has ever come up to me face to face to complain."

Wilkins looked astonished when I broke out laughing at that comment. Not too many Americans, I pointed out, are in the habit of ticking off bearded two-hundred-fifty-five-pound giants who win gold medals in Olympic-strength events!

"Good God," he said, "I am not violent. I have never fought with anybody."

For his part of it, Wolfgang Schmidt would like everyone to know, here and now, that he is not considering a political defection to the United States.

"What Wilkins says is true," he says. "We did meet in Cologne and talk of all those things, and we met again in Montreal and spoke of those things, but I could never support the United States political positions, particularly in the context of the Vietnam experience."

If he had said anything less, old Redsmith would have his head. Still, Schmidt admits he did have quite a time of it in Sudbury. The good news was that the town was pleasant, the facilities were excellent, and an admiring local girl increased his knowledge of the English language by at least 50 percent in six days. The bad news was

an attack of dysentery that kept him on the run for six nights. "By the
time we got to the Olympic Village in Montreal, the team doctors had
it under control," he says, "but I'm sure it had a negative effect on my
performance."

There are a lot of things about Schmidt the athlete that are out of
the ordinary.

Bruce Ogilvie and Thomas Tutko, the famed California-based sport
psychologists *(Problem Athletes and How to Handle Them.* Tafnews
Press, Los Altos, Ca.), can go on and on about the problems of
aspiring athletes crumbling under the pressure of parents who expect
more than their children are able to give. Behind every major leaguer
who turns away from a manager's glance down the bench for a pinch
hitter in the ninth, they say we can expect to find a father who put
undue pressure on a Little League star. Indeed, in the Montreal
Olympics when Hungary's Miklos Nemeth drilled the javelin to a new
world record of 94.58 meters exactly twenty-eight years after his father
Imre had won the hammer throw in London in 1948, there was a
huge sigh of relief expressed in the interview room. "Now," Nemeth
said with a deep tone of satisfaction, "maybe people will accept me for
myself rather than constantly describing me as the son of my father."

That is not the way it is with Wolfgang Schmidt. When the
youngster was first invited to join the Dynamo Berlin Club in 1966 as
a fourteen year old, "dad" was coaching an international shot putting
sweep at the European championships in Budapest and picking up a
new media nickname—"Medalsmith." As GDR weight-event performances have continued right on into the 1970s, he's even improved
on that. He is now known as "Goldmedalsmith." Wolfgang, with his
silver medal from Montreal, has finally started down the media road
himself. Now he's the one they call "Shotsmith." And he revels in it.
All of it.

"I prefer to compete with my father present," he says, "it gives me
an added incentive to do well. I love the biggest and most important
meets, particularly the ones with television. When the tension is there
for me, the performance is there, too.

"I know a lot of weight-event men like to get off their best
performance with the opening throw when they are strongest, but I
like to play it safe with the first one, and make it just good enough to
be sure of getting into the final rounds. Then I like to build my
performance as the competition continues. But I do hate to lose. In

Montreal, Wilkins was the best, no question about it. He deserved the gold medal. When I came into that competition, since it was my first Olympic-Games competition, my hope was to win some kind of a medal. Certainly I had some thought for the gold, but, really, when I look back at all the factors—the sickness, the time change, the noise and crowded conditions of the Olympic Village—I am satisfied with the silver. It was a good competition for me."

Schmidt says he will certainly continue to throw the discus through to the Moscow Games of 1980, but after that he is not sure. "There are many possibilities," he says, "for a permanent job in sport in this country, as a coach, a functionary, a teacher, many things. Or, since I am now a member of the Dynamo (police-financed) sports organization, I may very well end up being a policeman."

Mac Wilkins will be disappointed to hear that.

7

Roots

Without the aid of Horst Schiefelbein this book would have been a lot stronger on ski jumping than on historical perspective.

We first crossed paths in mid-January 1977, in the tiny mountain town of Laucha, a midweek stop on the annual East European Friendship ski jumping competition. Our group—consisting of myself, driver Dieter Maschke, interpreter Regina Krombholz, DTSB head office official Gitta Mueller, and DTSB local boss Joachim Oeler—had come directly from lunch to the middle of the competition and found our way into the athlete-press area where introductions were politely exchanged all 'round.

The scene epitomized the advantages and disadvantages every Western reporter encounters when conducting investigative work in East European countries. On the one hand, the organization is splendid, the hospitality marvelous, and the friendliness self-evident and sincere. On the other hand, from the perspective of the interviewee, the situation can be totally overwhelming.

Just imagine a foreign reporter coming to visit the Miami Dolphins in the early Seventies when they were a Miracle Machine, and sitting down to talk with Larry Csonka, Jim Kiick, or Paul Warfield in the presence of an interpreter, a tape recorder, Coach Don Shula, the Mayor of Miami, and a representative of Pete Rozelle's office.

What if, right out of the blue, the reporter asked the player if there was any truth to the rumor he was considering jumping to the World Football League? You think the player wouldn't have been as nervous and intimidated as I could see Wolfgang Schmidt was when we began discussing his private conversations with Mac Wilkins? You think the player wouldn't feel intimidated? Of course he would. Anyone would. And it proves a continual frustration to North American reporters who are used to slipping off to a bar with an athlete for a quiet evening's open-ended discussion.

As a result, one can often learn more in East Europe by shutting up and observing the general goings-on. Just watch carefully for the little things. Sometimes one small phrase, or even a wink, can carry more meaning than an hour's worth of taped interview.

On this day, for instance, former ski star Manfred Wolf was on the scene in his new duty as *Gruppenleiter, VEB Sportgeratewerk Schmalkalden*. The translation of that means he's the man responsible for relations between Germina skis—the label for domestic products turned out by the People's Sports Equipment Factory in nearby Schmalkalden—and the elite international athletes.

You don't have to ask. You can see the pride as he directs his platoon of equipment mechanics checking harnesses, waxing, and whatnot; the same men who sent chills up the spines of the great Austrian ski manufacturers when Hans-Georg Aschenbach won the Innsbruck gold on GDR-produced skis.

"Everyone wants Germina skis," says Wolf with a smile, "but they aren't going to get them. Our label isn't for export"—and now comes the wink—"at present."

The sports-equipment development work going on in Schmalkalden and other GDR locations could be the tip of an incredible iceberg, international tariff laws willing. As the GDR economy improves, permitting the acquisition of better equipment for what, by Western salary standards, has to be the cheapest high-quality craft labor market anywhere in the world, there is no reason why the GDR cannot unnerve every Western sports-manufacturing concern from gigantic Adidas on down.

In actual fact, they probably won't take that course at all, but will simply continue to subcontract work for Western concerns, giving the Western companies high-quality components at a low cost in exchange for desperately needed hard currency. This is one of the ways in which the GDR investment in sports excellence is already starting to pay dividends at the political level.

You could see all of that on a January afternoon in Laucha while watching Wolf and his men move among the top ski jumpers of the GDR, Poland, Czechoslovakia, and the Soviet Union. But you wouldn't have had it explained by asking probing Western journalistic questions. What you do is save the observation for another day at another time, when you meet someone knowledgeable in GDR sport and actually find yourself sitting across from each other at a table, sharing a beer or two. Then it might be a different matter.

Which is why, after an hour of ski jump viewing, I quickly accepted Schiefelbein's invitation to a journalist-to-journalist early-morning cup of coffee. This meeting couldn't have been more opportune, since, although I had a general idea what I was trying to do in researching this book, I was short on specifics of what, where, when, why, and how.

Schiefelbein sat and listened patiently, with only a few incredulous blinks of surprise, while I outlined the aspirations of the project.

"Why have you got three days of ski jumping on your itinerary?" he finally asked.

"Well," I explained, "the DTSB thought it would be a chance to meet athletes and see international competition in progress within the GDR."

"You'd get more for the book," he suggested, "by going over to Schnepfenthal and seeing the GutsMuths museum. It's no more than a thirty- to forty-minute drive from here, and without it I don't know how you'll ever understand the traditional background of sport in this country."

It seemed a first-class idea.

To Regina, the interpreter, it seemed dubious. Regina, and all other interpreters assigned throughout the research, had the ability to say nothing while taking on the countenance of a sad basset hound whenever there was a hint of a change in the preplanned schedule.

This is another important lesson of journalism in the GDR. It isn't that changes in the schedule aren't possible. In fact, as I said before, the GDR sports officials were more than eager to cooperate with every phase of this project as long as it didn't infringe on the territory of other government departments, military matters, or areas of restricted research, particularly in the sports medicine field. It was just that no changes were possible without permission from on high. That meant phoning Berlin and tracking down a boss of the DTSB, who would often be in a meeting or otherwise unavailable, before proceeding on the new course.

"Schnepfenthal?" asked Regina, who obviously wasn't that up to date on her GutsMuths.

"Schnepfenthal?" asked Dieter, the driver, reaching for the People's Road Map that sits under the dash of all State cars. "It's not even on my map!"

"It's supposed to be about two-thirds of the way between here and Eisenach," I answered knowingly, "and, in fact, it has been suggested that the Wartburg Castle in Eisenach might be the place to stop for lunch after we finish up at the museum."

Regina finally acquiesced, although I am still not sure whether this was because Berlin was in accord, or the more basic fact that her boots were not designed for snowbanks and ski jumping.

Getting there proved much easier said than done. For starters, a pea-soup fog had blanketed the GDR winter sports capital of Oberhof that morning, a condition that seemed to afflict the area for at least part of the day, almost every day.

Dieter, overnight, had learned that if we proceeded out of town in a north-by-northeast direction we couldn't miss Schnepfenthal. With that information in hand, we three—driver, writer and interpreter— headed off cautiously with varying degrees of confidence.

What an adventure! Schnepfenthal was not only off Dieter's map, it was off all the area road signs, and a blank in the minds of most passers-by we stopped along the road. Asking directions in Germany, even for those who speak German, can be a trying experience amidst clashing area dialects. "Did he know the way?" Regina asked once as Dieter returned to the car after speaking with an aging pedestrian. "Possibly," came the answer, "but I didn't understand a word he said."

German Autobahns, West or East, are excellent four-lane divided highways, certainly among the best high-speed roads in Europe. But once you get off the beaten track, GDR back roads are all first cousins of the Yellow Brick Road in the Wizard of Oz. They wind, and twist, and turn, and every few kilometers you come to a fork with a couple of directional arrows, neither of which make mention of the place you are seeking.

It isn't just Schnepfenthal, either. This exercise was to repeat itself six months later when I went with another driver–interpreter team to find the final resting place and museum of Ludwig Jahn, the father of modern gymnastics, in Freyburg.

"What now?" Dieter asked in despair as we reached yet another foggy fork in the road.

We turned to the right and soon came across a man who beamed an ear-to-ear smile and said, of course, he knew where Schnepfenthal was. It was "just two kilometers ahead, straight down the road. Keep going and you'll run right into it."

Not a quarter of a mile farther on, there we were facing yet another fork in the road without a road sign! Not a hint. By now I was convinced it is a Russian military master plan. If there's ever another conventional war in Germany, the Western armies have no chance. They will be constantly lost.

Once again we took the right fork, traveled five kilometers, gave it up, came back to the intersection, turned left, and drove down a hill and around a bend right into downtown Schnepfenthal.

"GutsMuths?" we asked the first available pedestrian.

"Yes, certainly," he answered, "turn right at the corner, drive to the top of the hill, turn left a hundred yards and you're there."

"There" turned out to be a building that appeared to be a German version of an English pub, with a place to eat, a place to drink, and perhaps even a place to stay. It didn't look at all like a sports museum.

"It's around the back," someone said with a wave of the hand, sending us off down the lane behind the building where we came to "it."

At first I didn't know what "it" was, as I looked at a collection of primitive, playground-styled equipment, obviously centuries old, protected by a small fence with a GutsMuths memorial plaque. Then slowly, and with delight in sensing something unexpected and worthwhile, the realization started to sink in. Without risk of too much exaggeration, one could say that Regina and Dieter and I were at that very moment staring at the nativity scene of modern physical education.

Though Jahn gets the credit for the development of gymnastics as a sport in the early years of the nineteenth century, the most extensive early attempt to put the idea into practice took place here in Schnepfenthal under the hand of Johann Friedrich GutsMuths in

1793. He, in turn, owes his inspiration to Johann Basedow and the Dessau Philanthropinium.

GutsMuths was a teacher in the Schnepfenthal school, a building that, amazingly enough, stands today much as it did in the eighteenth century, and he was appalled by the class system of education prevalent in the Germany of the late 1700s. So appalled, in fact, that he sat down and wrote a treatise called *Some Thoughts on Education* published in 1793.

Education, he figured, taking up an argument that is used even today, had to be physical as well as mental. Book studies and the development of the mind were not enough, there had to be a physical balance. What's more, since he had the power of a school in which to do it, he would do it. The students of Schnepfenthal would pursue the ideal of a sound mind in a sound body.

"Turn" is the German word for it, and as the idea of GutsMuths and the work of Jahn spread through the land, the German Turner Society was on its way to becoming not only a major power in the development of sports federations, but a major one in the development of German military nationalism as well. Today, the "T" in the "DTSB" stands for "Turn." Although England can rightly take its historical place as the birthplace of modern games, with the genesis of football (soccer), rowing, track and field, horse racing's Derby, and more, Germany deserves credit as the birthplace of modern organized exercise.

As another matter of historical fact, it was Baron Pierre de Coubertin's envy of the military might of England and Germany— which he credited to England's sporting and scholastic traditions of Eton and Harrow, Oxford and Cambridge, and Germany's national devotion to fitness and exercise—that directly led to the baron's plan for the re-creation of the modern Olympic Games in 1896.

If only the French, de Coubertin thought, would turn to exercise and sport, their military humiliations would come to an end. The French educational system, alas, thought de Coubertin daft—and quite probably GutsMuths, too. Education to them is a matter of the development of the mental processes. Later, when he saw his Olympic idea becoming a booming international success that was never fully accepted in France, de Coubertin shifted over to Switzerland and ran his International Olympic Committee from Lausanne.

I was still standing there daydreaming, and pinching myself at this unexpected stroke of historical luck, when Regina returned with the information that this was not the museum at all. The museum was back down the road on the other side of the town in the school.

It proved to be a total joy. Although the ancient school, now a twelve-year comprehensive university prep school for students from all the surrounding area, was in session, the principal assigned a couple of teenagers from a study period to show us the rounds.

The life of GutsMuths and the history of the school were delightfully presented in several small rooms. There were paintings of life in the 1790s, explanations, art work, old school uniforms, diagrams of the early gymnastics equipment, all tastefully presented and laid out.

For the better part of an hour we puttered around these schoolrooms, engrossed in their offerings. For the sports enthusiast, the feeling generated here is not unlike that followers of various religions must get when they visit the Holy Land.

Just think of the institutions that have come out of these ideas of Basedow, GutsMuths and Jahn, and those who came in their wake. The military were certainly among the first disciples. There may be an argument about whether an education should aim for a sound body as well as a sound mind, but there can be no question that a sound body goes a long way toward the creation of a solid soldier.

When the Nazis first made their move toward power and the formation of a government in the early 1930s, the first large, meaningful, national organization to offer its support was the German Gymnastics Union—the Turners. And Hitler was more than quick to play up to them with a national slogan of "Let's Get Back to Jahn."

But if the Turners thought they were going to stay above the political upheaval with their support of the National Socialist Party, they were sadly mistaken. In short order, their officers were pushed aside, forced to resign, and forgotten as Hitler moved his own ideologues into power in an incredibly successful bid to turn the whole sports establishment to the job of developing a new army. The fact that the IOC had already granted the 1936 Olympic Games to Berlin played right into his hands on this score, setting the stage for a total national effort at fitness to give the Fatherland respectable representation in the Games.

Sport offered the perfect cover for the creation of a fit military machine, one that had to be built during the years when the Treaty of Versailles barred Germany from embarking on overt military preparations. Back to Jahn indeed!

8

The DTSB
and Mass Sport

There are more than 8,000 mass-level recreational sports clubs in the German Democratic Republic and I have visited two of them. So, while not quite an expert on the subject, I did, nevertheless, get a feeling for what goes on.

On my first night in Berlin, in October of 1973, I headed off through the fog in search of the Empor Brandenburg Tor, a sports club in the downtown core of Berlin.

An idle passer-by could walk past this building a hundred times without ever guessing its function. It was once a bombed-out brewery, but it was rebuilt after the War as a neighborhood recreational facility, something along the lines of our YMCAs. The main difference between the GDR Empor and a "Y" is that dozens of trained volunteer coaches and officials work in each of the ten or so sports offered by the club.

They had bowling, gymnastics, basketball, badminton, team handball, volleyball, indoor soccer and a small training track. There was a hall for boxing, another for weightlifting, a perfectly shadowless billiard room for older men, and a basement that was half bowling alley and half beer hall where most of the 2,240 members, all of whom live within walking distance of the facility, could go for a cold one, a sausage and a quiet time with friends after their sport. Some might prefer a table in the corner for a quiet game of cards or chess.

On this particular foggy Tuesday evening in October, more than 700 of the members were on hand, many entire families with parents in keep-fit courses and kids involved in age-group team sports. All met at the end of the evening, in the basement.

"How many clubs are there like this in Berlin?" I asked, thinking ten at most, maybe less.

"I'm not sure," said Wolfgang Gitter, my National Olympic Committee host, "but I would guess there might be fifty."

Fifty!

Imagine taking the New York Athletic Club out of its Central Park setting, eliminating all the pomp and ceremony that goes with our most elite private clubs, and setting it down in the Bronx, or Harlem, or Bedford Stuyvesant. How, one wonders, can any municipal recreation system afford such an effort? The answer, of course, is that none can, not in any country in the world. It can only become possible through an incredible amount of voluntary cooperation from the membership itself.

"The DTSB is responsible for the training of coaches and the provision of officials," Gitter explained, "but beyond that the members have to do everything for themselves. The government provides the land and the building, and removes the structure from the tax roll. What's more, when expansion is deemed desirable, the government will provide all the raw materials, but the clubs' members have to provide all the labor themselves.

"The feeling is that any club with around 2,000 members such as this one must have enough skilled workmen within its membership to do the physical work involved. These people in this club completely rebuilt one bombed-out wall and then roofed it over to create their own basketball hall. They had enough construction workers within the membership to get it done working only on weekends."

Hearing a story like that, you begin to understand the pride a worker takes in his factory or neighborhood sports club. In a war-ravaged city rebuilt so that almost everyone lives in apartments rather than private homes, what could be better than these sport clubs as a means of providing a safety valve for the release of urban pressures? It is certainly a step up from the corner lot basketball and stickball games of New York's inner-city environment.

Seeing all this, one begins to reflect on urbanization's slow, subtle destruction of collective pride in the democratic West, without our realizing it. We paid for our lack of insight with the urban violence that swept through the United States in the last half of the Sixties. Could a hundredfold increase in expenditure for inner-city sports development have possibly prevented it? It's something to think about.

By the time I got to my second GDR mass sports club, early in 1977, I was much better prepared, with questions to be aimed at a table full of hosts in the forest-surrounded clubhouse of the Factory Sports Club of the Leipzig Transport Union. By this time, the DTSB had been able to provide statistics on their national facilities, plus a breakdown of subtotals for their memberships.

Going into 1977, the DTSB had 2,690,701 active members on their rolls, accounting for 16 percent of the population. They had 8,114 enterprise sports clubs, 158,926 certified volunteer coaches, and 99,915 certified referees and officials.

Facilities tell an interesting story. At the end of 1976 they had:

Sports stadiums	319
Sports grounds	1,130
Sports grounds without running tracks	9,251
Covered stadiums	17
Sports halls with spectator seating	169
Sports halls without spectator seating	2,148
Swimming Facilities	
50-meter covered swim halls	19
25-meter public swim halls	80
50-meter swim stadiums with seats	23
50-meter open-air swimming pools	501
25-meter open-air swimming pools	156
Winter Sport Facilities	
Ski jumps 90 meters and larger	2
70-meter ski jumps	14
Middle-sized ski jumps	110
Small ski jumps for beginners	200

Artificial ice surfaces	14
Natural ice rinks	516
Small natural luge courses	120
International-class luge and two-man bobsled courses	2

Water Sports Facilities

Boat houses	455
Rowing and sailing courses	67
Yacht racing areas	18

Other

Bowling for competition	1,516
Bowling for recreation	1,218
Tennis courts	1,173
Cycling tracks	15

On the one hand that list includes a lot of facilities, particularly when talking about Olympic-sized swimming pools, ski jumps, luge courses and rowing layouts. With more than one thousand 400-meter running tracks they are well situated for track and field.

But there aren't many covered sport halls, stadiums with seating, or tennis courts, and a ridiculously small number of artificial ice rinks when you consider that their elite figure skaters have at least matched the North Americans while their national ice hockey team is playing at the same level as the best the United States can put on the ice. There are only two artificial ice surfaces devoted to ice hockey in the entire GDR.

The trouble here is that statistics never really tell the story. It's not a question of how many facilities any country has; it's a question of utilization. How many times have we in North America seen a jogging track empty, or an entire basketball court being used by two players in a lonely game of one-on-one? How many times have you seen an empty municipal recreation park, or one occupied by just a few kids on swings and teeter-totters?

In East Berlin, the neighborhood parks are jammed. Virtually all the women must work because salaries are generally low, and children are either placed in day-care centers from the age of three months on or they are cared for by grandmothers, who flock to the parks during the day and settle into the clubhouses to chat and play cards while park workers supervise the kids on the playground equipment.

Some of the parks have intriguing fitness-oriented games on hand, the sort of things that just beg you to climb up and give it a try. Can you touch your toes, for instance? If you can, all well and good, but in Berlin they have a platform with a measuring device built on the front edge so you can see exactly how far you can reach below your toes!

Another park I walked through had a basket full of balls and a tall hollow cylinder that could be regulated in height so one could just barely reach up on tippy toes and drop a ball into the funnel. The object of the exercise is to see how many times you can stoop over, pick up a ball, reach to full extension, and drop it into the funnel within a given time limit. To do it properly, you use every stretching muscle in your body, a great way to develop flexibility. And you have fun while you are doing it, unlike the rigors of most exercise plans. They have bowling lanes that can be rolled out in park settings, and then rolled right back up again when you are done. They have full-sized chess games with pieces three feet high, forcing the players to get up and walk all over the board while playing a game. They have concrete open-air table-tennis tables in many parks; all you have to do is go to the park office and pick up the nets and paddles.

And they have volleyball courts everywhere, even in the courtyards of the high-rise apartment buildings. Amazingly enough, where North Americans have a tough time getting a foursome together for doubles tennis, East Berliners seem to have less of a problem getting twelve people together for a volleyball game in a housing project. The advantage for community involvement is that volleyball can be played at any skill level and involves twelve people using an area that would be used by only two or four in tennis. When you see this while walking around any GDR city, town or village, then you see that there is a lot of recreational sport activity going on outside the bounds of the DTSB.

Indeed, the Ernst Thälmann Young Pioneer Clubs and the Free German Youth Organization promote sports, tourism, and hiking within their programs while the Society for Sport and Technology (GST) takes care of such sports as shooting, deep-sea diving and sports parachuting, activities that fall outside the organizational mandate of the DTSB.

But then, of course, we have sport within the school system. This is the most important difference between mass sport in the GDR and North America. Whereas, in our system, the school plays the central role in the development of youth sport through school teams in football, basketball, baseball, track, and more, the GDR has none of that. Or rather almost none. There are some school sports clubs, many of which take out affiliated memberships with the DTSB, but they are not really strongly encouraged. Within the GDR sports system organized team and individual sport is left pretty much to the DTSB sport clubs.

The role of the school is to promote physical education in three fundamental areas. Every student within the regular school system works on gymnastics, swimming, and track and field, from kindergarten on, with two or three required hours of study per week. The thinking here is that children need gymnastics for basic body control, and swimming and running for cardiovascular development, and these are the needs of everyone, not just the athletically gifted. Therefore everyone has to reach basic levels of competence—barring a medical excuse—by the age of ten. If they have not managed such things as learning to swim by that age they are placed in remedial courses until they do manage it, just as would happen in mathematics, language, or any other course in any other educational system. Thus, the school physical-education teacher, rather than being a football or basketball coach who dabbles in physical education on the side, is an expert in teaching the basics of running, swimming and gymnastics. And whenever he spots youngsters of exceptional, or above-average talent, he will be quick to channel them toward the sports clubs, where trained coaches can begin their development.

This is the basis of the entire GDR elite athlete-selection program. Starting with the educational system and working up through the sports clubs, you can be sure they get at least a passing glance at the sports talents of everyone in the country at least once—which is perhaps why a country of almost seventeen million people can produce as many top-flight elite international athletes as either the U.S.S.R. or the U.S.A., both of which have more than fifteen times as many people.

When running down a list of DTSB memberships, some Westerners are inclined to scoff at a couple of the larger federations, such as Angling with its 391,202 members, and Fitness and Exercise clubs with their 232,016.

"Hell," one Canadian physical educator grumbled in Leipzig during the Sports Fest, "if we counted all the fishermen in Canada in our federation statistics we would be the most active sports country in the world."

That may be true, but if sport in North America could ever get organized to the point of having all the fishermen and campers—to say nothing of the National Rifle Association—adding its voice to the lobby of amateur sportsmen, then the voice would be a little stronger than it is right now.

The most recent DTSB membership list shows the following:

Membership in the DTSB—January 1977

Angling	391,202
Basketball	8,799
Billiards	8,509
Archery	2,847
Boxing	20,598
Ice Sports	7,714
Fistball	7,848
Fencing	7,181
Badminton	17,200
Football	552,523
Weightlifting	11,479
Handball	153,233
Field Hockey	5,869
Judo	42,297
Canoe	24,978
Bowling	163,146
Track and Field	173,062
Motorsport	56,183
Equestrian Sport	32,717
Cycling	20,736
Wrestling	22,250
Roller Skating	5,005
Rowing	13,776
Rugby	878
Chess	37,770
Bobsled and Luge	2,729
Swimming	85,812

Sailing	21,283
Skiing	35,973
Tennis	33,442
Table Tennis	87,338
Gymnastics	348,534
Music Groups	13,341
Handicapped Sport	5,803
Volleyball	111,115
Mountaineering	35,106
Fitness Clubs	232,016
TOTAL	2,951,352

If you are wondering how many of those belong to more than one federation, the answer is 260,651 since the actual DTSB individual membership roll only shows 2,690,701 members.

Exactly 1,970 of them belong to the Factory Sports Club of the Leipzig Transportation Workers, just one of eight mass sports clubs in Leipzig boasting more than 1,000 members.

The clubhouse is in a wooded area to the south of Leipzig, and I am told it's a bit of an honor for the club to be located there since it is in the middle of the lignite coal fields and the GDR's need for coal has been putting a lot of pressure on all the available mining areas.

"We don't have a lot of raw materials," they say, "and thus we have had to cut into a lot of woodland. As a result, there is a lot of air pollution around here."

You wouldn't know it from the grounds of the Transport Sports Club. Their corrugated metal clubhouse sits in the midst of a beautiful layout of soccer fields and tennis courts. Other club facilities are spread all over the city.

The home club grounds has three football fields, four handball courts, including one with lighting, ten tennis courts, which are home to 368 registered tennis players, and a volleyball area.

Sports activities commence each day at 4 P.M. and usually run on until around 9 P.M. at night. The major sport is soccer, as it is in most GDR sports clubs, with a boys' team, a children's team, a student team, a youth team, a junior team, three adult teams, one veterans' team and a women's team. The track and field division has eighty-five members, and sixty regularly play volleyball. There are seventeen sections in the club altogether, when the other divisions around town, including canoeing, sailing, bowling, and chess, are added. The club has doubled its size in the past ten years and today approximately 50 percent of the membership are adults and 50 percent are children.

None of the current athletes in the club are at the national team level, they explain, since promising youngsters are culled out at an early age and directed toward the city's elite sports clubs where they can take advantage of special sport schools and a higher level of coaching. This club is strictly for people who do their sport for the love of it, like millions of Americans who trek off to the park every week for softball, touch football, sandlot baseball, amateur soccer, tennis, golf, and whatever.

Their funding comes from many sources. For starters, there are the monthly dues of approximately 71 cents per working adult, 44 cents per housewife and student, and 11 cents per child. That might sound like nothing, but when you've got nearly 2,000 members in your club it does mount up. The problem is that the club doesn't get to keep all of it. From every adult payment of DM 1.30, the DTSB taxes the club 50 pfennigs. Exactly half of a housewife's dues of 80 pfennigs per month goes to the DTSB, and one fourth of each child's 20 pfennigs heads off to the governing body.

The club could never survive on its dues alone. The advantages come from the tax-free land and the annual grant from the Transport Union's Cultural and Social Fund. This is the money that is put aside for day-care centers, sport, culture, and other union needs. The sports club gets 25,000 marks a year, a figure that translates into almost 14,000 American dollars.

They also get 8 percent of the money that comes in from each member's union dues, and this totals another 6,500 marks or about $3,575. Then there are additional incomes from the club's own fund-raising techniques. Also restaurant and beer profits can be considerable since most clubs have a licensed clubroom where the members can relax after their exercise with beer, sausages, cards, and fellowship.

The club's full-time workers are paid by the Transport Union, and this is no burden on the club's budget, freeing the income to be spent on improving the club's grounds, stipends to the coaches who have earned the higher levels of certification, and on travel for club members taking trains and buses to represent the club in away-from-home matches. The athletes get as much as 75 percent reductions in travel costs when they move about as a team.

Items such as tax-free land and subsidized travel make it very difficult to put any kind of an overall figure on total GDR sports spending, but that is a subject that might better be reserved for a more thorough study a little later on.

In return for the provision of so much low-cost sport, the club members are called upon to give of themselves. As with the sports club Empor Brandenburg Tor in Berlin, they all give a lot of free labor to the club grounds. In Leipzig in January 1977, the Transport Club was turning its fund-raising efforts to helping the city prepare for the Sports Fest, the first such event in the country in eight years. One of the quick ways to raise money for this purpose is to have workers put in overtime on the job and credit the money to the Festival. By the time I arrived, fully six months before the Festival itself, the members of this particular factory club had already raised 65,000 marks, or approximately 27,000 dollars for the cause.

GDR mass sports clubs have a very good record of taking care of themselves. And, as we move up the ladder, we find that when they take care of themselves, it's an easy matter for the elite international sports system at the top to take care of itself as well.

9

The DTSB
and Elite Sport

In the 1976 Montreal Olympics the United States, far and away the richest country in the world with a population of approximately 215 million, won 94 medals including 34 gold. On a per-capita basis, that comes to a medal for every 2,288,489 Americans and a gold medal for every 6,327,000 Americans.

The GDR, with a population of just under seventeen million, won 90 medals overall, including an astonishing and disproportionate 40 golds. That works out to 1 medal for every 188,888 people, and 1 gold medal for every 425,000 GDR citizens. One obvious interpretation of this comparison is that if you are born with raw athletic talent and share the fantasy of millions the world over about winning an Olympic gold medal, you would be about 15 times more likely to realize your dream if you were born in the GDR rather than in the United States.

That's the kind of statistic that American shot putter Mac Wilkins might have been thinking of during the Montreal Games when he said he'd be happy if he won his event and the GDR won all the rest. Wilkins did not wish to be disrespectful of the United States with that comment, but simply wanted to awaken people to the fact the children he was then teaching in the California school system— among the next generation of American athletes—do not have an equal chance to realize the dream Mac Wilkins was realizing in Montreal.

And it's not just in the United States, either. The GDR per-capita medal statistics humble every other country in the world.

Ever since the medal production started to soar, first in Mexico in 1968, then in Munich, and finally in Montreal, the world's sports analysts have been trying to find out why it has been happening and how it has been happening. In some quarters it has been fashionable to imagine a system where young children are forced into sport at an early age and literally flogged on down the path to medals. Some find that answer politically satisfying, but in fact it is a ludicrous proposition. Others point to the GDR's admitted lead in the field of applied sports medical research, and by so doing put their finger on a part of the answer, but perhaps not nearly so large a part as they suspect.

Still others point their fingers at the country's elite and secretive sports clubs, with the professional coaches, special sports schools, and special medical clinics. The DTSB has twenty-seven such clubs, nineteen such schools, and as many medical clinics, both on a full- and part-time basis, as are needed. Most in the West have a negative opinion of these, saying this is not a course the world should follow since it breaks the tradition prevalent here of sport as a hobby. And yet most people who say that have never seen an East European elite sports club, sports school, or sports medical clinic.

Christine Errath was first introduced to the most extensive of all such clubs in the world when she was five years old. She did not come as the result of any scientific selection program, or at the behest of any neighborhood baby snatchers on the payroll of State Sports. The girl who would go on to win the World Ladies' Figure Skating champion- ship in 1974 at the age of seventeen came to Dynamo Berlin at the age of five with a girlfriend.

She told me, in a two-hour interview in February of 1977, conducted in English so she could practice her student language skills, that "we came because we heard there was a chance to learn to roller skate.

"I remember the day clearly because I was so small and my feet were so small [when she was ten she advanced to an adult size 1] they couldn't find a pair of skates to fit me. I sat there and cried until finally one of the coaches took pity and said if I would return one week later he would personally find a pair of skates that would fit."

He did and she did and that's the basic story of how the young five-year-old daughter of a Berlin construction worker first came to the attention of the professional coaches at the largest sports club in the world.

Until I first visited Dynamo Berlin in 1975 I thought that title must surely have belonged to the Central Army Sports Club in Moscow, the most important club in the Soviet Union. It's not even close. The grounds of Dynamo Berlin, one hundred ten acres in all, dwarf those of Moscow's Central Army Club. There's a sport hotel, an all-purpose arena, an indoor competitive pool with diving tower, an outdoor 50-meter pool, every kind of small training hall, for boxing, wrestling, judo, fencing, weightlifting, and more. Soccer fields stretch off in all directions; there is an indoor skating rink for figure skating, another for ice hockey, both of which flank a 400-meter speed-skating track of artificial ice—and the gem of gems, the largest indoor track and field training hall in the world.

From the outside, the track hall, the hockey rink, and the skating rink could be mistaken for three airport hangars. In fact, the first time I saw it I suspected that's what they were, thinking perhaps this club, like the Olympic grounds in Munich, had been built on what was left of a World War II air base.

Not so. The track hall is built that way because it can be done at low cost while still allowing maximum indoor usage for field event training. For an indication of the size, try to imagine a ten-lane 120-meter-long straightaway. No conflict here when some athletes want to work on starts, while others are hurdling, and still others are using the inside lanes for serious training. The surface is rubberized with modern Western materials, and the infield is wide enough to accommodate several sports activities across the width. There are basketball areas, volleyball areas, and indoor soccer areas for five-man teams, none of which directly interfere with the multiple pole vault pits, high jump areas, or training strips for the long jump and triple jump. The roof is high enough to get good elevation with a discus, something that is all but impossible in indoor training in most other areas of the world, and the shot putters work at one end. There is no shortage of videotape equipment, blackboards, chalk, and all the other accouterments of the scientific approach to the training of athletes.

Any track nut in the world can sit in that hall all day and be happy, just sitting and watching.

Behind the track building the road winds gently down to the special sports school and beyond to the dormitories where young student athletes who do not reside in Berlin live in residence. Athletes in sweatsuits are everywhere.

Across the street from the indoor competitive pool sits the Dynamo sports medicine clinic, a research and treatment area where, I'm told, every doctor was once a former athlete, since they find that tends to lead to better applied medical practice.

On the other side of the new pool sits the old pool, and a little insight into the history of this club. The old pool is an outdoor 50-meter affair with a diving pool attached, and a huge corrugated metal shed on wheels that can be rolled aside in summer or pulled right over the top of the water in winter to make the pool available for winter training.

What's more, right across the street behind the sports medical clinic sits a brewery with its tall smokestack poking up into the dreary sky of industrial Berlin. When the old pool was first built, the stack was disconnected and pipes were run under the street so the excess brewery heat could be used to heat the pool.

"Today this is no longer necessary," my club guide informed me with pride. "Now we have enough turbine power here within the sports club to heat the entire brewery if we wished."

At the time though, they were undoubtedly just as proud of the cleverness of their solution to the heating problem—a solution, though, that probably wouldn't be welcomed in North American municipalities with similar shortages of funds.

"Of course, we could build that kind of heated 50-meter pool in North America," says Montreal's Gordon Berger, Canada's leading major swimming pool builder, with Commonwealth Games, Canada Games, and Pan-American Games facilities to his credit. "But we wouldn't do it. Those pools may be operational, but they look terrible, and there isn't a municipality in this continent that will accept something that looks cheap. If the neighboring town has a $6-million municipal pool, they want something as good or better. Since most of them can't afford it, they do nothing instead and in the long run it's sport that suffers."

What is the cost of such a massive sports club as this? That's a good question and one I'm afraid no Western journalist will answer, if for no other reason than that SC Dynamo Berlin is an elite sports club of the National People's Police and in the GDR police and military budgets are not matters for public scrutiny.

But its cost would probably not rival what would be spent in the United States on a small- to medium-sized college serving 1,200 students, which is the number of athletes training at SC Dynamo Berlin. They are managed by sixty full-time professional coaches, all Leipzig graduates, and that's where the cost comparisons of East and West would start to differ. Any coach in a Western country with the qualifications of a Dynamo coach would be earning $25,000 to $30,000 a year and up. By Western standards that would involve $1.5 million a year in coaching salaries alone, without even beginning to consider the salaries of the teachers in the special sports school, who work, not 9:00 to 4:00 like teachers in most regular schools, but whatever hours suit the sports training schedules of their students, be it 7:30 in the morning or 10:00 at night. (An advantage, though, for teachers and students both is that classes tend to include only four to eight students at a time.) In the West, all these would be major expenditures, but in the GDR, where the state deducts off the top for free social services to its citizens, labor costs in the form of salaries in cash are comparatively minimal. Whatever the actual GDR figure, its Western equivalent might easily be five or even ten times greater. These high costs almost preclude a Western copy of any East European elite sports club unless we opt for tapping the military budget and state security budget as they have done.

Not all of the elite sports clubs in the GDR resemble Dynamo Berlin, of course. After all, Dynamo is the elite crown jewel in the Dynamo federation, which includes 250,000 athletes (at both elite and mass sport levels). Of those, 90,000 are in the children and youth category. In all, the federation is served by 20,112 volunteer coaches working in 365 sports facilities.

Only the U.S. military has the wherewithal for that type of program, and at present there is just no way the U.S. military is about to give that sort of status to the development of U.S. amateur sport.

The total breakdown of all twenty-seven GDR elite sports clubs plus ten football clubs looks like this:

Large, All-purpose Clubs

TSC Berlin
SC Chemie Halle
SC DHfK Leipzig
SC Dynamo Berlin
SC Einheit Dresden
SC Empor Rostock
SC Karl-Marx-Stadt
SC Leipzig
SC Magdeburg

Medium-sized Clubs

SC Motor Jena (emphasis on track and field)
SC Turbine Erfurt
ASK Vorwarts Frankfurt (boxing and football)
ASK Vorwarts Potsdam (track and field)

Small Clubs

SC Berlin Grunau (water sports)
SC Cottbus (track and field, cycling)
SC Dynamo Hoppegarten (shooting sports)
SC Dynamo Klingenthal (skiing)
SC Dynamo Luckenwalde (wrestling)
SC Dynamo Potsdam
SC Dynamo Zinnwald (biathlon)
SC Motor Zella-Mehlis (skiing and wrestling)
SC Neubrandenburg (track and canoeing)
SC Traktor Oberwiesenthal (skiing and winter sports)
SC Traktor Schwerin (boxing and volleyball)
ASK Vorwarts Oberhof (winter sports)

ASK Vorwarts Rostock (rowing and sailing)
SC Wismut Gera (boxing and cycling)

Football Clubs

FC Carl Zeiss Jena
HFC Chemie
BFC Dynamo
SG Dynamo Dresden
FC Hansa Rostock
FC Lok Leipzig
FC Karl-Marx-Stadt
FC Magdeburg
FC Union Berlin
FC Vorwarts Frankfurt/Oder

What it basically boils down to is that the DTSB has placed its elite sports clubs all over the country where they are needed to serve the population and where they are adjacent to the best natural facilities. Since there is a large Army base near Oberhof in the Thuringian Forest, it seems only natural that the military would take over the luge and bobsled programs in that area. Since the Leipzig Institute has magnificent sports grounds it makes sense to create a separate elite sports club like DHfK Leipzig to utilize the services of the young coaches in training, graduate students and Ph.D. candidates, and to provide a possible competitive outlet for top athletes studying at the school.

A medium-sized club like Motor Jena in the southwest GDR has 300 members, 150 of whom are students in the special sports school, with 250 in serious training for international-level sport in track and field, wrestling, fencing and gymnastics. SC Motor Jena, with one of the great club track teams in the world, has twenty professional coaches.

SC Cottbus, over against the Polish border in the southeast, with four sports including boxing, cycling, gymnastics, and track and field—it's the home of world high-jump record holder, Rosie Ackermann—has seventeen professional coaches, 125 students in the special sports school, 200 athletes in serious training, and 250 members overall.

"The athlete," says skater Errath, looking back at fifteen years of Dynamo in her own twenty-year life span, "is well taken care of in an elite sports club. Everything is free. The equipment, the costumes, the lessons, the ice time, all of it. Otherwise it would be impossible for the daughter of a construction worker, like myself, to become an international competitor in a sport like skating.

"In the beginning, of course, I didn't even know that's what I was trying to do. After all, I went there as a five year old interested in roller skating. After some weeks, one of the coaches came up to me and said he thought I had talent. He asked me if I would be interested in coming back more regularly in the winter to try figure skating.

"In the beginning there were maybe fifty kids in the program who were invited to try figure skating. Six months later we were down to twenty, and three years later when I was nine years old, I was one of six young skaters asked to join the club's special sports school.

"This was a very big day for me because I was beginning to have difficulties in school. I had teachers who didn't understand the pressures I was under in the skating program, and coaches at the club who didn't seem to have much of an understanding of the problems of the regular school.

"Once I was enrolled in the special school everything was in place. We had exactly the same study course as students in the regular twelve-year school, but we could set our own pace. Sometimes during competitive periods, myself and the other skaters, like our pair skaters Manuela Gross and Romy Kermer, would miss classes for months at a time and just concentrate on skating. But then in the summer we could spend long hours in the classroom and catch up again. Even if your studies might fall a year or two behind it doesn't matter because there is no peer pressure of falling behind. When you are done with competition, as I am now, you can always stay at the school, finish your education, and go on to the university."

Errath finished her twelve-year preuniversity course in the spring of 1977, and then headed off for the Humbolt University to study and perfect her German, looking toward a career as a television sports journalist.

Although it might seem a little strange that a girl who can already conduct a two-hour interview in English and carry on every bit as fluently in Russian would have to perfect her German, Christine says this is not at all unusual.

"It's not just the foreigners who have trouble with German," she says. "It's a very difficult language and it takes a great deal of time to speak it with the degree of perfection required to be a television journalist. It will be difficult, but I know it is a field that I will enjoy."

Christine certainly enjoyed her skating career, particularly the opportunities to travel all over the world to more places than she can now remember off the top of her head.

The travel started when she was a twelve year old and she went to her first European championship, finishing 18th in a field of 23 in the women's singles event.

"That was a good beginning," she says, "but it was followed a year later by the low point of my career at thirteen when they left me home in 1970 and took a thirteen year old from Karl-Marx-Stadt in my place. Luckily for me, that girl got nervous in the competition, finished in the last place, and did not compete internationally again. In 1971 I was back on the national team and finishing in 7th place in the Europeans."

Although Christine personally gave no reason for her brief demotion at the age of thirteen, others were quick to point out that the system will not support young athletes, no matter how talented, if they start to get egotistical about their careers and show signs of losing interest in their education. The system that guarantees prized places in the universities and good jobs later on to anyone selected for the special sports, music, language, or science schools, does not give people free rides along the way.

It was a more sober young Miss Errath who finished 5th in the 1972 Europeans and 18th in the Sapporo Olympics before moving up to the European singles championship in 1973 and the World title in 1974. World champion at the age of seventeen! Since GDR skaters do not have the option of joining major North American or European traveling ice shows, her quick ascendancy to the throne could have been the beginning of a dynasty. Could Christine Errath be to singles skating what Irina Rodnina and Aleksandr Zaitsev have been to the pairs competition?

The answer to that is no. In 1975, with the World Championships set for Colorado Springs, all eyes were on the battle between Christine and the rising new American superstar, Dorothy Hamill, a girl from

Connecticut who had spent her formative years in Lake Placid before moving on in the wake of Peggy Fleming to train with the great Carlo Fassi in Colorado. But by the time it was finished, both girls had faltered and Dianne de Leeuw of The Netherlands had skated off with the title.

"That was a difficult competition for me," says Christine. "It was the first time I had been exposed to a North American crowd and it was all the more difficult since I was drawn into the position of being the final skater in the free-skating program.

"It's the first time I have ever been up against a really demonstrative crowd. It was not like Europe. Many of them brought huge banners urging Dorothy on in the competition. I sat there and watched the banners, listened to the crowd, saw the 5.9 scores go up on the board, and then had to think about my own program. When I came out on the ice the crowd was absolutely silent, no applause at all, and I found it a very disconcerting feeling."

The Olympic year was a disaster all around.

"Right at the peak of my training I fell on the ice and badly sprained an ankle," she says. "For three weeks I lay in the Dynamo clinic getting the best of care before I tried to return to the practicing. But no matter what I tried the performances just weren't there. I had the strength. All the skaters of Dynamo have the strength because the coaches see to it that we use the running track for a forty-five-minute to an hour run as much as three times a week, every week, right up to our departure for a major event. But my ankle never did get 100 percent strong again. I was in trouble at the Europeans, and also in the Olympics where the best I could manage was a bronze medal while skating a restricted program.

"When the Games were over I sat down with my coaches, my doctors, and finally the officials of the federation as well. What I needed was a complete year off from all serious exercise to let the ankle come back to full strength. But I have always had a weight problem and a year without exercise would certainly aggravate that as well. We looked at the problem from every angle and we came to the collective decision it would be best if I retired from active competition. If I had decided to continue I think I might never have regained the full form I was showing in 1974, so there are no regrets.

"And besides, now that I have retired I can enjoy my food a little more! That was another aspect of life at Dynamo. We had a very carefully planned nutrition program with full individual diets. You'd be surprised at the differing diets they gave us even within the skating group. After all, it's important for the male in a pair's team to have great strength for lifting the girl. Conversely, it's important that the girl stay as light as possible. With a singles skater like myself, there was a need for strength for the triple jumps, and also a need to keep off the fat and maintain an attractive figure.

"In my case I have a very small mother who herself had early sport success as a gymnast before the War, but my father is a heavy-set man, and if I ever let myself eat all I want I will soon be that way, too. At Dynamo I used to have a lot of fruit for breakfast, a big lunch, but often no supper at all after training, perhaps just an apple or two, in the continuing effort to keep my weight down.

"Now, even though I am retired, a lot of that has rubbed off and I am very careful about my calories, even if it's only because I don't wish to outgrow my pants and dresses. For exercise I have started to play a lot of tennis, at least three times a week in the spring, summer and fall, and I skate three times a week while teaching the latest crop of five and six year olds who are starting out just as I did back in 1962. I find that teaching work very satisfying indeed, and it certainly makes me feel like I'm still a part of the sports club."

On the question of whether she ever wishes, even secretly, that she were free to follow the Dorothy Hamills, Janet Lynns, Peggy Flemings and Karen Magnussens into the world of show business, Christine just pointed at a copy of Billie Jean King's *WomenSport* magazine, which was lying open to a picture of Miss Hamill cavorting in a clown costume.

That entire issue of the magazine had been full of Dorothy Hamill, everything from Billie Jean's editorial on down. The editors had planned a big splash on the new pro star, only to be turned down in their request for an interview by her managers—managers who were very carefully protecting the professional Hamill position as a millionairess on ice and the advertising stylist for Clairol's Short 'n Sassy look.

The Dorothy Hamill of 1977 was giving no press interviews whatever, except for a preselected few in the way of specific show promotion. This was the managers' way of making absolutely sure that nothing could possibly be said that could endanger the public's image of that girl in the hairstyle ad.

Billie Jean wrote an editorial saying that she understood the pressures the Hamill management team was feeling, because she had felt them herself when she was on top of the tennis world, but she added that she did hope Dorothy would find a way to come out of the constraint occasionally, just to feel a little more human.

"I can't imagine that Dorothy Hamill likes to live that way, money or not," says Christine. "She was always fairly outgoing. Perhaps not so outgoing as I remember Karen Magnussen and Jo-Jo Starbuck [now Mrs. Terry Bradshaw] as being on one post-World Championship tour, but, still, Dorothy was always friendly and a good mixer. Now she has all that money and can look forward to perhaps a decade of traveling from city to city, living out of a suitcase, in one hotel after another. And then what will she do with herself?

"I found the United States a fascinating place to visit, particularly after the 1975 World Championship when we stopped for three days in both San Diego and New York. I really appreciated that because usually on the postchampionship tour you just flit in and out of one city a day for a single performance. Even at the championships the pressure is always on the women because we are the last division to compete. In New York we had three whole days, and I have never in my life seen such contrasts. We saw Broadway, and the Empire State Building, and it was really exciting. But then I also went around with a friend and looked at some of the less impressive sights of the city. I saw people lying on the street in a drunken state not far from our hotel right across the street from Madison Square Garden. I saw the lines at the welfare and employment offices. In the evenings we had some parties at the homes of prominent New York skating families. I have never imagined, much less seen, such amazing apartments as these families possessed. I will remember it always.

"But, as I was flying home from the United States, I also realized that if I had been born in New York and my father had been a construction worker just as he is in Berlin, I would never have had the opportunity of becoming a figure skater. When I got home I felt glad to be there.

"So, personally, I don't think I would ever want the life of a performer in a professional ice show. I think I am much happier doing what I am doing right now, studying and teaching and working toward a career in television. It will not be a job I will be getting simply because I am an athlete, it will be a job that I will be getting because I am qualified to get it."

Indeed. The GDR's system for providing elite athletes with later careers outside sport has to be seen to be believed. From what I have seen it is unique even to Eastern Europe. And yet it is eminently sensible. If one of the "perks" of the Communist system is the rewarding of international performance with virtually "the job of your choice" after retirement, then it is sensible to make every effort to assure that athletes are indeed qualified to hold such jobs. It's better for the athlete's self-esteem and better for the State as well.

Christine Errath will be a television commentator, but only after she has completed the years of training and apprenticeship anyone else in the field would have to complete. Several U.S. Olympic stars, Mark Spitz, John Naber, and Bruce Jenner, to name the most recent three, have gone into television commentating, too, to capitalize on their Olympic fame. Some of them are good at it. Most though, would never get such a job but for their gold medals. One wonders, occasionally, if a U.S. Olympic silver medalist might not have had more talent as a broadcaster than some of the gold medalists. If they could try calling a major television network.

"Who's that?" they'd say.

And the skating battles go right on. Christine Errath and Dorothy Hamill have gone their way, only to be replaced by Annett Pötzch and Linda Fratianne, once again from the GDR and the USA, who have traded the world championship back and forth in 1977 (Fratianne), 1978 (Pötzch), and 1979 (Fratianne). On the ice it's a safe bet they spend the same number of hours doing the same number of things, and off the ice they suffer many of the same sacrifices when it comes to outside social life and diet.

And yet, when compared to Errath and Pötzch, Hamill and Fratianne had to make far greater personal sacrifices to get there, if only because the U.S. educational system is not hooked up to handle their particular needs. Also involved is a far greater financial sacrifice: the minimum family outlay for a serious U.S. figure skater now surpasses $10,000 a year for lessons and private ice time alone.

In this light, it's clear the special sports school would be a very responsible addition to any country's elite training plans for the future. The Canadian Government has already begun tentative studies of how such an idea could be applied to hockey. If the United States Olympic Training Centers develop as planned they will be needed there, too. The situation where excellence in sport can only be obtained at the price of an education cannot be deemed acceptable for much longer.

10

Those Amazing Fräuleins of Swimming

Swimming officials in the GDR are so thorough, that whenever a new national or world mark is set in a meet, they list the time of day alongside the performance—just in case someone does a better time elsewhere on the same date, raising the question of who held what for how many minutes and hours. Since the record keepers were on duty at the 1975 GDR International Age Group Invitational in East Berlin, I know it was at precisely 5:44 P.M. on Saturday, March 1, 1975, when Canada's Nancy Garapick, a thirteen-year-old youngster from Halifax, hit the final turn in the 200-meter backstroke, a mere finger tick behind Liane Stier of the GDR Empor Rostock club.

From that moment on the German athletes in the packed Dynamo Berlin pool could do nothing but stare in silence as the Canadian swimming star pulled clear by an arm's length, a half-body length, then a full length, and finally more and more and more.

"There's the world record right now," said her startled coach, Nigel Kemp, as Nancy flailed under the warning flags 5 meters short of the finish wall, "she's only going to be that far off."

Indeed, just four seconds later this girl, who would go on to win 2 bronze medals in the Montreal Olympics, touched the electronic timer in 2:21.61, the eighth fastest 200-meter backstroke in swimming history to that time.

While Nancy's ten Canadian teammates, aged fifteen and under, waved their towels and jumped around in glee, coach Kemp and team manager Walter Price sat back and jotted down some more startling notes in their diaries.

Two days earlier, this North American swim team, the first ever invited to compete in the GDR, had crossed through the Friedrichstrasse subway station check point. Nancy Garapick had stood on the street corner blinking in amazement at the contrasts between East and West Berlin.

"What happened to all the billboard signs," she wondered aloud.

Walter Price looked surprised. The Edmontonian had been selected to manage this team because he had been born in Germany and spoke the language and also because he was a professional chemist whose knowledge, thought the Canadian swim federation, might come in handy in a first-hand check of the GDR sports medicine scene. But now, sensing the cultural value of first trips abroad for thirteen-year-old athletes, he settled back to a short explanation of the history of Berlin, the divided city. Soon everyone within earshot knew why West Berlin had flashing lights and neon signs and East Berlin did not.

"It has been that way ever since the War," said Walter.

"What war?" asked Nancy.

With that, Walter Price's eyes glazed over as he sat contemplating generation gaps and the educational shortcomings that befall young girls who spend up to five hours a day training in a swimming pool. This was to be Walter's first surprise in a big weekend of surprises.

Months earlier there had been real elation in the Canadian swim offices when the mail had brought the invitation to send a team to the GDR Invitational. After all, the federation had been trying—without success—to get someone into the GDR for more than a year for a first-hand look at the system that had produced the miracle of the 1973 Belgrade world championship.

Before Belgrade, no one in the world of swimming had been terribly interested in what was or was not going on in GDR swimming. In the Munich Olympics of 1972, their women hadn't won a single gold medal. There were signs of a coming breakthrough with 4 silver and 1 bronze medal, but the U.S. women were still firmly in command.

In Munich, the U.S. girls had won the 400-meter freestyle relay by just ³⁶/₁₀₀ths of a second with 3:55.19 against 3:55.55. In the Belgrade relay, every one of the four GDR girls broke the individual 100-meters world record on her leg, and the team swept home with the gold medal with approximately one third of a swimming pool to spare.

What's more, they did it in a shocking new, semi-see-through, skin-tight, rubber swimsuit. It was nicknamed the "Belgrade suit," and became the forerunner of the model now used by every competitive swimmer in the world.

The GDR swimmers swept the pool, and within a year went on to break every women's world record on the books in their overnight rush to the top. Kornelia Ender, a thirteen-year-old surprise silver medalist in Munich, became a fourteen-year-old superstar known everywhere in the world.

But, before the Belgrade meet was even over, the rumor mill that always accompanies sports breakthroughs of this nature was hard at work. Some tried to make a scandal about the new swimsuits, until the word came down the line that they were actually invented and manufactured in the West German Federal Republic, not in the East German Democratic Republic.

"The company came to us with the product shortly after the Munich Games and asked us to try it out," says Manfred Ewald. "We did, and we liked it. Then we made some small suggestions for changes, and they made the changes. One of the problems at first was that the material was a little revealing in the areas of the breasts, but later we had them made out of colored patterns and that solved that problem. When all the headlines first broke about the GDR's new miracle suits, the manufacturer demanded to know why we were taking credit for his swimsuit. I told him we had nothing to do with it. So the company held a press conference to explain where the suits came from and that was the last we heard of that complaint."

No sooner had the suit sensation died down when others started to claim that several of the GDR girls had deep masculine voices and extremely well-developed muscle structures, which were deemed proof positive, they said, that male hormone anabolic steroids were the secret behind the miracle. In the coming months everything a fertile imagination could imagine was imagined. In retrospect it seems strange no one got so excited when they were only winning silver and bronze.

Did Canada want to send a team to the GDR? Did she ever! Within weeks, eleven of the country's top fifteen-and-unders were selected and Kemp, a one-time British butterfly champion, educated in Oregon, picked up the coaching assignment. Between the professorial coach, and Price, the analytical German-speaking chemist, so the thinking went, the truth must out. North American swimming would await their report.

North America, one hopes, wasn't holding its breath. The host swimmers did not look at all overwhelming. And they certainly hadn't been using any muscle-building compounds. As a matter of fact, many of them looked so slim and shivery sitting around the pool, the Canadians even came to the conclusion that they hadn't even been lifting many weights. It was obvious that in the fifteen-and-under category, North American swimming programs were ahead of the program in the GDR, both in technique and in talent.

Although Garapick's victory in the 200-meter backstroke was certainly the most impressive Canadian triumph on the weekend of March 1 and 2, it certainly wasn't the only one. Canadian girls walked off with no less than seven events against a like number of swimmers from Sweden, Czechoslovakia and Hungary, and at least 100 youngsters from the host GDR.

At the inevitable party that concludes all such international events, GDR coaches were full of congratulations for Kemp and Garapick and full of curious questions on her training techniques. They arched their eyebrows when told that thirteen-year-old Nancy was on a full training program at the national team level, spending as many as five hours a day at the pool and swimming up to 12,000 meters a day.

"How do you maintain her interest when you work that hard at such an early age?" one asked.

"How much mileage are your athletes putting in," asked the Canadian coach.

"Oh," said the German, "about half as much as yours."

The Canadian management team simply did not know what to make of it. But, noticing that the GDR national team had been swimming a dual meet that same weekend against the Soviets—with two young GDR breaststrokers who would have been eligible for the

Age Group Invitational—the Canadians concluded that they had not been swimming against GDR national team candidates at all.

"I suspect we have come over here with our top swimmers to swim against their club swimmers," said Kemp. "I did not see one GDR girl in this meet capable of swimming in the Olympics in Montreal in sixteen months' time."

This seemed like an entirely logical conclusion. Walter Price concurred, and so did I. I put it out of my mind completely until I was cleaning out my desk sixteen months later after the Olympics and came across the story and results from that March weekend in Berlin. Out of curiosity I started to work through the lists event by event, and name by name, checking with the Olympic results with growing astonishment. Would you believe that *seven* of the sixteen girls selected to swim for the GDR in the Montreal Olympics came straight out of that meet in Berlin? To be technical, perhaps only five, since two of those eligible missed the meet through injury. What's more, those who actually did swim amassed 3 of the 10 gold and 4 of the 5 silver medals while breaking, or helping relay teams to break, three world records.

In the Berlin butterfly events, Andrea Pollack finished second in the 100-meter with 1:07.29, and third in the 200-meter with 2:28.68. The Canadian girls who finished ahead of her, Debbie Sojnocki, Jennifer Frain, and Janka Samuhel, did not come close to qualifying for places on Canada's Olympic team. Yet in the Games, the fifteen-year-old Pollack swam a sensational 1:00.98 in the 100-meter butterfly, second only to the world record of 1:00.13 of teammate Ender; she won the 200-meter butterfly with a new Olympic record of 2:11.41, and added a silver and a gold in the relays.

Petra Priemer, who was nowhere in the sprint in Berlin, and whose best time in the 100-meter in all of 1975 had been only 1:02.14, came through in the Games at age fifteen to win the silver medal with an astonishing 56.49. She then picked up a silver medal in the relay.

And then, *über alles*, there was Petra Thümer, one of the few girls who did score close victories in the Berlin meet. Just sixteen months before the Games, fourteen-year-old Thümer won the 400-meter freestyle with 4:30.90 and the 800-meter freestyle with 9:11.17, the latter a GDR age-group record. Good age-group times, yes, but certainly not world-class times. And yet, in the Games themselves, Thümer blew past world-record holder and world champion Shirley

Babashoff to set two world records of her own with clockings of 4:09.89 and 8:37.14 in the 400- and 800-meter freestyle. That time in the 400-meter would have beaten Don Schollander's men's winning time in the 1964 Tokyo Olympics with three seconds to spare. Mike Burton's winning time in Mexico City in 1968 was 4:09.0, less than a second faster.

As for the rest of the GDR age groupers at the Berlin meet, Birgit Treiber won 2 silver medals in the backstroke, Carole Nitschke, just a fourteen year old in Montreal, finished 4th in the 100-meter breaststroke and 6th in the 200 with 1:13.33 and 2:38.27 respectively; Regina Jaeger finished 7th in the 800-meter freestyle with 8:50.40; while Antje Stille, who had rushed up to set a 200-meter backstroke world record of 2:13.60 just before the Games, faded back to 2:17.55 and 6th place in the final itself.

When you consider the fact that Canadian national-level swimming coaches pride themselves on being competitive at the world level today the obvious question is What happened? Only two of the ten conquering Canadian age-group swimmers from 1975—Garapick and Thunder Bay's Joann Baker—qualified for the Canadian Olympic team, and only Garapick medaled, winning 2 bronzes. The girls from the GDR who competed in the Berlin meet won 3 gold and 4 silver. The GDR coaches created these champions in less than sixteen months total time.

To get the answer we had to obviously go back to the source at Dynamo Berlin. Over luncheon, on a pleasant January day in 1977, Andrea Pollack settled down to talk about it all.

She talks about the thrill of the aggressive butterfly motion, easily the most taxing of all swimming strokes, with the body undulating like a dolphin's while the arms slice through the water as if they were scythes. It's almost as fast a stroke as the freestyle, but it requires much more strength. Anyone who can master it has to have great reservoirs of power and fine technique. It's a monster of an event.

And yet, the 5'4" Andrea Pollack, sitting down to lunch at Dynamo Berlin, dressed in jeans and a loose sweater, looks more like a typical fifteen-year-old high school cheerleader than the barrel-chested swimmer that had been impressed on my memory in Montreal. There was no deep guttural voice, just a very pretty baby-faced smile. It's a funny thing, how, in the heat and passion of all the Olympic action, you can get caught up in so many imaginings, all so convincing at the time.

"Yes," she said, responding to my opening question, "of course I remember the meet here in Berlin in March of 1975. I remember those Canadian girls too. We were surprised. They were very, very strong."

Not wanting to sound too much like a prosecuting attorney, I nevertheless pressed on.

"Did you do an awful lot of weightlifting for shoulder development between March of 1975 and the Games in 1976?"

"Some, but not so much."

A noncommittal answer. It was obvious, as is so often the case with GDR athletes and visiting journalists, there weren't going to be many yards made through intimate discussion of training habits.

"Did you have any idea, back then in March of 1975, that you would be competing in the Olympic Games, much less winning gold medals?"

"Of course not, I wasn't a member of the national team in March of 1975. There had been no indication I would be selected."

"When were you selected?"

"There was one more major meet after the one in Berlin, a big European junior meet. When that was finished they came and selected several of us for the national team. From that day on our lives changed completely. The training was much more difficult, at least twice as hard as anything we had done before.

"I had the advantage of training with Rosemarie Gabriel, then the world-record holder. Right from the start this gave me a point of comparison, and a target. But it was difficult and I was never sure I would make it. Even during our own Olympic trials I was only dreaming of making a place on the team and perhaps winning a bronze medal in the butterfly. It wasn't until I was in Montreal that I realized I had a good chance to win."

Andrea's answers almost exactly paralleled the statements of Kornelia Ender just before the Montreal Games, when she was asked to think back on her own performance as a thirteen year old in Munich in 1972.

"I had no idea of winning anything," Ender explained. "It wasn't until I climbed out of the pool after qualifying for the final in the individual 200 medley that I thought of winning a medal. My coaches took me aside and told me they thought I had a chance." In that Munich final, Australia's superstar, Shane Gould, just did nip the thirteen-year-old Ender by 52/100ths of a second with a 2:23.07 against a 2:23.59. The Belgrade miracle was on the way.

Andrea Pollack had the same uncertain expectations in 1976. Just the same, her modesty, though genuine, belies nine years of preparation by the GDR swim coaches, working under the direction of national coach Rudi Schramme.

Like Ender, who was first introduced to a swimming pool as therapy for a hip problem, Andrea was sent off to a pool in her hometown of Schwerin when she was six, for treatment of a back defect.

"I was good at it," she says, "so I was invited to swim with the swim club after school. When I was ten I was promoted to the special sports school."

She was promoted, undoubtedly, because of the results of several tests that would have been conducted while she was swimming, once, twice, and then three times a week at the local club in Schwerin. In the GDR they do not train hundreds of random youngsters with the intensity of the North American age-group program, they bring them along slowly and gently, always looking, always testing, and always evaluating.

"We look for a variety of things," says Schramme. "We look at their size, their style, their ability to glide in the water. We check closely on their attitudes and intelligence. While we are doing this the sports medicine experts are testing oxygen-uptake capabilities, tendon structure, and their overall health."

What they are all looking for—and this is a process that in the case of Pollack, Thümer, Priemer, Nitschke, Treiber, Stille, and Jaeger was just nearing completion in March of 1975—are the athletes that have the best chance of standing up to the tremendous pressures of an intensive-training drive. To a large extent this can be told through testing. Blood samples are taken every time the training load is altered, sent to the Leipzig Institute and analyzed thoroughly for patterns.

Other tests are run by placing the swimmers in a so-called "flume tank," a Swedish-designed testing device where the swimmer can duplicate the situation presented by a runner on a treadmill. The swimmer just lies in the tank and swims against a controlled current of water, swimming on the spot as it were with the coach in a position to regulate the pressure of the water against the swimmer. They can test respiration, blood pressure, and much more with this device as they quickly work an athlete into a state of exhaustion.

When I asked Kornelia Ender how much she used this machine she said: "A lot more than I liked to use it. I never did care for it much, but the coaches depended on it."

The GDR coaches, and their sports medical support team, are seeking the athletes who have the metabolisms that will take world-class training loads without suffering breakdown. Physiologically they can find these potential stars fairly quickly. But then there are the psychological factors to consider, too.

Once a girl like Andrea Pollack has been selected for this process, her life is in for a big change. Now her coach, in this case Dynamo's Rolf Gläser, who had three Olympians in Montreal with Nitschke and Gabriel in addition to Pollack, will start working with the national team's sports medical personnel. She will have her computerized file in Leipzig, and a medical-coaching book will be prepared, one copy for the coach and another for the doctor listing everything from training objectives to medical and diet-nutrition reports.

Had Andrea been dropped from the program before this final stage, she would have likely dropped out of the special sports-school setting and gone back to the regular school system in her hometown of Schwerin. Unless, that is, there was a prospect for her to excel in a sport other than swimming. Once she had been designated as an international-level athlete, however, it was as if a compact had been signed. Her career and future both within sport and without would be assured, and in exchange she would place her physical well-being in their hands. From the time of national-team selection on, the athlete, doctor and coach work as a tight unit dedicated to the task of making it to the top.

All of this brings us to the problem of the human metabolism. Once sports medical people and scientific coaches begin to understand some of the functionings of the human metabolism, it's rather natural they will want to alter and improve it in the interest of better athletic performance.

Blood-testing and muscle biopsies are certainly the most potent research weapons in sports medicine's scientific arsenal. Doctors follow the athletes like puppies at high-level competition and in training camps, at least twice a year taking smears from little nicks in the earlobe. By frequently testing to determine an athlete's nutritional needs and oxygen-carrying capacity, scientists can easily design a program for each swimmer based on the swimmer's day-to-day training capabilities. There is a fine line, however, between training—building strength and endurance—and overtraining, which can actually break down muscle tissue. North American swimmers, who are just now starting to take the first baby steps toward blood-testing analysis, can easily undertrain or overtrain. As a result, some of our swimmers often swim greater daily yardage than their GDR counterparts, but benefit less.

When Schramme and his team arrived in Montreal they knew they had girls capable of breaking the world record in every event, and yet right up to the last minute they feared the U.S. girls might take half the gold medals. The results show that their fears were well grounded. Although Andrea Pollack and her amazing young friends won 11 of the 13 women's swimming gold medals they won 5 by less than a second and lost the dramatic 400-meter freestyle relay to the U.S. by less than a second after placing Ender on the leadoff leg instead of the anchor. The GDR girls broke their own world record by 4.30 seconds, but they still lost when Claudia Hempel couldn't catch Shirley Babashoff in the last 100 meters.

Schramme did not second-guess that strategy.

"I'd do the same thing again," he insists. "The American team simply swam the better race, a much faster race than we thought them capable of. Perhaps if we had had Barbara Krause [who missed the Games with a throat infection] she'd have led off and Kornelia would have swum the anchor, but with the swimmers we had, there was no fault in the planning. The credit must go to the Americans for a simply wonderful effort."

Which is another way of saying the GDR girls met their objective even though they finished second. The objective wasn't high enough. And besides, with 11 golds out of a possible 13, Rudi Schramme could afford to be magnanimous.

But not for long. In the 1978 World championships in West Berlin, the amazing American girls were right back on top under the leadership of a whole pool full of new young talent. Nashville's Tracy Caulkins had surpassed the retired Ender to claim easily the swimmer-of-the-year title. Linda Jezek had pulled ahead of Treiber and Stille in the backstroke. Joan Pennington won the 100-meter butterfly from

Pollack, and Caulkins upset the GDR Olympic champion in the 200-meter butterfly. Caulkins dominated the 200- and 400-meter individual medleys over Ulrike Tauber. The American girls won both the relays. The Soviet girls were more dominant than ever in the breaststroke. And, the Australian pair of Tracey Wickham and Michelle Ford were the class of the world at 800 meters. The domination of the GDR women was, at least momentarily, at an end. Rudi Schramme was quietly replaced at the top of the national swimming program.

Once again, as in Montreal, the figures were a little misleading in that many of the races in the world championships were closely contested. Where the GDR had been winning all the close ones in the Olympics, the United States was now winning them in West Berlin. No one, thankfully, brought up the subject of anabolic steroids. The GDR team did not accuse the Americans of their use, and the American girls and coaches had certainly proven to themselves that anabolics are not necessary to win swimming championships. It's a question of setting the training objectives high enough and then finding the athletes that can meet them.

"It's partly a cyclical thing," Rolf Gläser admitted, while relaxing after the U.S. Women's International Swimming competition in the Harvard pool in January of 1979. "When a swimmer like Kornelia Ender retires, the replacement is always right there to step in. Same for Ulrike Richter in the backstroke. Then you get an injury, or someone gets sick, and suddenly the momentum is all going in the other direction. When one country wins most of the medals their entire national program gets the credit. But often just one or two swimmers carry most of the load. The 1980 Olympics could well come down to a question of whether Tracy Caulkins dominates our young Petra Schneider, or whether it's the other way around."

Some American coaches, in the interim between 1976 and 1978, have copied some GDR techniques, particularly when it comes to testing the quality of workouts by measuring the lactic acid buildup in muscles during training.

"That's the test," says Gläser, "that lets you know scientifically just how close you are coming to maximum output in training. With it you soon know if you are working at or near the swimmer's potential."

Some U.S. swim coaches now use it, others do not. But all U.S. coaches now advocate strength work and out-of-the-pool dry-land training. They are starting to set much higher training objectives than could even have been imagined prior to the GDR "swimming miracle" of 1973 through 1976. The 1980 battle in Moscow's Olympic pool should be memorable.

"And we'd all better watch out," warns Gläser with a smile, "for the Soviets."

11

The Etiquette of Sportsmanship

Two very poignant moments were recorded in the swimming section of the official film of the Montreal Olympic Games, moments that say more about the European and North American approaches to sport than could be said in the entire length of this book.

The first came in the final of the women's 100-meter freestyle, first of the much ballyhooed confrontations to prove whether Kornelia Ender of Halle, GDR, or Shirley Babashoff of California, U.S.A., would be the swimming queen of the Games of XXI Olympiad.

Swimming side by side in lanes four and five, the two girls churned along in the sprint event, which is almost always decided by the unerring exactitude of the electronic eye, cutting through the spray to gauge hundredths of a second when most humans see only a thrashing blur. The two hit the finish wall, rocked back, and glanced immediately for the electronic news on the scoreboard, news that gave Ender her first Olympic gold medal and yet another World record with an incredible clocking of 55.65; Babashoff a disappointing fifth in 56.95.

For a moment their eyes locked as the two great swimmers stared into each other's faces, and then Shirley turned her head away and placed her forehead sadly downward against the edge of the pool. Ender shrugged and in a flash was diving over lane dividers on her way across the pool to congratulate her silver-medal-winning teammate, Petra Priemer.

Babashoff's disappointment was more than understandable. Four years earlier as a fifteen-year-old sensation in Munich, she had won the silver medal in this event, finishing in 59.02, second to teammate Sandra Neilson, with both girls getting home ahead of the world-record holder from Australia, Shane Gould, who wound up with the bronze. Now in 1976 Babashoff had come to Montreal as the big U.S. hope, the *Sports Illustrated* pre-Games cover girl, the one relied on to prove that the GDR women's domination in swimming would disappear once the really big show was underway.

Faced with the reality of the final moment, she could only turn away.

The next minute of the official Games movie brought the counter to this anecdote. Now it was the men's 100-meter backstroke final, with the GDR's Roland Matthes, double gold-medal winner in Mexico in 1968 in the two backstroke events, double gold-medal winner again in Munich in 1972, back in Montreal for an incredible third attempt, but this time against John Naber from the University of Southern California, the most happy-go-lucky superstar of the Games.

The scene was the same: Two swimmers in adjacent lanes driving for the finish, water flailing, crowd roaring. They touched the wall, they bounced off, again with eyes searching for the electronic scoreboard, which this time showed Naber with a new world record of 55.49, shattering Matthes' 56.58 that had stood as the world standard since 1972, and leaving the GDR star who had dominated the event for more than ten years with just the bronze in 57.22.

Once again the eyes locked as the two stared at each other, and then, with a broad grin, Roland Matthes reached over and tousled John Naber's hair in friendly congratulations.

In the press conferences afterwards, Babashoff's bitterness again surfaced when she made derogatory comments about the GDR women swimmers, comments like "at least we look like women," and "I don't really think they enjoy swimming, it's more like a job to them." After each ensuing event, with Ender racing on to 4 gold medals and 1 relay silver, Babashoff scoring 4 silvers and 1 relay gold, Shirley refused to shake hands or offer congratulations to anyone from the GDR. On the medal ceremony stand when the U.S.A. won the relay gold, she even went so far as to turn her back when the girls from the GDR tried to congratulate her.

Shirley received so much press criticism for this behavior that on August 21, 1976, her mother penned a letter to the Los Angeles *Times* to try to tell the other side of the story of a girl who won 4 silver and 1 gold and did "badly" at the Olympics. She chastised the reporters who credited Kornelia Ender with "class" when she said she was happy with a silver medal and "criticized Shirley for saying the same thing." She said that kids are "not trained for the tricky questions put to them by reporters." And she reminded everyone that Shirley Babashoff was a teenager who got up at 4:45 every morning for four years to train for the Montreal Games, giving up the social life enjoyed by other teenagers.

The GDR's Roland Matthes, on the other hand, was better prepared for handling the press. When he showed up for the 100-meter backstroke press conference alongside Naber, a reporter looking for a clinical analysis of the race asked him if he had been aware of the lead Naber had built up when the field made the turn at the 50-meter mark.

"No," said Matthes, "thankfully I was not."

"Why do you say 'thankfully'?" the puzzled reporter persisted.

"Because had I seen how far he was ahead," said Matthes rather impishly, "I would have had to stop and applaud his effort and then I would not have been able to win the bronze medal."

Every reporter in the room within earshot of that remark used it in the next day's stories. Reading it one had to come away with the feeling that Roland Matthes is a young man with poise and class—a young man indeed trained to handle the tricky questions put to him by reporters. This is not to say that he is handed scripts, mind you, or that he has writers hovering offstage at these press conferences thinking up the bon mots, but that, from his initial involvement in elite sport, he was trained in the basics of the etiquette of sportsmanship. Just as a young golfer in North America quickly learns not to leave his bag on the green when he is putting, Roland Matthes and Kornelia Ender learn how to go about congratulating an opponent after an international event.

When I spoke with him in Erfurt a year after the Games, Matthes had an easy recall of his action in the pool at the finish of the 100-meter backstroke, even to the point of why he had broken into a smile.

"Ever since I was eleven years old," he says, "I can remember my coach, Marlies Grohe, telling me how to behave when I lost a race. We have sayings that are taught to young athletes as they approach the Spartakiad competitions (just as with Boy Scouts in North America), and one of them is that you will always win graciously and lose with dignity, because to do anything else is an insult to sport, and, after all, you are trying to become a sportsman.

"But the reason I smiled at the finish in Montreal is because as far back as I could remember in the backstroke I had never ever lost a race. When I looked up and saw Naber's time, the first thing that came into my head were those admonitions from Marlies. 'So this,' I told myself, 'is what losing feels like.' I couldn't help but laugh at it as I reached over to congratulate Naber.

"The other reason for relaxation is that when I saw that time on the board of 55.49, I absolutely knew that John Naber was a better swimmer than I was. When we started our preparation program for the 1976 Games, we looked at my record of 56.58, considered my training capabilities, and set an objective of 55.70 or 55.80 for the Games. I knew even then from Naber's performances in the U.S. championships this might not be enough to win, but I really wanted to compete in my third Olympic Games and I did have a slight hope that 55.70 might be enough to win again.

"But then in January I was playing water polo and someone hit me in the ear with an elbow so hard there was damage to the inner ear. I was completely out of training and out of the pool for eight weeks. Then, six weeks before the Games, my appendix burst and I was rushed to the hospital to have it out. I wasn't able to get back in the water in time for the GDR championships, the Olympic trials meet.

"Under these circumstances the bronze medal for me was a personal triumph. If Naber had won the gold medal in 56 seconds or slower, I might have felt disappointed, but when I saw that 55.49 on the board I knew I would have been beaten in Montreal no matter what. No matter how good you think you are, you always have to be prepared for the fact someone better may come along. When that happens you have to honor and respect them for their ability. That's what sport is all about."

In Europe, perhaps. But aside from lip service, this is not always the case in North America, where the professional influence and emphasis on the importance of winning has become dominant. When teams win big games and championships in North America, they and their supporters are expected to run around the field with a finger lofted in the air shouting "We're Number 1." When professional teams win championships they are expected to rush into dressing rooms and pour champagne all over each other and toss the coaches into the showers. They are the winners.

Losers are expected to shut the clubhouse door. To cry in front of their lockers. To be down on themselves. In the 1978 Super Bowl postgame scene, Denver quarterback Craig Morton was scorned in some newspaper accounts when he spoke of the joys of being a Christian, said he felt "blessed" by the entire season, and refused to accept the big game loss as anything other than just another football game. Many of the same reporters who sat in the pressroom in Montreal and thought Roland Matthes had a lot of class, walked out of the Denver room in New Orleans thinking Craig Morton was weird.

I like Craig Morton. And I like Roland Matthes and now that I know them both, I'm not in the least bit surprised he decided to ask Kornelia Ender to be his wife rather than any one of thousands of other GDR girls who might have been interested in a man who is esteemed in the GDR the way Joe Namath is in the U.S.A. And I like Shirley Babashoff, who, as her mother so eloquently points out in her letter from the heart, did not have the foggiest notion how to behave when two individuals named Kornelia Ender and Petra Thümer stood in the way of the realization of the dream of her lifetime, a dream that had been so widely promoted in the papers by writers who chose to overlook the performances Ender had been putting into the record books for three solid years.

But I did wonder what effect Shirley's bitter Montreal comments had had on Ender personally, both during and after the Games, and in anticipation of that I was very much looking forward to interviewing her.

But when the moment finally came I nearly missed her entirely. What a difference a year made!

We had arranged to meet in the lobby of the Interhotel in Halle, so I was certainly on the lookout. And, since we had been together twice in Montreal, I thought I knew exactly what she looked like. Yet when the moment came, all I did was glance briefly at the tall and slender blonde who walked past me in the hall heading for the lobby. She had gone at least twenty yards before I turned and looked again. She was blonde. The height was approximately correct, and there was something slightly familiar about the face. So I padded along in pursuit, watched while she stopped to glance around the lobby as though she, too, were looking for someone she vaguely remembered, and then made my move. "Kornelia?" I asked in a most tentative voice. "Hello," came the reply, "how are you?" I felt foolish.

This was exactly one year to the day from the historic night when she had set an Olympic mark that may never be matched, by winning the gold in the 100-meter butterfly in a time equaling the world record, resting twenty-six minutes, and then coming back to beat Babashoff decisively in the 200-meter freestyle, again in world-record time—and this time reversing the strategy she had always used in the past. Until Montreal, Konni had always blasted out the first 50 meters, tried to build as big a lead as possible, and then hoped to hold on the final 50 meters coming home. This time she lay back and let Shirley carve out the record-setting fractions for the first 100 meters, drew relentlessly even in the third 50, and then sprinted for home to remain the first woman ever under two minutes for the distance with a 1:59.26. Babashoff, who had won the silver behind Shane Gould in Munich with 2:04.33, finished in 2:01.22 this time, but it was still only good enough for second.

It was a swim that is certain to be long remembered in Olympic history, and here, just a year later I almost didn't recognize the swimmer. A week later in Leipzig, I was to take some solace from the fact that all the other foreign visitors to the Sports Festival didn't recognize her either. Just seven months after she had shocked her own swimming federation with her decision to retire while right at the top of her career, she had lost fourteen pounds and changed her appearance completely.

This change was all the more dramatic when you consider most athletes face a major problem keeping their weight in line in the immediate months after they stop serious training at the international level. Those who swim or run thousands of meters per day burn up a lot of calories along the way. After they cut back on training it's difficult to stop eating the amounts they have become accustomed to, and, if anything, they usually indulge their drinking habits further. The result is almost invariably an immediate weight gain.

Now, here was Kornelia Ender, in her last year of high school prior to embarking on a premed course and a hoped-for career as a pediatrician, losing fourteen pounds and seemingly well on her way to becoming one of the most attractive former athletes in the world. She had even defeated my first line of questioning by showing up in one of Dorothy Hamill's wedged haircuts.

The thought had come to me in a shop about a week earlier when I passed the pop record stand and saw an exact duplicate of the Ender face of 1976 staring out from the jacket of a long-playing album. It was so close a likeness that I went closer and checked, only to learn it was a picture of a Danish singer named Gitta. Kornelia Ender, sad to say, had not been able to capitalize on her Olympic fame by making a record. But, I thought to ask, had she prompted a new trend in European hairstyle—shoulder length, soft and natural, with a little flip in the front? Konni thought it was a great joke, the idea of her being a model for women's hairstyles, but she was just as quick to point out that this is not the way things are done in the socialist states.

"We have an institute of hair dressing here," she said, "and they have the designers who work out the new hairstyles. Once they have them planned they write articles that are printed in the newspapers and women's magazines with explanations for how we can do them at home. Most of the people here just adopt one of these styles. This one is a new one this year and it is simply called 'Chic '77'. For a swimmer it is perfect. I can do my training, and then when it dries out it is ready to go. I don't have to do anything with it at all."

Her training?

"Certainly. Now that I have finished competition I am in my two-year down-training phase. Right now I am swimming around 2,000 meters a day at a graduated step-down pace under medical supervision. This is a standard practice for all the international athletes in this country."

It is also yet another example of the world's most thorough national sports medical program at work. The Leipzig-trained GDR medical specialists may take it upon themselves to change an athlete's metabolism in order to improve performance, but they also accept the State's responsibility to reverse the procedure at the other end of the program. All the blood-testing and computer analysis used to get the athlete to the top in the first place is then used in reverse to bring him or her back to normal.

This is the kind of thing, when you see it in practice, that makes you rethink basic political precepts. To the Western mind the capitalistic system is supposed to be the one interested in the rights and interests of the individual. The socialist societies are supposed to be the ones that honor the collective well-being at the expense of the individual interest. And yet the President's Commission on Olympic Sports has recognized the need for U.S. legislation to protect the athlete's basic rights. What's more, beyond the problems of the amateur lie those of the professional athlete in North American society.

Every year, in every training camp, we have the story of the aging veteran who knows he's nearing the end of the line. He battles through one more off-season in an effort to maintain the highest level of fitness possible, and then he sweats through a training camp right up until the final cut when the coach or general manager calls him in and tells him he has been placed on waivers without recall. He has been cut, told the system doesn't need his services anymore. The career is over. Most coaches say it is the toughest, dirtiest, and most difficult job they must do. Even the legendary Lombardi, toughest of the tough, used to assign the task to someone else. (All the Green Bay Packers knew when it was coming though, because Lombardi would suddenly avoid speaking to the player who was about to be cut at least forty-eight hours before it happened.)

The last thing in anyone's mind at this point is the player's metabolism. No one, including the orthopedic surgeon who usually serves as a team doctor at the pro level, has even told him he might have an unnatural metabolism. No one tells him that if he gains weight sharply over the next ten years and cuts back sharply on his exercise level, he could be facing as much as eight times the average risk of serious heart trouble once he reaches his mid-forties. Of course not, and at least part of the reason is that, if a club did make a big thing of it, some court might well decide the teams had a continuing responsibility to all their players to advise and assist them in the aftermath of their careers. Some clubs are already facing suits from athletes who claim they were forced to take drugs and are now suffering side effects from having followed orders and done so.

The medical profession can take a little heat on this issue as well, of course. Preventive medicine has always been given lip service. And most Western governments go beyond that with extensive public service advertising campaigns directed toward the promotion of physical fitness. But concrete programming has always lagged far behind the good intentions.

The GDR is taking very good care of Kornelia Ender even though she will probably never win another sports medal for them as long as she lives, and her retirement did catch the GDR swimming federation flat-footed. In Montreal during the Games she was showing no indications of retiring at all, at least not before at least one more round of European championships and world championships in 1977 and 1978.

"I think with swimming," she had said then, "it is a matter of seeing the progress of the opposition. Most people think swimmers are very young when they retire, but that's not really true in terms of experience. Most girls start their training so young that by the time they are approaching twenty years of age they have put in as much time on their sport as other athletes in other sports. I myself can feel that there will come a time when I wish to put my full attention to something else. That's when it will be time to quit."

That time, it turned out, was only a few months away.

Her husband, Matthes, thinks the big problem with swimming is fighting the boredom. "Swimming is a boring sport," he says quite matter-of-factly. "The training is boring, and after a time even the competitions can get boring. Not the Olympic Games, of course, because that's where the best in the world all come together at once to create an experience every athlete will treasure for a lifetime. But the rest of it can be boring. This year I attended my first national championships as a spectator in more than a decade and I nearly fell asleep."

Asked if it had been love at first sight between him and Konni, Matthes broke into a broad chuckle. "Hardly," he said. "The first time I was ever aware of her was at the time of the Munich Games when she was only thirteen years old. I thought she was a very young girl with a high opinion of herself. I didn't care for her at all. But then after her successes in Belgrade in the World championships of 1973, we wound up traveling and competing together quite a lot. By the time of the European championships in 1974 we had started to become quite friendly. By the Cali [Colombia] World championships in 1975, I guess you could say we were going together. But it was something that just developed and happened, not something that was planned."

Matthes expresses puzzlement at Western newspapers, some of which were quick to speculate that the state had arranged their marriage to produce future sports champions.

"Before the news of our engagement was known," he says, "some of them had written stories saying Kornelia would never be able to have children because of the changes the doctors had created in her system. Then, when they heard about the engagement they started to say this was something arranged by the government for the purpose of producing future athletes. How can they make up such nonsense?"

They make it up, quite simply, because some of them have a hard time relating the amazon-like seventeen-year-old Kornelia with her broad shoulders and immensely powerful arms, to the playboy image of Matthes, whom you might expect to see in the company of movie stars, fashion models, and the rest of the "beautiful people" set.

One look at the 1977–78 Kornelia and they will certainly change their minds. Most of the fourteen missing pounds seems to have melted from her upper body. Her face is slimmer, her nose is slimmer, and the powerful shoulders that created such total dominance in butterfly, crawl, and backstroke have been trimmed back as well.

And besides, Matthes was told, any country that was really interested in an experiment in selective breeding would follow the exact system in use at horse- and cattle-breeding farms all over the world. They would marry Roland Matthes to all the women on the GDR national swimming team.

"That," he agreed, "is a very interesting idea."

But instead Roland got married to just one girl early in 1978, completed his coaching certificate in Erfurt, became the proud father of little Francesca in September, and enrolled in medical school where he will work toward a career in sports medicine. Konni will head to university in the fall of 1979 to start her premed courses. In the meantime, with full state support, they share a small apartment in a large block in Erfurt, one wall covered with a Peter Fonda "Easy Rider" poster, the other with posters of Roland's favorite racing drivers Carlos Reutemann and Emerson Fittipaldi, in action.

"It's a good thing we live where we do," says Konni with a shudder, "or he would be driving a racing car." Instead they settle for a small sedan. Most athletes in the West would live at least as well, and probably better in a material sense, although they would certainly have to take care of their own university expenses if they intended to spend the next several years engrossed in their studies. No U.S. athletes have ever received a swimming scholarship to medical school.

Marriages between athletes are common in the GDR, but they are obviously the result of the special sports schools. Just as men and women who attend the same university in the United States tend quite often to get married, so it is with those who attend the sports boarding schools in the GDR.

Matthes also had some interesting observations about why the GDR men's swimming program lags so far behind the women's. The fact that it does so has been used as proof by GDR swimming officials that the women's program is not developing as a result of any medical breakthroughs. If we could sweep women's swimming with drugs, this argument goes, why couldn't we sweep men's swimming the same way?

"I don't think the men of the GDR will ever catch up to those of the United States in swimming," he says, "mostly because our program is not competitive enough. We just don't have enough top swimmers to make things interesting for each other.

"The United States has thousands of high schools with competitive swimming programs and the best swimmers then get into tough programs in dozens of the best universities. An American swimmer is able to develop himself against world-class competition every time the school has a meet.

"In our case you can take Roger Pyttel for example. I thought he might have been the best butterfly swimmer in the world coming into Montreal, but in Europe he is never pressed and always in a class by himself in major races. In the Olympic final he was suddenly in against three Americans who were all battling him for the lead coming into the final 50 meters, and it was just too much for his nerves. Americans are always ready for that.

"And, there's another factor. In swimming, women develop much more quickly than men. It takes a male swimmer several more years to mature. In the United States the universities are perfect for this. In all of Europe we don't have enough pools or enough swimmers to match this, and, personally, I don't know how we will ever catch up. We will always have a few individual stars but not much depth."

How does he account for his own decade of complete domination in the backstroke?

"I was a special case," he admits, "a special physiological case. I am quite tall (6' 2¼") but I only weight 165 pounds. One of the reasons is because right from the start I had a condition that would translate into English as something like hollow bones. My bone structure is very light for my body size and as a result I can maintain my position higher in the water than most people. In backstroke this is a very big advantage."

A funny thing: John Naber has the same build, with one exception. He's about two-and-a-half inches taller!

And Kornelia Ender's feelings toward Shirley Babashoff and the others in the Western swim contingents, whose comments, perhaps unthinkingly, seemed like such a blatant attempt to undercut her accomplishments? It was such a disagreeable subject she really didn't want to get into it.

"I can understand someone who was unsuccessful and angry," says Konni, "but I cannot understand someone turning away and refusing to shake hands on a victory platform or after a race. Occasionally we have behavior like that in the GDR, too, from the ten year olds. When it happens their teammates straighten them out on the matter very quickly. It is simply a matter of having some consideration for others."

On the matter of consideration, the real Konni Ender had a moment all of her own in Montreal. Since she had been on the program every day during the swim meet, she had not taken the time to drop in at the Village service counter to see the videotape replays of the races, a service the Organizing Committee was making available to all athletes. After her final swim, a couple of GDR reporters thought they might get a story out of watching the tapes with Konni and recording her comments. She agreed, only to find on their arrival that the employee at the counter didn't recognize her and refused to make the effort to get any tapes out of the file that were more than twenty-four hours old.

Just as the reporters were about to make a scene, she intervened on behalf of the clerk by telling the reporters that if those were the rules then they would simply have to abide by them without making a big fuss. With that she headed back to her room followed by one of the reporters who was still looking for some kind of a story.

"Do you know what she was going back to the room to do?" he later related in amazement. "She was going back to write a letter to the family she had stayed with when she competed in her first Spartakiad. She told them that, no matter what they had seen on television from Montreal, she wanted them to know the biggest thrill of her life as an athlete had come when she had stayed in their house and won her first national youth championship as a child."

It's a letter one GDR volunteer family will treasure for some time to come.

12

Tales of Two Villages

Lake Placid and Oberhof—villages as alike as peas in a pod and yet as different as night and day, capitalism and Communism, or, the United States and the German Democratic Republic.

Up until now only a handful of people have had the opportunity to visit both America's Olympic Village in the heart of the beautiful Adirondacks *and* the capital of the GDR winter sport program tucked away just as scenically in the midst of Germany's Thuringian Forest. And that's a shame. On the other hand, anyone who has visited either can consider himself fortunate, if only for the resulting enhanced appreciation of man's relationship to nature.

But as far as winter sport is concerned, nature's possibilities weren't appreciated before the turn of the twentieth century, in Lake Placid, Oberhof, or anywhere else in the world.

It was back in 1904 when Melvil Dewey, the founder of the exclusive Lake Placid Club and the inventor of Dewey Decimal System for the categorization of library books, decided to keep his club open in the winter in hopes of drawing New York society to the little recognized delights of skiing, sledding, and hockey. Most people thought he was crazy. The Adirondacks were a great place to visit—in the summer.

But within less than a decade he was proven right and they were proven wrong. A generation later, when Melvil's son, Godfrey, set out to bring the 1932 Winter Olympic Games to Lake Placid, a tradition had begun. This tiny village of just over 3,200 souls was on its way to world sporting fame with a ski jump, the continent's only bobsled run, and an arena that would have been the pride and joy of many cities in the 1930s. The 1932 Games spread Lake Placid's name so far and wide that, when immigrants poured into the United States from a Europe suffering depression and soon to be ravaged by war, the two places they really wanted to see were Niagara Falls and Lake Placid.

The resort business at first boomed, but then faded when the new sport of alpine downhill skiing caught fire (there had been no alpine skiing in the 1932 Olympics) and turned attention to more exciting mountain resorts like Stowe, Vermont, and Sun Valley, Idaho. It would be years before permission was granted by the environment-conscious Adirondack Park Authority to cut into Whiteface Mountain for the creation of challenging downhill trails. Lake Placid became a central training base for North American bobsledding and United States figure skating training schemes.

The early days of Oberhof were similar. The Thuringian Forest has no hills high enough for downhill skiing, but they are simply perfect for sledding and tobogganing. The world skeleton (single) sled championships were held there in 1931 just prior to their being dropped from the Olympic program in Lake Placid. Oberhof was a village of huge homes, estates, and guest houses, most of which were foreign-owned.

The restrictive practices and exclusiveness of both Lake Placid and Oberhof in the 1920s and 1930s stand today as stark testimony of the times. In the days when the B'Nai B'rith were filing court actions to block the use of government funding for the construction of the Olympic bobsled run at Mt. Van Hoevenberg, land owned by the elitist Lake Placid Club (Godfrey Dewey simply gave the land to the State of New York and cleverly ducked out of responsibility for the post-Olympic maintenance of the run), Europeans were still accepting such organizations as Britain's Public Schools Alpine Sports Club. The PSASC, a forerunner of the modern day travel agency, booked resort hotels throughout Europe, for the entire season, to make sure that class-conscious British would vacation with none but class-conscious British when they trekked off for their winter sport. Germans and Swiss would simply have to go elsewhere, even in their own country, unless of course they qualified by virtue of having once attended a British private school. As preposterous as all this seems today, it was quite accepted at the time.

In Lake Placid, upper-class domination began its decline soon after the government came up with the idea of the graduated income tax. In Oberhof, in spite of the outcome of the War and the placement of Thuringia within the Soviet Zone of Germany, things didn't change all that much until 1950. During the military occupation between 1945 and 1950, the large guest houses became favored spas for the officer classes. The transformation of Oberhof began shortly after the new German Sports Committee came into being in October of 1948. The committee had to start somewhere and one of the first GSC organizational decisions was to hold a winter sports festival in Oberhof. At first the private hotel owners were delighted, only to become quite perplexed when word was passed along that the maximum room rental for the period of the Festival would be only two marks per night.

Gerhard Sprafke was the GSC official in charge of the organization of the Festival, a twenty-three-year-old Manfred Ewald was in charge of the sports events, and Klaus Huhn was a youthful press chief. They had a problem. The hotel owners had banded together and taken their complaints over room rate control to the town council. What's more, they had packed every chair of the public section at the council meeting.

"Gerhard was a fair-haired man of at least two hundred pounds weight, even in these times of hunger, but he had about four hundred pounds of energy," recalls Huhn. "The hotel owners were very polite, and keeping their temper in the belief they would surely be able to control the room rates. Gerhard knew they would be hard to convince, but he also knew it was out of the question for the Festival organizers to back down. So he mounted a filibuster.

"After he had spoken for two hours, they tried loudly to intervene in his speech. He pointed out that democracy gave one the right of free speech. After four hours, they were shouting for beer, but the speaker explained that one couldn't have beer during a democratic meeting of the municipal council. After six hours of Sprafke's talk they finally agreed to the proposal of reducing the prices to two marks a bed as a tribute to the first winter championships of the new sports movement.

On the following morning they all had their photographs taken for the newspapers."

Godfrey Dewey, whose pleas for government financing of the 1932 Olympic Arena were turned down by both Washington and Albany, and also by the first of two plebiscites of his own local voters, would appreciate Gerhard Sprafke.

A year or so later, in 1950, the private hotel and resort owners of Oberhof found themselves facing expropriation. The new government of the GDR stepped in, compensated them for the property, and created the Free German Holiday Service, a most important step in the master plan for the renovation of Oberhof as the country's winter sport capital.

A constant problem for Lake Placid today—and one that was immediately faced by the Oberhof of 1950—is the boom-and-bust economy that goes with all holiday-resort centers. Throughout the year, with the exception of the school-holiday summer months, Lake Placid is a boom town with more than 100 percent capacity from Friday night through Sunday night, and a ghost town the rest of the week. As part of the massive Adirondack Park, the village of Lake Placid lies in a 6.5-million-acre mountain region. The entire area has a population of 112,000 people. Essex County is the second largest in the state in area, but the second smallest in population with just 35,000 people. Lake Placid is the second largest village with 2,731, some 500 less than were living there at the time of the 1932 Olympic Games. For winter sports enthusiasts, back-packers, hikers, and nature lovers who can trek ninety miles southwest from town without crossing a single road, it's one of the great natural park sites in the country. For those interested in trying to develop a viable village economy, it's a never-ending problem. Unemployment, particularly in the winter months, is rampant. Any visitor driving into town and parking on main street gets an immediate idea of the real level of economic deprivation. Lake Placid still has the one-cent parking meter!

The National Holiday Service has solved this problem for Oberhof. Trade unions now own most of the hotels and make them available on a rotation basis for low-cost subsidized vacations for their workers. Since they are able to spread these throughout the year, the entire village operates at more than 75 percent capacity 365 days of the year.

"Since 1950 we have doubled our rooming capacity," says Oberhof Lord Mayor Rolf Hackel, "to the point where we can now take care of 4,500 guests per night in a town with a population of just 3,000. Before 1950 the annual guest figure never topped 47,000; now, with most of the visitors coming for planned and prepaid thirteen-day vacations, we have more than 100,000.

"They pay a fixed rate from 310 marks (about $130) per week for the new international-class Panorama Hotel, down to 130 marks ($54) per week for the guest houses, and that rate includes room plus all meals. Children pay just 30 marks ($12.50) per week."

The Panorama Hotel is as modern as any in North America, with its twin pyramid-shaped towers rising majestically out of the hillside, the only grumbles occasionally coming from those with children. It was initially designed strictly as an Interhotel catering to mostly foreign guests, but then changed halfway through with 80 percent of the rooms going to the domestic Holiday Service, and just 20 percent for the rest of the public at large. Thus, because of the initial planning, it is a little short on facilities for children.

It's a small problem, though, considering the amount of time most people spend outdoors in a winter resort setting like Oberhof or Lake Placid, where everyone has access to cross-country ski trails, sledding, hiking, climbing, and a host of night spots and restaurants that do a booming business all the year round. One of the most popular activities, however, is heading over to the ski jumps and luge-bobsled course to watch some of the leading athletes of the world in daily training sessions.

Oberhof has five ski jumps in the area, and the pride of them all is the 90-meter giant atop a hill with enough outrun (or landing area on the downhill slope before hitting the flat ground at the bottom) to have permitted a hill record of 120 meters, one of the longest in the world short of the sport of ski-flying. Coming down the scale they also have an 80-meter jump, a 50-meter jump, a new 45-meter jump for teenagers competing in the Spartakiad Games, and a 20-meter jump for beginners.

But the real pride and joy of Oberhof is the artificial luge run, a training facility that is to luge and two-man bobsled racing what Disneyland and Disney World are to amusement parks. It is a remarkable facility, with fourteen curves, including the world's first 360-degree "gyroscope," all packed into 1,032 meters. Equally remarkable is that luge racing—whose mass popularity in Europe makes possible such an elaborate setup—is almost unknown as a competitive sport in North America.

In Canada and the northern United States, sledding and toboggan-ing are certainly not unknown, but they are generally practiced by children who ride along sitting, kneeling, or flat on their tummies, with no competitive aspect whatever. Not so in the GDR, where the fun is to lie flat on your back to cut the wind resistance while sliding on a preconditioned and iced course. All that's needed to make this sport popular in North America are the facilities. When Canadian national coach Bjorn Ivorsen constructed a recreational luge course in the suburbs of Toronto, "eight kids were waiting to try it before I had finished it and the next day there must have been a hundred of their friends."

Because there are no high mountains in Thuringia or in the Harz mountain regions of the country, sledding has a much better chance than skiing. This is particularly so when you consider that most of the people who live in the villages and hamlets of these snowy regions do not own automobiles. The family sled, then, is a basic necessity, if only to pull groceries home from the store in the winter.

After school the sleds fall into the hands of the children who head for the nearest hill, which has, often as not, a small makeshift toboggan course with two or three molded curves. Where the North American parent might flood a backyard ice rink, the German parent sets up a few curves on a hill to create a luge course. The next step, predictably, is organized competition through the Spartakiads, which are held annually up to the county championship level, and biannually up to the national championship level.

Although the population of the entire snow availability region is just 700,000, at least 15,000 children annually take part in the Spartakiad luge competitions at the village and hamlet level. The best of these, perhaps 200 competitors of both sexes in all, are invited to Oberhof for the championship. The most promising can count on being invited to stay on and see if they have the aptitude for serious lugeing, a sport that, at the top levels, is not nearly so simple as it may look. Not that lying flat one one's back a few inches off the ice at speeds up to sixty miles an hour looks simple, mind you, it's just that most untrained observers would never suspect it takes a well-developed athlete to do it. It takes a great athlete to be a luge champion, and yet the very best of them, athletes like Oberhof's world and Olympic champion Margit Schumann, have physical builds that could make it tough to get to the top in any other sport.

"Margit has the perfect body for the luge," says Andreas Estel, one of the GDR junior coaches, himself a refugee from the GDR's attempt in the early 1960s to develop alpine skiers in spite of the lack of mountains. "She's not too tall [5'5"] and fairly stocky [154 pounds], but most of all very strong. If you were looking to another sport, you might say she had the perfect build for a discus thrower, except she's not tall enough to be a world-class discus thrower. Strength is everything in this event. The fastest sled is one that can maintain the tightest course without rising too high up on the curves. The way to hold a sled low is to use your muscles to constantly fight against the centrifugal force."

"Of course there is also the matter of fear," adds Hans Hofman of the Trakton Oberwiesenthal club, "but that is usually not a factor for us because the ones who are fearful will not pass through the early Spartakiad competitions. In addition, Oberhof was purposefully designed to make it the safest luge course in the world. We have never had a serious accident. This factor should be of prime importance to any country thinking of building such a training course. It has to be safety first. You can't run a program from September through to May if you are going to have ambulances pulling away from the run every other day."

There are ninety-four tobogganers in the junior and senior men's and women's program in Oberhof, and a like number working out on a natural ice run 137 miles away in Oberwiesenthal, for a grand total of about 200 in the elite program. The Oberhof course is in operation as much as twelve hours a day, for both luge and two-man bobsled, with all groups working on a strictly regimented program. One group starts off for an hour on the run, with every inch of training recorded by the closed-circuit videotape television system, and then while they retreat to the film room for post-training analysis with their coaches, the next group will be at work on the slide. When that's done, they head off to school, or to their jobs, only to return for another session in the afternoon.

If anyone is interested in duplicating an Oberhof, this may be the time to mention that it takes twenty-four full-time employees to operate it and it cost thirty-five million marks, or approximately fourteen million dollars at the time, to construct and equip fully. If there is local taxpayer resentment of that kind of an expenditure I didn't see it amongst those watching the practices and junior national championships while I was there. No matter what the initial cost of a sports facility anywhere in the world, most people don't resent it when they can see that it is being used. In Oberhof, 10 percent of the entire budget comes from the small fee paid by tourists to watch the practice sessions.

"The annual maintenance budget for all the winter sports facilities here is 1.8 million marks ($990,000)," says Lord Mayor Hackel, "and that comes to us directly as a grant from the State Secretariat through the County Committee to the Village. The entire sports project employs fifty-eight full-time people in the community."

Oberhof's special sports school was under construction when I was there in 1977 and was scheduled for completion some time later in 1978. When this system is in place and operating, there will undoubtedly be a great increase in the local elite cross-country skiing program at the youth level, a development that will take some of the pressure off the nearby Oberhof Army base. Until now the Army Sports Club ASK Vorwarts Oberhof has been home to such senior cross-country ski stars as Gerhard Grimmer, and the incredible bobsledders who arrived on the scene in time for the 1976 Innsbruck Olympics and revolutionized the entire world's approach to bobsledding in just one year.

Grimmer is a legend all over Thuringia and easily one of the half dozen most popular athletes in the entire history of the GDR, in spite of the fact that his name will never appear even once in the Olympic record books.

He was born in Katharinaberg in 1943, right in the middle of the War, and grew up in the small Thuringian town of Selingenthal. He displayed an early natural affinity for cross-country skiing at a time when the now-expanding Scandinavian sport was of only minor interest in central Europe. In the days before Vermont's Bill Koch was even born, Swedes, Finns, Norwegians, and the Soviets had a lock on this traditional sport of style and stamina. And then came Grimmer, who in the course of an eighteen-year career would give GDR competitive cross-country skiing the same lift Koch gave American cross-country skiing with that startling silver-medal performance in Innsbruck in 1976.

Grimmer is a monument to the years of effort it takes to develop the cardiovascular system of a top-notch cross-country skier able to contend at a distance of 50 kilometers, or more than 31 miles. He entered competition in 1958 but says that, even ten years later at the 1968 Winter Olympics in Grenoble, he "wasn't ready for that level of competition."

Then came a world championship silver medal in the 30 kilometers in 1970, and victories over the 50-kilometer distance in Norway's legendary Hollmenkollen events in 1970 and 1971. Surely Sapporo would be his Games in 1972.

But they surely weren't. "I got the flu," says Gerhard with a wry smile. "I was sick as you can imagine, and although I skied in the relay on the final day all I could do for the rest of it was watch on television."

On the way home, thoughts of retirement were heavy on his mind, but when 30,000 people came out and greeted him on his return to Thuringia, "greeted me as if I was returning with the gold medal, I knew I would go on some more."

He went to Falun, Sweden, for the 1974 Nordic World championships and had the greatest week of his life. A gold medal in the grueling 50 kilometers, his first world championship, and then another in the 4 x 10 kilometer relay with Gerd-Dietmar Klause, Gerd Hessler, and Dieter Meinel, who had come on as a last-minute substitute for an injured Axel Lesser. He also finished second in the 15 kilometers to wind up as the top individual skier in the championship. In Innsbruck it looked like this team, particularly with Lesser back in form, would contend for the gold and win a medal for sure.

Indeed, Gerd Hessler had a fine opening leg of 34:44.44, just two seconds back of the leading Swede, and on leg two, Lesser swept into the lead. Gerhard Grimmer, adrenaline pumping like always in such situations, moved to the starting line. And then, a minute later, he took off his skis and walked away. Alex Lesser had broken a ski while leading and was out of the competition.

"As much as you would like to dream of owning an Olympic gold medal," says Grimmer, "you can't just write ahead and have them reserve one for you. You have to go and win one in the competition.

In my case this was simply not meant to happen, not even in the 50 kilometers. I tried my best, but I could do no better than 5th."

When he came back to Thuringia the whole town turned out to cheer for him again. But this time he retired anyway. "I'll always ski," he says, "but now only for the recreation."

The younger athletes around Oberhof would call Grimmer the "Old Man" if it wasn't for the fact that bobsledder Meinhard Nehmer also operates out of Oberhof and has already laid claim to that sobriquet.

Nehmer was a long-in-the-tooth javelin thrower of thirty-three years, back in 1973 when it was announced that Innsbruck would hold the 1976 Olympic bobsled events on a luge course rather than build a course for each sport. At that time the GDR knew nothing about bobsledding, which was not a mass sport at all, a fact underlined by the federation rules that prohibit anyone under the age of eighteen from even attempting it. But they knew almost everything about luge. Once they heard the bobs would race on a luge course, they put the scientific approach to work.

Their studied conclusion, and it's amazing no one had thought of it before, was that three of the four members of any four-man bobsled team had to be strong and very fast, while the fourth had to be a good driver. If he was also strong and fast so much the better. The two-man sleds needed one of each.

Nehmer, who shows no emotion whatever when he races, gets a bit of a chuckle about the stories about his "scientific" selection to the bobsled team. "When they came around to the track club and asked who was interested in trying bobsleigh," he says, "I was the one who held up my hand."

Since it is not possible to run a four-man bob down the Oberhof course, the GDR officials built a start nearby to practice the first 50-meter runups, and then began training all their new recruits on two-man sleds, which did fit their course. They were an amazing group. Nehmer the javelin thrower. Bernard Germeshausen, who had once scored 7,534 points in the decathlon for SC Turbine Erfurt (that's 1,084 points less than Bruce Jenner scored in winning the Montreal gold, but it's not a bad decathlon). There was Raimund Bethge, a six-footer who once ran the 110-meter high hurdles in 13.4 (as against a world record of 13.2) and finished 5th in the European championships in 1969. Jochen Babock, who had his ice-hockey career cut short through injury; Horst Bernhard, who had toiled for eleven years as a middle heavyweight weight lifter; Bernhard Lehmann, straight out of the Army where he had won a military all-around competition consisting of running 3,000 meters, rope climbing and hand-grenade throwing; Horst Shonau, who was quick to move up from the luge program, since right from the beginning he had longed to drive either bobsleds or racing cars; and Harald Seifert, a so-so decathlon athlete with the Chemie Halle Sports Club. A couple of coaches named Erich Enders and Horst Hoernlein were given the job of shaping them into a team. Or rather a series of two- and four-man teams.

The results were dramatic to say the least. As far as the experts were concerned, the great drivers in Innsbruck were Switzerland's Erich Schaerer and the German Federal Republic's Wolfgang Zimmerer. And yet, driving on a luge course that drew nothing but scorn from veteran bob drivers who were not impressed with the lack of challenge, Meinhard Nehmer won both gold medals, beating Zimmerer by half a second in the two-man and Schaerer by close to a second in the four. What's more, young Shonau finished 4th in the four-man and 7th in the two. But just wait, the traditionalists said, until these newcomers see a real bobsled course rather than a converted luge slide.

That happened in St. Moritz, possibly the grandest bob course of them all, in the 1977 World championships. Meinhard Nehmer won again. In Lake Placid in the second week of February, the old man finally had his troubles, and finished third. Teammate Shonau won the gold, however, while Switzerland's Schaerer, who finished second again while driving the final sled down the last run of the competition, just chucked his helmet off into the snow in disgust, hardly satisfied with narrowly edging Nehmer for the two-man championship a week earlier.

The old man of Oberhof would love to hang it up right about now, going into his thirty-eighth year, and turn his full attention to his profession as a meteorologist. It has reached the point, he says, where it's hard to keep getting psychologically up for each competition. That's some admission for a man who appears to have the nerves of a surgeon, or perhaps of a Willie Mosconi or an Evel Knievel. Barring injury, he will hang in there for the 1980 Olympic Games.

"I honestly don't know how he does it," brakeman Bethge said after the two-man event in Lake Placid in 1978. "Going into that final run we could have finished anywhere from 2nd to 6th and we finished 2nd. I don't know what he does, and if I don't know what he does nobody will, because I am sitting behind him in the two-man sled. He is the steadiest man I have ever seen in my life."

Makes you wonder if there isn't a Meinhard Nehmer throwing the javelin somewhere in the United States in a vain hope of making the U.S. Olympic team. If there is, Lake Placid will be ready and waiting following the 1980 Olympic Games.

If sport had had a different priority in the United States, according to the secretary general of Lake Placid's Olympic Organizing Committee, Rev. Bernie Fell, they'd have been Oberhof before Oberhof. And, in future, they hope to rival their GDR counterpart.

Bernie Fell is a man who usually does what he sets out to do. Once he was a policeman, until he got shot in the stomach investigating a robbery. As he lay there wondering if he would make it, he prayed to God and promised to turn to the Church if he lived. True to his word, he was soon off to seminary school and a career as a Methodist minister. Since that's hardly enough to make ends meet in the Adirondacks, Bernie also took on the duties of directing Lake Placid's recreation department. That led to the job of organizing the Olympic bid for 1980, which in turn led to the job of second-in-command of the Organizing Committee. Ron MacKenzie, the founder of the National Ski Patrol, is the president. Art Devlin, the former U.S. ski jumping champ, is a vice-president.

Jack Shea, hometown hero of the 1932 Games when he won gold medals in the 500- and 1,500-meter speed skating as a twenty-one-year-old collegian, is now the chief elected official of the Town of North Elba. Lake Placid, in the strange maze of Adirondack politics, is actually a village incorporated within the Town of North Elba. In 1932 Jack Shea stepped to the dais in the opening ceremonies to take the athlete's oath of Olympic purity, and then twenty minutes later won his first gold medal. In 1980, more than forty years later, he'll be right in the thick of the opening ceremonies again as the town's top elected official. As great a thrill as that may be, even he knows that Lake Placid's future as a winter sport area is not going to be entirely measured by the performance in the Games.

"With two artificial ice arenas, a refrigerated speed skating track, and refrigerated bob and luge runs, we are going to have more artificial ice-making capacity than any single city in the world," says Shea. "Post-Olympic maintenance costs are going to be substantial, or at least far beyond the support that can be given from the taxation base of Lake Placid and North Elba."

What Lake Placid is banking on is a state-wide lottery to raise $100 million for operational costs after the Games. They dream of a school expansion plan that will not only support, but tailor its programming around the needs of figure skaters, cross-country skiers, ski jumpers, Nordic-combined (cross-country plus ski jumping) hopefuls, biathletes (cross-country plus shooting), and bob and luge performers. They speak of a school that can train future coaches for the American winter sports effort, and a development program that can bring the United States back into the front rank of competitive winter sports nations.

"The ideas of Oberhof are not new," says Bernie Fell, "we had them here in Lake Placid twenty-five years ago. At one point it looked as though a request to the State of New York for money for a small sport-oriented liberal arts college might go through, but then the Russians put that first Sputnik up in the sky and the priority suddenly went to science. They built a school in Plattsburg instead."

There was no money from Washington or Albany for a proper winter sports training center between 1932 and 1976, simply because it wasn't high on the list of governmental priorities. So instead, they will spend more than 100 million government dollars to stage the 1980 Winter Olympic Games, and then seek another $100 million to carry on from there in hopes of turning Lake Placid into an American Oberhof—and in hopes of creating a couple of hundred jobs to help a very depressed economic region in northern New York State, and finally coming up with a U.S. winter sport training center with a sensible educational support system so that the U.S. winter sport athlete of the future can, at last, himself have some hope. "Oberhof-West" may eventually make it after all.

13

Aschenbach: Miracles of Medicine

When I was making up the first rough sketch of an outline for the research into this book, I knew that the key to the absolutely essential section on GDR sports medicine would be my finding out how Hans-Georg Aschenbach had made a miraculous recovery from knee surgery to win the gold medal for Olympic 70-meter Jumping in Innsbruck in 1976.

But, if it hadn't been for an unexpected and totally unplanned illness of my own, and the luckiest and rarest of accidental meetings while recovering, the sports medicine door might have remained closed throughout the entire research. It's a story that has its genesis in Moscow's Central Institute of Physical Culture in the spring of 1974, when I accompanied a group of touring sports officials and physical-education students on a rare look inside a Soviet sports medical research center. We saw an impressively equipped laboratory of applied science with room after room of testing equipment, closed-circuit television systems, and data centers manned by researchers in white smocks.

I wound up with a small group ushered into the lab of Dr. Yakov

Kots, a Soviet neurophysiologist credited with the development of a new system of applied electrical stimulation of muscles, a system that was claiming gains of up to 50 percent in muscle strength and performance after as little as two weeks treatment. We sat transfixed as one of our group had the electrodes wrapped around his arm. Dr. Kots turned up the power, creating a strong involuntary muscle contraction in the student's arm, held it for ten seconds, and then turned the dial back, allowing the arm to relax again. The student said the whole area felt "a little warm, but with no sensation of pain."

As far as the field of sports medicine is concerned, there is absolutely nothing illegal or immoral about the use of electrical muscle stimulation. It has been used for years in the rehabilitation of severely atrophied muscles that, after operations, cannot be quickly restored through exercise. But the thought of increasing muscle fiber mass in a healthy athlete was indeed news, at least in North American medical experience.

Attempts had been made in this direction as far back as 1947, but they had all been unsuccessful. Furthermore, the athletes tested found the treatments very unpleasant. Since Dr. Kots would reveal none of his data to such casual, if curious, visitors, we returned with no hard information other than the general guideline that a treatment consisted of ten shocks of ten seconds' duration with each shock spaced between fifty-seconds' rest period. This was continued every other day until twenty treatments had been completed.

Reports of this intrigued researchers at both the University of Toronto and the University of Western Ontario, and they conducted their own research on university athletes. Both studies, however, were unable to confirm Dr. Kots' findings. The result led to skepticism, since the Canadian findings tended to uphold the earlier Western research studies of Millard in 1947 and Massey in 1965, which indicated electrical muscle stimulation in training was not more effective than normal training techniques using isotonic and isometric exercises.

The Canadian studies had left me with mixed feelings on the subject, and it was more or less out of mind until the day of one of the most prestigious events of the Innsbruck Olympics, the 70-meter jump, scheduled for Sunday, February 7, 1976. Most people—and there were thousands jamming all approaches to the hill on a simply gorgeous, sunny afternoon in the magnificent Tyrolean setting of Seefeld—were out to see the anticipated Austrian sweep. With Karl Schnabl, Reinhold Bachler, Rudi Wanner, and the amazing young Toni Innauer on their side, most competitions had been falling to the host country jumpers in late 1975 and January of 1976.

There was some slight concern about the GDR's Jochen Danneberg, who had won a pre-Olympic tune-up event just before the Games, but not much. And nobody was giving Hans-Georg Aschenbach a chance at all in spite of the fact that two years before in 1974 he was the awesome world champion, a man dominating ski jumping as it had seldom, if ever, been dominated before.

Aschenbach, after cleaning up in '74, had wrecked his knee in an accident in June, 1975, while jumping on a man-made artificial plastic jump in the Harz mountains, and, following an operation, had entered just one major competition since, limping badly and finishing far down the line. After that he had dropped out of competition and most of the world's jumpers, and jumping fans, were surprised to see him entered in the Innsbruck field at all.

For almost two months the Austrian jump team had been brimming with confidence, as had the Fischer ski company, which had the Austrian team contracted at the equipment level. Nor could the arch rival Austrian ski company, Kneissl, have been more depressed. Winners mean a lot to ski companies.

When Danneberg became a hopeful, the Kneissl ski company headed straight for the GDR ski federation with an offer to put him under contract to their product for the Games. The offer must have been an interesting one, because the GDR accepted it and from that moment on a vehicle was constantly at Danneberg's beck and call throughout the final training period, something the jumper found personally embarrassing since his teammates didn't have such luxury. And Kneissl was a little loath to use their advertising supply vehicle to transport Danneberg's friends with the GDR Germina equipment. "Either they get rides or I don't use it," said Danneberg. Faced with that, the company relented and started lugging all the GDR ski jumpers around Innsbruck.

Finally, the competition started. The names of the fifty-five jumpers had been put in a draw and pulled out at random, with the baby of the GDR team, twenty-two-year-old Henry Glass, first on the starting mark. Henry popped an 80.0-meter jump with moderately good style points for a total of 118.3 and the crowd wondered how that would stand up against the rest of the field.

A dozen jumpers later, they had some idea. That's when the first Austrian, Rudi Wanner, landed a 79.5-meter jump for 116.6 points. That disappointment had barely settled when the GDR's Berndt Eckstein, another twenty-two year old, took the lead with 80.5 and a score of 118.6. Six jumpers later Switzerland's Ernst von Gruenigen hit 80.5 and 119.1 to move on top in a surprise to all, and within the next ten jumpers Reinhold Bachler and Toni Innauer both landed just 80.5 jumps with scores of 118.1 and 115.6 respectively. For Austria, it was all up to Karl Schnabl, waiting to be the fiftieth jumper down the hill.

Aschenbach was to be the fortieth jumper, and by the time his head appeared at the top of the run, blue helmet glistening in the sun, the crowd was in full voice. Throats that had been turned skyward shouting *"Toneeee, Toneeee, Toneeee,"* when Innauer had stood in the same spot, where now hurling forth the jeering whistles that take the place of booing in European sport. Here was a man putting his life on the line in one of the world's most dangerous sports, attempting a comeback after a knee operation, and thousands in a crowd of 50,000 were trying to rattle his nerves. At the bottom of the hill GDR coaches, manager and equipment representatives stood silently, outfitted in the same shades of light blue, and squinting up the hill to the sunbathed summit.

Suddenly Aschenbach was rocketing down the run, out of sight for a brief second and a half at the bottom of the curve, and then out into the open air, skis perfectly parallel, arms flat at the side, offering nothing to affect the aerodynamic perfection. On down the hill, down, down, and then *whump*, the landing, one foot slightly ahead of the other as he streaked down the out-run and headed up the hill on the other side, losing speed, listening all the while for the voice of the announcer with the distance.

"84½ meters," came the word, as Aschenbach glided soundlessly back across the out-run. And then, when style points ranging between 18.5 and 19.0, the highest of the day, were flashed, "and 128 points."

The crowd stood awestruck. In an event that can be decided by fractions of a point, Hans-Georg Aschenbach, the master of '74, now was leading by 8.9 points. As he flung his skis over his shoulder and

The International Bicycle Race for Peace of 1952 wound through a Berlin still showing the ravages of war *(Neues Deutschland/Moll)*.

Olympic dynasties in the making? Discus thrower Wolfgang Schmidt, silver medalist at Montreal, defeated gold medalist Mac Wilkins of the U.S. at the Dusseldorf World Cup of 1977 (*Neues Deutschland/Behrendt*). But as early as 1949, Schmidt's father Ernst (**above right**) was breaking national shot-put records, though East-West politics prevented his competing in the 1952 Helsinki Olympics (*Zentralbild/Hoff*).

Wolfgang Behrendt boxed his way to the GDR's first Olympic gold medal in 1956 . . .

...while today his son Mario is rising in the ranks of candidates for future Olympics, shown here defeating Renard Lorenzo Ashton of Great Britain in a junior international meet in October 1978. Father Wolfgang, now a photographer with the GDR's national newspaper, *Neues Deutschland*, took the photo.

In 1949, thousands of members of FDJ (Free German Youth) worked for nearly a year to transform a bombed-out slaughterhouse (**above**)—then the only site available—into what is now the main indoor sports complex in the city, Werner Seelenbinder Hall (*Neues Deutschland*).

Twenty-seven years later, the national devotion to sport was even more apparent in the festivities accompanying the Sixth National Sports and Gymnastics Festival and Sixth Children and Youth Spartakiad Games. **Below:** Opening ceremonies before Leipzig's Town Hall (*Panorama DDR*).

The Spartakiad Games in Leipzig included elite international competition as well as national-level contests. **Above:** A GDR participant in international women's track and field (*Panorama DDR*).

Young athletes from sports clubs around the country compete at the Spartakiads, held every year at the district level and every two years nationally. Jörg Pasemann of Halle's Chemie Sports Club is on his way to victory in the 10,000-meter walk, 16- and 17-year-old category (Panorama DDR).

Involvement starts early for the serious contender, including this 13-year-old from Potsdam (ADN/Zentralbild).

The term "mass sport" is unfamiliar in the West; not so in the GDR, as illustrated by the table tennis and volleyball finals at the Leipzig festival. These and other sports attracted contestants of all ages from more than 8,000 local sports clubs throughout the country (*Panorama DDR*).

(Photos: top left, middle left—*Neues Deutschland/Behrendt*; middle right—*Panorama DDR*; bottom right—*Christoph Hohne*)

The Sportshow concluding the festival featured performances by
the police-sponsored Dynamo Sports Club—and a contingent
of 1,100 local kindergartners *(Panorama DDR)*.

In attendance at the festival: Erich Honecker, the GDR head of state (left), with Manfred Ewald, president of the German Gymnastics and Sports Union (DTSB). The friendly alliance of these men has helped keep sport high on the list of national priorities (ADN/Zentralbild).

The Sportshow fielded more than 14,000 performers, not including the 12,500 participants in a vast, carefully rehearsed card section, which transformed one entire side of Leipzig Stadium into a spectacle of color and pattern (Panorama DDR).

Above: The 360-degree "spinning top" of the Oberhof luge run *(Panorama DDR)*. **Right:** The gold-medal-winning crew of Nehmer, Gerhardt, Germeshausen and Bethge *(Joachim Kuphal)*. **Below:** A section of the bob-run overlooking the Thuringian hills *(Panorama DDR)*.

Left: In the early seventies, the medal-winning efforts of cross-country skiing champion Gerhard Grimmer inspired a new generation of GDR world-class winter sportsmen (*Panorama DDR/Dressel*).

Below: Hans-Georg Aschenbach, whose amazingly quick comeback from knee injuries to win the gold medal in the 70-meter jump at Innsbruck testifies to the advanced state of GDR sports medicine (*Panorama DDR*).

Kornelia Ender and Roland Matthes, both Olympic gold medalists in swimming, married in 1978; Francesca was born in September 1978. Both athletes now study medicine with full state support *(Doug Gilbert)*. **Below:** Ender's teammate, Andrea Pollack, in action *(Panorama DDR)*.

Christine Errath, winner of the World Ladies' Figure Skating Championship in 1974 and bronze medalist in the Montreal Olympics in 1976 (Panorama DDR).

Waldemar Cierpinski came out of nowhere to win the gold medal in the marathon at Montreal. Here he has a try at slalom foot-racing in kicking off the national "Start With Bronze" fitness program (Neues Deutschland/Behrendt).

Despite duties as a parent and as a representative in the national assembly, Gunhild Hoffmeister found time to train for a silver-medal performance in the 1,500-meter run at Montreal (Panorama DDR).

Below: Helmut Recknagel, ski-jumping gold medalist in the 1960 Olympics, was, with Henry Glass and Werner Lesser, one of the "three musketeers" of GDR ski-jumping.

Rosemarie Ackermann, gold medalist in the high jump at Montreal *(Panorama DDR)*.

Below left: At Montreal, Renate Stecher took the silver medal in the 100-meter dash, and the bronze in the 200-meters; **right:** Christina Brehmer, silver medalist in the 400-meter dash *(Panorama DDR)*.

Klaus Huhn, sports historian, writer, and sports editor for *Neues Deutschland*.

started heading back up the hill, the GDR managers started to permit themselves the first little smile of the day.

Ten jumpers later the great Schnabl threw everything he had into his effort with the crowd setting up an incredible supportive din from all over the hill, but could only manage 82.5 meters and 121.8 points. The smiles grew a little wider. And then it was Danneberg, off and sailing in the number-fifty-three spot, almost a perfect copy of Aschenbach himself, thumping down at 83.5 meters, and settling into a very solid second place with 124.4 points. At the halfway point the GDR skiers were solidly 1st and 2nd.

Now strategy took over in the coaching area. Youngsters like Henry Glass and Berndt Eckstein, sitting 6th and 7th in the field, threw caution to the wind in hopes of climbing up into medal contention, lost both form and balance, took tumbles and dropped all the way down to 32nd and 44th place. Still, as they picked themselves up off the hill, they did so in the knowledge they had tried for the brass ring rather than settling for a conservative jump and a sure spot in the top ten.

As the second round progressed, everyone waited for the big three late in the round. Switzerland's von Gruenigen exactly matched his first-round distance of 80.5 and moved temporarily into the lead with 238.7, a lead not even he could have hoped would hold up. When the day was finished he would be in 5th place.

In point of fact, the lead lasted just six jumpers before Czechoslovakia's Jaroslav Balcar hit a fine 81.5 to go with his first round 81.0 for a point total of 239.6, good enough for 4th place.

That's when the GDR coaches started to go to work with their pocket calculators on the sidelines. Since they knew what Balcar had done, and they knew approximately what Schnabl could be expected to do, all manner of possibilities were computed before coming to the decision a jump of 80 meters would be enough to win it for Hans-Georg. As soon as that decision was reached at the foot of the hill, a walkie-talkie came out of a pocket and the coach flashed the word to another GDR coach close to the top of the hill. He signaled the message on to Aschenbach minutes before the jump and everyone at the bottom of the hill took a deep breath and steeled themselves for another round of the terrific whistling.

As in the first round it came, louder than ever, as the shiny blue helmeted head, face almost totally obscured by goggles, poked over the top of the jump tower. Down the in-run, off the end of the jump with good power, the forward lean, the ski tips rising parallel to the shoulders, and the landing accompanied by the involuntary gasp from the thousands who seldom realize they have all been holding their breath since the jumper became airborne.

"82 meters," droned the loudspeaker, and this time Aschenbach waved both fists overhead in triumph while the coach who had been computing the necessary times raced to get the winner's GDR-manufactured skis aloft and in place for the still photographers and television cameras. He did it almost as an in-joke, because, while the Austrian-manufactured skis are virtual advertising billboards with the name printed everywhere, including all over the bottoms where they can be photographed while in flight, Aschenbach's "Germinas" from Schmalkalden had no promotional lettering whatever. The very idea of a pair of bald, almost homemade-looking skis in the hands of an Olympic champion in 1976 seems utterly preposterous. But it does add to the GDR sports mystique.

Ten jumpers later, faced with Aschenbach's insurmountable point total of 252.0, Karl Schnabl, pride of all Austria and the Fischer company, jumped 81.5 meters, scored 242.0 points, won a bronze medal, and looked absolutely disconsolate. Even Kneissl had cause to celebrate when, two jumpers from the end of it all, Jochen Danneberg hit 82.5 to take the silver with 246.2.

A week later the Austrian team, taking home-court advantage of Innsbruck's huge 90-meter inner-city Bergeissel jump, regained some lost prestige. They came up with the idea of coating the bottoms of their skis with gas to remove the wax and gain speed down the run on a warm day when the snow began to melt on the in-run. Finally, the whistles would turn to cheers as Schnabl finally won his gold, with young Innauer picking up the silver, leaving Glass and Danneberg in 3rd and 4th.

But in Seefeld, on February 7, the joy had belonged strictly to the GDR, particularly to two officials standing directly in front of me, who clutched each other with emotion close to tears, pounded each other on the shoulder, and said: "We did it. It worked."

What worked? I wondered, and put the question to a friend who was standing right at my elbow while all this went on.

"I'm not sure," he said, "but those are the team doctors and it has something to do with treatments they gave him for his knee. Some kind of electric-shock treatments."

My mind flashed back to that lab in Moscow, the claims of 50 percent increases in muscle mass in short periods of time, the Canadian scientific disclaimers, and then back to the incredible performance we all had just seen in Seefeld.

When Aschenbach, alternately hugged and tossed aloft like the victim at a picnic-blanket toss, got back to the doctors, there were more embraces and another interesting quote from the skier. "I'm just as good as I was in 1974," he said. "Thanks for everything." The doctors grinned.

Here it was, I thought: a positive example of how applied sports medicine can take an athlete and push him back to the top at a time when his confidence, so necessary to every champion in every sport, has been shattered through injury. The GDR doctors had taken a knee that would have kept most competitors out of the Games entirely and built its owner back to full physical and psychological strength in less than a month.

Eleven months later I arrived in Oberhof looking for Aschenbach, hoping to confirm my supposition in an interview. By this time Aschenbach, sad to say, had had yet another accident, yet another knee operation, and had decided to call it a career at the very tender age of twenty-six. Apparently there are limits to the miraculous, even in the GDR.

In the morning, with the great Oberhof 90-meter hill completely shrouded in fog, I decided to get my first close-up look at just what is involved in their daredevil sport. Those who fear roller coasters and heights can only marvel at the people in this world who dive off 10-meter diving towers, drive bobsleds, slide on their backs down luge runs, and hurl their bodies down 90-meter ski jumps. They are very special people.

I found out just how special they are on that first morning in Oberhof after getting permission to walk up the hundreds of steps that lead a jumper from the base to the top, in hopes of getting close-up pictures of the takeoff area with my camera. I was only halfway up the stairs when a great whooshing sound—a cross between that of a passing airplane and a dozen startled geese—passed by out of sight but seemingly within feet of where I stood on the stairs. Instinctively I found I had ducked and grabbed hold of the railing. Surely, I thought to myself, they are not ski jumping in this fog.

They were indeed. *Whoosh . . . whoosh . . . whoosh,* as bodies crashed through the still air, creating this incredible noise, a sound I have never heard captured by a microphone on any televised ski jumping competition—also a sound that escapes the thousands of spectators at the bottom of the hill. It's one of the strangest, most startling noises I have ever heard.

By the time the morning session was over I was no longer feeling sorry for the GDR team with its loss of Aschenbach, and Jochen Danneberg, who would miss most of the 1977 and 1978 seasons with recurring injuries. Their depth is amazing. Henry Glass is steady, Harald Duschek is not so steady, but remarkably talented, and a young, fearless teenager named Mathias Buse could easily be the best of them all since Aschenbach, who, after all, is still something special.

He is special, as much as anything, because of his style. Style points for most ski jumpers run between 15 and 18 or 18.5. Style points come from the way one takes off, the arch of the body, the positioning of the skis in flight, the movement or lack of movement of the arms, and the attitude of the body on landing. A score of 20.0 is perfect, and it is every bit as rare in ski jumping as it was in gymnastics before Nadia Comaneci appeared on the scene at the Montreal Olympics. Hans-Georg Aschenbach twice received style point scores of 20.0 in ski jumping. To compare other ski jumpers of this decade to Hans-Georg Aschenbach is like comparing hockey players of this decade to Bobby Orr when Orr was at his best with the Boston Bruins.

It would be more to the point, perhaps, to contrast Aschenbach, retiring at the top of his career after three knee operations, to Orr, struggling on until the fall of 1978, a shadow of his former self, still attempting to play hockey for the Chicago Black Hawks after five operations. Once again, it's a case of two different superstars and two different systems.

"I quit," Aschenbach said that afternoon, "because it seemed like the sensible thing to do. I had been at the top in ski jumping, I am twenty-six years old, and I am planning to go to medical school and study to be a doctor of sports medicine. Considering the number of years of study that are involved in this, I am already behind schedule as a student."

The switch in career goals takes him out of the army, where he had reached the rank of lieutenant purely on the basis of his ski jumping success. "I did three months of basic training," he says, "and after that my duties here at Oberhof were training and competing in sport and very little else. I was a sergeant but I received my promotion as an officer after winning the World championship in 1974."

During the course of the next hour, Hans-Georg spoke fondly of his sports beginnings as a youngster in Brotterode, where he says, "Almost everyone I knew took a try at ski jumping. We had a small jump there that was very popular with all of the kids. In our area ski jumping has become one of the most popular sports of all."

Indeed, with some 1,200 jumpers active in the country every year it is not surprising everyone who reaches the international level is a threat in major tournaments.

Aschenbach was quite willing to speak of all this when I interviewed him, but he was just as obviously not willing to talk about anything specific in his own medical file. Actually, this seems to be true of all GDR athletes, particularly when they are being interviewed by foreign journalists. Knowing that, I tried to direct the discussion onto the subject of electric muscle stimulation through the back door. Did he, I asked thoughtfully, give any credit for the Seefeld gold medal to the ski team's medical support system?

"No," was the one word answer.

Was there nothing at all unusual in his rehabilitation program?

"Nothing," came the reply, and by now I could see he was getting a little suspicious at the direction of the questioning. "My operation and rehabilitation were very routine."

As I listened to that answer I had a sinking feeling. The story behind the story of GDR sports medicine was going to be even harder to pry loose than I expected.

As a matter of fact, I don't know what I would have done if I hadn't, to my total astonishment, gotten seriously ill less than a week after the interview.

14

The Back Door

It happened at lunch just outside of Dresden.

A pain in the side: anyone who has ever had a kidney stone knows all about it. For anyone who hasn't, it's almost impossible to explain. One minute you are sitting there feeling fine, and the next all of the color is gone out of your face.

The first attack passed in about an hour and a half or so, and as I went out and wandered window-shopping through the rebuilt malls of the great traditional cultural capitals of Germany there was the hope the pain in the side had been nothing more than an intestinal reaction to a differing diet. During the night there was one little stab, enough to wake me up, but then in the morning, minutes before we were planning to depart for Cottbus, it came back worse than ever. The hotel doctor was summoned, then an ambulance, since there were fears of a possible attack of appendicitis, and finally I was taken to what must be one of the oldest hospitals in Europe, a former estate that was surely posh when Napoleon stayed there, and strongly built to have survived the fire-bombing of World War II that virtually leveled the whole city, but it was definitely showing its years by 1977.

If the building was outdated, the staff in the emergency room certainly wasn't, however. Within ten minutes there had been a urine test, a blood test, and an X ray. Within thirty minutes, thanks to the results of the tests, I was admitted.

Once these arrangements were finalized, Dieter, my driver, headed back to Berlin; Regina, my interpreter, headed home to Halle (since it was Friday there wasn't much either one of them could do to help out over the weekend); and there I found myself, flat on my back in a three-bed ward in the company of two seventy-five year olds named Otto Lieberwirth and Georg Shrader. Otto and Georg, like the hospital, had survived the Dresden bombing—they weren't home at the time—but now they were having their problems, too, Otto with a stomach operation and Georg with a leg in traction. They didn't speak a word of English, my few words of German were next to useless, and that was that as I lay there without a clue as to what was wrong with me, hoping against hope it wasn't serious.

"Well, one thing's for sure," said a doctor who stopped by a few minutes later, "it's not appendicitis. It looks like what you have probably got is a kidney stone, but we won't know for sure until we take another set of X rays on Monday. If everything is clear then and your tests come back to normal, you can probably get on your way."

Minutes later a nurse came into the room armed with a needle and spoke to me in German. When she saw that I was uncomprehending, she pulled aside the covers and drilled the needle right into the heart of my left thigh muscle like a dagger, emptied it of its contents, and wordlessly left the room. For the next three minutes, while the drug battled to diffuse itself in my thigh, the discomfort in that area surpassed what I had felt in my side with the kidney stone. I hoped the nurse had found the right bed.

It turned out she had indeed. The next time I was hit by an attack, which happened that evening at the start of the night shift, I signaled for the nurse, who came in looking distressed to see my lying there clenching my teeth.

"*Schmerzen?*" she asked, inquisitively.

"Ow," I replied, pointing to my stomach, under the cold packs they had been applying all day.

"*Spritz?*" she asked.

I groaned, a response that sent her padding back out into the hall only to return with the needle to drill another shot right into that same thigh muscle. After five minutes of massaging that aching thigh, the pain from the shot finally subsided and it was only then that I noticed the pain in the stomach had gone away too. Amazing, I thought. *Schmerzen* was obviously the word for pain and *Spritz* was the magic word to request a shot. It's amazing how fast you start to learn a foreign language when you have to. After yet another *Spritz* that evening I finally got an explanation of what it was. They were injecting a drug called Spasdolin, a strong relaxant that opened internal passages and made it easier for small objects to pass through the system if that was indeed what was happening.

I also picked up a little tidbit on the sports medicine front when my English-speaking doctor stopped by before going home, to check on my condition and ask what I was doing in Dresden in the first place. His expectation was that I was most likely a member of a tourist group, but when I explained that I was a journalist gathering research for a book on GDR sport, he chuckled and said I had come to the wrong hospital.

"Just about ten kilometers down the road from here there's a special hospital in Kreisha reserved just for athletes," he said, "that's where you should have gone to do research on a sports book." In response to what must have been my incredulous look, he continued: "They have a lot of equipment, imported from the West, that is simply not available in the regular hospital systems in the GDR. Kreisha has the best of everything."

Manfred Ewald seemed taken aback when I brought this subject up during our interview in Berlin two weeks later. He had inadvertently brought the subject up himself by asking why Westerners keep having fantasies about the size of the GDR sports budget. I had replied that I knew of no other country in the world where the Health Ministry would consent to provide a hospital with the most up-to-date medical equipment in the world, and allow it to be restricted to athletes.

"What hospital are you talking about?" he asked in a tone of surprise. When I said "the one in Kreisha," there was a moment of silence before Ewald looked over and said, "that isn't a hospital, it's a rehabilitation center. We have a problem with rehabilitation. As you know, one of the features of this country is that medical services are provided free of charge, as a basic right, to everyone. The theory is a good one, but in practice we still do not have enough polyclinics to provide quick service to the entire population. When a worker has to go for physiotherapy, the waiting time is considerable and the employers simply have to allow for it. When we eventually have more clinics it will be a better system.

"Within sport we have the need for a considerable amount of physiotherapy. Faced with the need for building either small clinics in nineteen sports centers throughout the country, or building one in a central location, the obvious economic decision was to build just the one clinic in Kreisha. Now, when an athlete needs extensive rehabilitation he can have the operation at a hospital near his home or club, and then go straight to Kreisha for the rehabilitation in a controlled setting.

"It is a better atmosphere than a hospital, and it is also considerably less expensive than creating nineteen mini-centers all over the country. Once all the options were explained to the appropriate government departments, there was no problem getting an agreement for this sort of project."

Ewald makes an interesting point. When you consider the fact every professional sports franchise and major college campus in North America has full—and duplicative—sports medical, research, and rehabilitative equipment on hand you wonder how much could be saved through sharing, even within a city. Furthermore, a common facility gives the added advantage of complete control of diet and nutrition throughout the rehabilitation process, a time when an athlete can easily pick up a lot of pounds if he isn't careful. And yet at the moment it is socially impossible. Football players would not be happy if separated from their families for several weeks, particularly when injured and insecure. Also, the colleges and universities traditionally do not pool resources. The social and financial problems defeat an otherwise pragmatic course of action. But in the GDR the specialized, seemingly extravagant extra facilities of Kreisha prove both sensible and practicable.

Whenever you are in any hospital you expect to get up early in the morning, but from all the checking I have done since, my Dresden hospital has to be in a class by itself. When the night nurse popped in, flicked on the light, threw open the window, plopped a washbasin down at the bedside, and went around the room greeting everyone with a cheery good morning, I groggily leaned over and stared at my watch. Then I shook it assuming it must have stopped. It was 3:30 in the morning! The first thing I did was close the window. After all, it was the end of January. Then I went back to bed. But by 4 A.M. tea was being served. A half hour later it was breakfast, and then the floors were being swept. By shortly after six the doctors were making their first rounds, and by 7 A.M. patients were being wheeled off to the operating rooms. Compensation came at the end of the day with everyone getting off to bed between 8:30 and 9 P.M.

The problem was a lack of nurses. I was in a postoperative ward, and at night there was one nurse on duty for approximately sixty patients, almost any of whom (including myself with the occasional need for a shot of Spasdolin) were apt to be needing help. The rest of the time there were two nurses to handle everything, including the supervision of the kitchen. Of course they couldn't cope with it, but that, I soon realized, was part of the beauty of the system: the patients, when they were able, were expected to pitch in and help out with the chores. Patients on the recovery road helped to prepare the meals in the kitchen and then washed the dishes after the meals were finished. They swept up the floors when young student volunteers weren't available for that duty, and through it all they developed a camaraderie totally missing in North American hospitals.

They were astonished to learn that this is not the way hospitals were run in Canada and the United States. I tried to explain that we had signs on the doors of the kitchen warning patients to keep out, first because of stipulations in the staffs' union contracts, and also for fear a patient might injure himself and possibly sue the hospital. They listened, laughed, and thought we were a most curious society indeed to allow, nay insist, that our patients lie around feeling lonely and sorry for themselves.

The most fraternal act of all came about late in the evening a couple of times a week when a friend of the night nurse who worked at a brewery down the street would drop in after his shift and bring along a case of beer. This would often be around midnight, and the nurse would then make the rounds of the ward and ask anyone having trouble sleeping if they'd like a brew. Otto Lieberwirth and I had an agreement to wake each other up on beer nights. In the morning when the doctors made their rounds the wastebaskets in the rooms would be full of empties.

"Technically it may be against the rules," one doctor explained with a wink, "but it's really good for cleaning out the system. It's even better than the tea you are supposed to be having."

Otto Lieberwirth was a gem. All day long, every day, he would be visited by a procession of workmen, some of whom looked like chimney sweeps, others resembling sewer workers covered in grime and wearing huge rubber boots. None of this was explained until my interpreter visited on Sunday, three days after my arrival, and formal introductions could be made. Otto had been the man in charge of all the hospital maintenance departments for twenty-five years until his retirement in the early 1970s. Now he was back as a patient, but since he still knew the building better than anyone else in the world, the workmen were flocking to his room to try to solve their problems.

"This whole building is kaput," he said with loving finality. "The elevators stop between floors with patients on their way to and from operations, the hot water might work one day, and only the cold the next. The heat has a habit of going off and on. As a building, it should almost certainly have been phased out after the War, but at the time there was nothing else. One day, I suppose, they will finally close it down. In a way that will be a good thing, and in a way it will be sad."

Whatever they do I hope they never lose the spirit of community involvement.

When my Monday X rays—an awful set of things that required four massive injections of dye to be passed through the veins—came back clear of kidney stones, they decided I could be on my way as early as Wednesday. True to their word, come Wednesday Dieter was back from Berlin with the car to drive, Regina was back to interpret, and I had the bags packed and ready to go. Only to have yet another attack of whatever it was in the car enroute to Berlin. When we arrived in Berlin I was whisked straight to the Weissensee Hospital emergency room, given a shot of pain-killer, more tests, and then wheeled down the hall and into yet another hospital room—this time a small single. Perhaps, I thought as I drifted off to a short nap thanks to the drug, I shall write a book about the GDR public-hospital system.

When I awoke it was to the gentle prodding of a smiling, pleasant-faced surgeon by the name of Dr. Heinz Wuschech, who was still attired in his operating-room greens, minus the rubber gloves and cap. For a full fifteen minutes he prodded and poked, gently pummeled the kidney region, got an interesting reaction from the area of the gall bladder, and then sat back on the end of the bed and ordered up both an internist and a complete set of blood tests.

"Are you a sports journalist?" he finally asked right out of the blue.

When I nodded, he continued, "I thought so. I met you once, at last year's Olympic Games."

"Where?" I asked, completely mystified by this turn to the questioning.

"At the 70-meter jump in Seefeld. I'm the doctor for the Nordic ski team and you were there with our coaches and journalists. I am Hans-Georg Aschenbach's doctor."

"Are you the one," I said, hardly able to believe this stroke of fortune, "who did the operation on his knee?" When he nodded, I crossed my fingers and pushed on to the next question. "Are you the one who did the electrical muscle stimulation in the rehabilitation program?"

"Sure," he said with an even bigger smile, "are you interested in that? If you are, I'll go and check the medical records on that case and we can talk about it tomorrow." I would have laughed—except that it hurt too much. So I just lay there and thought about needles in haystacks. The story behind the story of GDR sports medicine was starting to unfold.

"Aschenbach had his operation in July," Dr. Wuschech explained, "and was sent to Kreisha for six weeks of rehabilitation. He did some cycling exercise, of course, and other normal rehabilitation on the leg, but no jumping whatever.

"And then, when we did get back to jumping it was only with tiny exercises where he would jump off a small box a few inches off the floor just to get the muscles working again. The big thing at this point was to make sure that all the exercise was of the straightforward type. We wanted him exercising, but we didn't want him putting any sideways strain on the knee. By November in St. Moritz he was ready, in the opinion of both myself and the coaches. This wasn't like his first operation, where we had used the electrical muscle stimulation to try to speed up the process. This time there had been plenty of time for a normal recuperation.

"In spite of that, in that first competition in St. Moritz, he looked just terrible. He wasn't getting any lift off the jump at all and he was limping around when he was walking. I can remember Walther Steiner, the Swiss jumper, coming over to me and asking me what was wrong with Aschenbach. He wondered what we were doing with a cripple out there on the jumping hill. Personally, I was astonished. Although there was no physical reason for Aschenbach not to be jumping well it was obvious that he had lost his confidence because of the second operation. He said he didn't feel he had any strength in the knee at all, but physiologically that shouldn't have been the case.

"So we went right back to Oberhof and started all over again on the smallest jumping hill, but it was obvious he had no self-confidence in the knee. That's when we thought of trying the electrical muscle stimulation again. Right away, Hans-Georg was enthusiastic. We continued the stimulation program, along with his regular training, and you could just see the confidence returning. I don't know for sure if it was helping, but you could tell that he was convinced it was helping. By the time we got to Innsbruck, Aschenbach was his old self again. As far as I am concerned, this was more of a psychological treatment than a physiological treatment, but that only goes to point up the importance of that phase of medicine, too. If you are going to have a scientific approach to sport it is very important that both the coaches and the medical specialists be well grounded in sports psychology."

The GDR does not, however, regularly assign full-time sports psychologists to work directly with the athletes on their national teams. This is in general contrast to the trend in the West over the last decade ever since a pair of California professors named Ogilvie and Tutko came on the scene with intensive athlete-related studies, and books such as *Problem Athletes and How to Handle Them*.

I had once been reading a copy of that book myself while covering the Chicago White Sox in the mid-Sixties, and had shown the chapter on "The Withdrawn Athlete" to Manager Eddie Stanky, who was then having a terrible time trying to convert a just-acquired veteran infielder from a loner role into that of a team leader. Stanky needed a holler guy to take charge of the infield, as he would have done himself in his day as a player. He felt his new second baseman Jerry Adair was just the man. But Adair demurred, told the manager if that's what he was looking for he had traded for the wrong player, and had left the office nonplussed. As Stanky read Ogilvie and Tutko's analysis of why loners are loners and how to handle them he got angrier and angrier until he could finally stand it no longer, and, rising from his seat, threw the book back at me in disgust, an act that intrigued third-base coach Grover Reisinger, who then came by my hotel room to borrow the book and read it for himself. The next day he returned it in chagrin. It seems Stanky had caught him reading it in the clubhouse and had blown up all over again. If he didn't change his reading habits Grover got the impression he might just be subjected to a fine.

And why did Eddie Stanky, one of the most knowledgeable baseball teachers in the game, react this way? I don't think it's so much the fact he was a fire-and-brimstone ballplayer who was best suited for managing eager kids in college (for whom he has all the patience in the world), or pros cut in his own image, although that's certainly part of it. The real reason is that Ogilvie and Tutko are academics and not baseball men. Old-line pros who feel they know the game best want to learn from their peers, not from psychologists.

The opposite attitude prevailed in preparing the Canadian swim team for the Montreal Olympics. Dr. Brent Rushall from Lakehead University in Thunder Bay was on hand throughout the final days and was the last official to speak to the swimmers before they went to the starting blocks. Knowing that the Canadian swimmers were performing before an audience full of parents and friends, Dr. Rushall worked on a system that would demand total concentration and positive thinking. Since Olympic swimmers must qualify in morning preliminaries before the evening medal finals, he had every swimmer tell himself or herself that "it was going to be a great day, as soon as they woke up in the morning, before another single thought could enter the mind." Once they were at the pool he had them mentally transforming themselves into animal figures, such as lions, bears, tigers, or whatever animal suited their personality. Forget the parents, forget the friends, forget the opposition, just be a lion, and while you are at it, of course maintain your concentration. When they reached the starting blocks for an Olympic final, it's a wonder the Canadian swimmers weren't growling.

But when I was explaining all this to Kornelia Ender one day in Halle, her eyes just grew wider and wider as she stared at me in amazement. "Lions?" she asked, not quite knowing whether to laugh or take it seriously. "They went to the starting block thinking of lions?"

I asked her what she was thinking of in the very last seconds before the start. "I am thinking about the start," she said, "amd I am thinking about the technique of the first few strokes of the race that is to come."

Part of the difference in approach, of course, is that the Canadians were trying to produce a lifetime best performance in the Games, hoping for the kind of amazing result an American Indian named

Billy Mills produced for the U.S. in the Tokyo Olympics when he won the gold medal in the 10,000-meter run, running it more than a minute faster than he ever had in his life. In the GDR the athlete comes to the competition with a realistic goal that has been set as a result of scientific planning and carefully monitored preparation. He knows what he's ready to do and thus appears less emotional and less frenzied, which can be a valuable asset since extreme nervousness often creates tension, which in turn uses energy and is counterproductive to top performance. As one Canadian coach succinctly put it:

"They come to the competition with the big studs trained and ready to go. When you've got 'em it doesn't matter if you are the Montreal Canadiens, the Oakland Raiders, the Cincinnati Reds, or the GDR women's swim team. You are going to win most of the time."

But Dr. Wuschech is not alone in the GDR in recognizing the importance of an athlete's state of mind. In fact, the top sports psychologists in the country work at the Leipzig Institute teaching the basics to all the coaches and doctors who will eventually work with the national team athletes. The coaches themselves, rather than full-time psychologists, have the final personal relationship with the individual athletes and influence their states of mind.

The only GDR voice that even mildly questioned this practice was, of all people, Hans-Georg Aschenbach. "I have seen other teams with their psychologists," he says, "and I have spoken to other athletes about them. Personally I think team psychologists are a good idea. I know I wouldn't have minded having one with our ski team."

Then he might have growled at all those whistling Austrians in Innsbruck!

15

Dr. Wuschech: More Revelations

The first few days in the Weissensee Hospital were testing ones indeed. Blood tests, X rays of the kidney, X rays of the gall bladder, X rays of the back, urine samples, and all manner of gentle poking and prodding. All of which seemed inconclusive.

Through it all, Dr. Wuschech's bedside manner was reminiscent of the good old days of American family medicine. In the hospital by 7 A.M., he was often still making his rounds as late as 9 at night, talking, chatting, touching and offering friendly encouragement all over the ward. When Christine Errath came to visit, they greeted each other like long lost friends, with Wuschech pushing a few strands of her hair back in place with the admonishment that "world champions don't give interviews without perfect makeup."

"He's a wonderful doctor," Christine said after he had left, "one of the most popular we have. When I was eight years old he treated me at the Dynamo clinic for a knee problem and he was marvelous."

I wholeheartedly agreed—until the evening he decided to chuck modern science and revert to old tried-and-true methods to find the real source of my problem. I was bundled down the hall to the bathtub and submerged to the neck in the hottest water I have ever endured in my life. I was immersed in it for more than fifteen minutes, and then immediately wrapped from head to toe in heavy blankets, arms pinned inside, for a full hour. The feeling came close to that of a steambath as the sweat rolled off my body.

When the blankets were removed I went straight to bed and slept for about four hours, then suddenly awoke with the most painful attack of them all. This time it took at least ten minutes for the injection of Spasdolin to end the suffering. Worse than the pain was the thought that I had suffered a complete relapse and would perhaps need an operation after all.

First thing in the morning, though, there was Dr. Wuschech asking me if I had enjoyed a good night's rest. When I told him of the pain, he immediately brightened and asked me to show him the exact location. When I pointed it out he smiled again. "Good. That proves there is nothing wrong with your gall bladder. Heat of that nature will always create pain directly in the trouble spot. Now we know." Terrific, but with a little warning the night before I could have been prepared for it.

From then on it was downhill to recovery. Within two days I was allowed to use the hospital more as a hotel, with a pass to leave every day for book research and interviews, returning in the evening for medication and rest. One night after finishing his rounds, Wuschech poked his head in the door and asked how I was feeling. When I told him I felt fine, he nodded at the closet and told me to get dressed. Within minutes we were seated in the front seat of the biggest Italian made Fiat you can buy, and heading out of the hospital parking lot.

An Italian Fiat is a great trophy in a country where most of the minority who can afford a private car at all drive a GDR-made two-cylinder plastic Trabant, a Wartburg (the pride of Eisenach), a Polish Lada or Polish Fiat, or perhaps a Soviet Saporoschez or Tschaika, all of which can only be purchased at high prices and after long periods of waiting. Western cars, for most GDR citizens, are beyond possibility since they have to be bought through the International Intershops with Western currency.

Wuschech has a comparatively modest apartment, since he prefers living close by the hospital rather than perhaps having something nicer much farther away from work. But he does have a large screen color TV set. His two children are in the elite athlete program: the daughter swims and the son is a judoka with Dynamo Berlin. Both attend the special sports school.

His wife was born and raised in West Berlin, and the evening I was there, was fussing over the problem of sending flowers to her ailing father across town. Because of the divided city, the seemingly simple task required a friend to come from West Berlin, take the money for the flowers, fill out forms declaring how much money he was taking out of the country and why, and finally go to a West Berlin shop to place the order. "Only in Berlin," they say with a sigh, "could such a situation exist."

Their situation is not uncommon. Back in the 1950s when they met and married, Heinz Wuschech was a first-division soccer player in a city where access between the Berlin military zones was just a formality. And then one morning in 1961 they woke up and found out that a wall was built all the way around West Berlin. Things have not been the same since. By then Wuschech was well into medical school and on his way to being a doctor of sports medicine.

"It took a long time," he says. "First, there was medical school, and then, since I wanted to study sports medicine, I had to take the entire Leipzig coaching certification course on a correspondence basis while working as an intern in the hospital. This is a standard requirement for sports medical doctors working with national teams. Your training in sport has to be on the same basis as the coaches' training."

Once the training was completed, he went to work in the Dynamo Berlin clinic, where, among other things, GDR sports medical specialists have been conducting an ongoing fifteen-year research program into all facets of the question of anabolic steroids.

"It would be interesting to work in sports medicine full time," says Wuschech, "but, since my primary work is as a surgeon, for me this is not possible. Thus I carry a full load of work at the hospital, with the exception of the time I take off to work with the Nordic ski team."

A lot of North American surgeons would undoubtedly love the opportunity to do the same thing, but they find it financially impractical. Tucson, Arizona's Dr. Ted Percy, one of the most respected orthopedic surgeons Canada has ever produced, is a perfect case in point. In his years as surgeon to the Montreal Canadiens hockey club, Ted Percy has been credited with all but miraculous work. He saved Lou Fontinato's life when his spinal cord literally hung by a thread after a head-first crash into the boards at the Montreal Forum. He rebuilt at least twenty-five pieces of Dickie Moore's kneecap after an industrial accident when the easy thing would have been simply to remove the kneecap altogether and end his hockey career. He surgically fixed harness race driver Del MacTavish, Sr.'s wrist in a locked position so he could hold the reins and continue driving, and much, much more. On the amateur scene, Dr. Percy served as the medical member of the Board of Directors of the Canadian Olympic Association. He was chief medical officer for the Canadian team in the Commonwealth Games in 1974 in New Zealand and also with the Canadian Olympic team in Montreal.

"The Canadian sports federations would like to have the same doctors working with their teams all the time," he says, "but this just isn't possible. We have the expenses of an office to consider plus the salary of a secretary, and the factor of all the operations we do not do while traveling with an international sports team. A month away from home for a Canadian or American surgeon can easily run to as much as $7,000 in lost revenue."

Percy made a series of proposals to Montreal's McGill University with the thought of opening a full-time university-level sports medical program in Canada, and, when that idea brought little response, accepted a similar post with the University of Arizona and left Canada in February of 1978.

Berlin's Dr. Wuschech has no such problem. As a doctor in the GDR he is on salary whether he's working in his current position as chief surgeon at Weissensee Hospital or traveling around the Nordic world with a ski team. With top doctors like Wuschech working regularly with coaches and athletes, the results for the GDR have been dramatic to say the least. And yet, when you examine the basic methods of operation, the whole procedure is a remarkably simple and well-organized application of science to sport.

Dr. Wuschech, for instance, maintains a total performance "book" on every athlete under his care, just as do all the other doctors working with GDR athletes. These files are most central to the successful practical cooperation between doctors and coaches and the athletes themselves. They contain everything. Health records, training performances, and long-range plans and objectives. These files are among the most important in the GDR sport system, infinitely more valuable

than the playbooks that are carried around with such care—up to
$1,000 fine if lost—by football players in the National Football
League.

The contents of the training books, are, of course, confidential.
They do, after all, give an indication of the level of performance top
athletes will be expected to achieve with their current training
programs.

The questions that had started this discussion had been supplied me
by Carleton University's Dr. Don Johnson on the off-chance that
such an opportunity as this would present itself. Dr. Johnson had
been taking first steps toward clinical blood-testing with cross-country
skiers by taking a sample at the beginning of a training session, and
others at each succeeding 5,000-meter mark. Under analysis the
blood samples had shown that the serum potassium levels had been
dropping, sometimes precipitously, during the workout, and then
coming back to normal levels a day or so afterwards. "That's
interesting to know," says Dr. Johnson, "but the next question is, just
how important is this information? Does it mean coaches should be
adding potassium to the diet to counteract the temporary loss, or is it
of no real importance at all?"

According to Wuschech the answer lies somewhere in between the
two. "It is an indicator," he says. "When the serum potassium level is
dropping in the blood what is actually happening is that red plasma is
leaking out of the blood cells as a result of overexertion. In the short
run it is not important, but in the long run it is a clear indication the
athlete is training at a level higher than his metabolism is ready to
accept comfortably. In the short run, if a competition was approaching, it would be a good idea to supplement the diet with potassium,
but in the long run, the indication is to cut back on the intensity of
training and work on increasing the athlete's endurance capacities.
The alternative, if you continue to press ahead in the training in spite
of the serum potassium warning sign, is injury. Not immediately,
perhaps, but certainly before you go too much further in the training.
One thing I can promise you is that the Olympic champion in the 50-
kilometer cross-country ski race does not suffer from serum potassium
depletion in the course of his racing."

Wuschech said this does not mean you cannot push ahead quickly
with some young athletes quite early in their competitive training, it
just means that it's important to know the individual metabolism you

are dealing with before you begin to try it. A living example of all this, he explained, is Ulrich Wehling in the Nordic combined.

Nordic combined skiing—an event that requires the competitor to ski 15 kilometers of cross-country and then combine that result with the best two of three jumps on the 70-meter ski jump—is not highly appreciated in North America, but in the long tradition of skiing as a sport there is absolutely no event that carries more prestige. At the first formal ski competition in modern history, held in Norway's Hollmenkollen in 1892, there were two single events, a 17-kilometer cross-country and a ski jump, but the prestigious King's Cup went to the performer who had the best combined total in both events. The tradition has lasted ever since. Back in the 1920s, before the advent of alpine skiing as a serious sport, to ski at Hollmenkollen was the equivalent of playing tennis at Wimbledon or rowing in the Royal Henley. The great jump was used on only one day of the year— Hollmenkollen Day. From the sport's first inclusion in the Olympic Games in 1924 until the beginning of World War II, Norway won every single medal, gold, silver and bronze, in Nordic combined skiing.

But in the 1972 Olympics in Sapporo, Japan, the winner was an amazing nineteen-year-old skier from Oberwiesenthal named Ulrich Wehling. A teenager winning the Nordic combined gold medal was absolutely unprecedented, and he did it by skiing some 4,000 kilometers (that's about 2,500 miles for the metrically uninitiated) and sailing off no less than 850 ski jumps in the pre-Games training year.

That would have all been written down in Dr. Wuschech's books, entered just as neatly as withdrawals and deposits in your bankbook. Except that in this case the training totals are listed right alongside nutritional balances, results of blood-testing, and a host of other data computed by the GDR central sports computer in Leipzig just as regularly and automatically as your bank computes the interest on your savings account.

"In 1972," says Wuschech, "that's all the training Ulrich Wehling was physiologically prepared to handle. If he had been pushed beyond that we would have been heading toward probable injury through metabolic breakdown."

The upgrading came in time for the World championships in Falun, Sweden, in 1974. This time Wehling and his support team, knowing that the world would be taking dead aim on his title, had gradually upped the training ante. In preparation for Falun, Ulrich, now a twenty-one year old, trekked through 4,500 kilometers (2,796 miles) of cross-country skiing and completed 1,000 ski jumps. He won the World championship.

And then it was on to Innsbruck where he would be a maturing twenty-three-year-old defending champion. Once again, the load was slowly increased throughout the training period until in 1975 and the early weeks of 1976 Wehling completed 5,000 kilometers (3,107 miles) of skiing and an astonishing 1,300 ski jumps, thanks mostly to the possibility of jumping on those plastic hills Hans Renner had invented in 1955 during the summer months. In Innsbruck both of Wehling's jumps were beyond the 80-meter mark, a distance that would have made him a contender in the individual jumping competition in the Games. He needed every bit of it, too, as the best he could manage in the cross-country was a 13th place, two minutes and twenty-seven seconds behind the other Germany's Urban Hettich, who dominated the cross-country part of the event just as solidly as Wehling dominated the jumping. But no matter how you cut it, there it was, yet another gold medal.

Those results show that Wuschech and the coaches were in fact making a superb Nordic combined performer out of a man who was an excellent ski jumping talent and only a slightly better than average cross-country skier. One's ability in cross-country skiing at the international level is almost entirely dependent on lung capacity and oxygen-uptake capacity, both of which can take only so much development. After 1976 in Innsbruck, in a physiological sense, there wasn't much more that could be done in the development of Ulrich Wehling as a cross-country skier, a fact that became completely obvious in the 1978 World championship in February of 1978 in Lahti, Finland, when he finished 3rd behind his younger teammate, Konrad Winkler. The twenty-three-year-old Winkler had been 7th in the cross-country phase in Innsbruck, and 4th in the jumping, and a kind of balance any coach would love to see.

Dr. Wuschech was not about to speak of Winkler's pages in the GDR sports medical futures book. But he was willing to answer the last three of Dr. Don Johnson's Canadian medical questions.

Q. Are small doses of anabolic steroids harmful to adolescents?

A. No, or at least not in the vast majority of cases, but only if you are talking about very small doses given under close supervision in a manner so as to support or correct a possible imbalance in the metabolism rather than to change it or overwhelm it. There are side effects to the use of anabolics, as any doctor knows, but generally they do not occur much more often than would be the case with women taking birth control pills. In both cases there are dangers, but they will not affect more than a small percentage of those taking the drug, and, if you test properly, those side effects will become apparent in time to stop the use of the drug. On the other hand, unsupervised use of anabolic steroids on adolescents could be very dangerous indeed. I don't think anyone would recommend it.

Q. What is the youngest age that endurance training should be advised for young children?

A. We have found that it is possible for young children at the age of four and five years to handle what could be classified as endurance work. However, for psychological reasons I wouldn't recommend any special training program at that age. What I am saying is that it is possible for someone that young to ski a long distance, but you wouldn't put them in training for it. You should just encourage them in this direction in their play.

Q. Does faradic (electrical) muscle stimulation improve the strength and endurance of normal muscles?

A. We do not make use of it in that fashion. Our results show that it is an effective treatment of atrophy (shrinking through lack of exercise) of a muscle following an injury or an operation, or to correct an imbalance wherever one muscle has become weaker than the corresponding muscle on the other arm or leg for any reason. But we have also rejected the use of electrical stimulation in the technique events. In high jumping, for instance, the technique is the most important thing, even more so than strength. Therefore, we would not want to stimulate an athlete's quadriceps (front thigh muscles) in such a way that we might alter the athlete's balance and thus force a basic change in his technique.

This apparent rejection of electrical stimulation for strength enhancement is intriguing, if only because it is in contrast to the attitude at the Central Sports Institute in Moscow, where Dr. Yakov M. Kots holds forth as one of the prime miracle workers of Soviet sports medicine. Considering the close relationship between the Soviet Union and the GDR, one would have imagined that any breakthroughs would be shared. Taking the Soviet data into account, it could be that Hans-Georg Aschenbach's complete recovery and return to form in ski jumping was primarily physiological, with the regaining of confidence following on that. I can say this with some personal self-confidence after having undergone eight treatments with Kots' amazing Stimul One machine myself.

16

Stimul One

Gymnast Olga Korbut writes him a letter saying she wouldn't have made it to the Olympics without him. Tennis star Olga Morozova stops in at his apartment for treatment before she heads for major tournaments in the West. He travels with the Soviet national ice-hockey team to training camps and World championships. He lists Valery Kharlamov as one of his best friends in sport. His field, ostensibly, is neurophysiology. One day, some people think, he might win a Nobel Prize. Who is this Dr. Yakov M. Kots?

In the foreword to a NASA-sponsored English translation of Kots' book, *The Organization of Voluntary Movement* (Plenum Press, N.Y., 1977), Dr. Edward Evarts, chief of the Laboratory of Neurophysiology of the National Institute of Mental Health in Bethesda, Maryland, describes Dr. Kots as "One of the most productive members of the Nikolas Bernstein Group," a group with grounding in mathematics, cybernetics, and kinesiology rather than straight physiology, and somewhat apart from the great Russian tradition in the study of the nervous system originating with Pavlov.

He is, in short, one of the modern giants of sports medical research and the developer of Stimul One, the most amazing development in the field of electric muscle stimulation in three decades, a machine that one day might revolutionize the treatment of back and muscle injuries all over the world.

He came to Montreal in December of 1977 under an exchange arrangement worked out between Montreal's Concordia College and Moscow's Central Sports Institute. He came, with his small machine slung over his shoulder like a portable typewriter, to show the doubting Thomases of Canadian research who had published studies casting suspicion on his results, that they were about three decades behind the times in their machinery.

The test would be straightforward and simple. Sixteen Concordia student athletes would have a muscle biopsy drawn from the thigh. Then they would undergo ten treatments of Kots' electrical-stimulation machine over a period of ten days, and then a second biopsy would be taken from exactly the same spot as the first and sent to the biochemical labs of the University of Montreal for microscopic analysis. Dr. Bert Taylor, Canada's top sports biochemist and director of that lab, said he would gladly cooperate even though his knowledge and research led him to the conclusion that electrical stimulation could not possibly increase the size of an individual muscle fiber in a ten-day period. The Russian insisted that it not only could, but it would. Since he had no control over the laboratory study, it appeared he was taking a pretty big risk. He did not look perturbed in the least. He even brightened, during a first interview, when I mentioned it was too bad his machine couldn't do anything for a curved spine (my own) that had been giving me grief through pinched nerves and muscle spasms. The local doctors, including Ted Percy, had suggested I needed a lot of exercise, which is a nice idea, but all but impossible when you have a sore back.

"Have you got an X ray available?" he asked.

When I returned with more than a dozen a day later he studied them carefully, nodded, and said he was sure he could help. In fact he said it was only a small problem, since backs were relatively easy. Some day this could prove to be the best news millions of North American chronic back sufferers have ever heard.

In spite of all the assurances, however, I still felt nervous the next afternoon as I sprawled on a lab table in front of the inquisitive eyes of Canadian doctors, researchers, physiotherapists, and lab technicians who were crowding around the table. Many were skeptical. Dr. James Sullivan, president of the Canadian Association of Sports Medicine and a top surgeon at Montreal's St. Mary's Hospital, had a few questions that didn't make me feel any better at all.

"What does it do to the heart?" he wondered.

"Nothing," replied Kots, "his pulse rate will remain normal throughout the shock treatment."

"But the blood pressure, surely there has to be a worrisome effect there?"

"No," said the Russian, "not so."

"But what of the pain?"

"The stimulation current will have a total anesthetic effect on the area where it is applied," said Kots, "the treatment will not be painful."

"After a couple of days," Don Johnson offered by way of an aside, "your back muscles ought to turn completely black and blue."

While all this talk had been going on, Dr. Kots had rubbed a damp cloth across my back, then put two electrodes in place, both of which were covered in a gauze that had been dipped in a saline solution to prevent skin burning, and finally placed heavy buckshot bags over the whole area to assure a tight and constant contact between the electrodes and the skin. And then it started.

At first I stiffened in anticipation, not from the pain but from the unknown. Sensing this, Dr. Kots spoke quickly in Russian to his assistant, Dr. Ivan Babkin, a Soviet sports medical cardiologist who had come along as an interpreter. "Dr. Kots wants to know what you are feeling," he said. What I was feeling was a pins-and-needles effect, similar to what you get if a foot or hand falls asleep, and incredible pressure as if the very life was about to be squeezed right out of me.

"I feel," I said, "as if Vasily Alexeyev were standing on my back about to attempt a World record in the clean and jerk!"

"What you should be feeling," said Dr. Kots, "is the sensation of a steamroller moving across your back."

In short order we were into a constant and steady flow, first twelve seconds of shock intense enough to force you to tighten with resistance, cease talking, stop the normal breathing pattern, and then eight seconds of rest and recuperation. Kots explained that an athlete getting an exercise workout would get ten seconds of shock and fifty seconds of rest spread over ten repetitions. I was getting twelve and eight—three thunderbolts a minute spread over twenty minutes, for some sixty shocks in all. After about five minutes the pattern became so regular there was a deep sensation of heavy drowsiness.

My pulse rate was checked. It was approximately normal. My blood pressure was checked. That, too, was normal. Everything was just fine and the Canadian medical people crowded around looking like you'd expect people to look when they are trying to figure out how a magician pulls a rabbit out of a hat. As they checked the strength of the muscle contractions in the back and discussed my almost complete lack of pain, it was clear they were impressed. After the session there was a period of approximately twenty minutes when my back felt every bit as anesthetized as your jaw feels when you come home after a shot of Novocain from the dentist. But this was soon followed by a sensation of complete relaxation, as if I were coming out of a dry-air sauna.

I took the Kots treatment for eight days, or half of the fifteen treatments he says he would have prescribed had I been attending his clinic in Moscow. The results were absolutely astonishing. Before we had started I was able to reach about mid-thigh in an attempt to touch my toes. After seven treatments I could almost get all the way down to the ankles without pain. The back muscles, among the hardest to exercise in the entire body, were now as taut as a jockey's. I had almost recovered a full range of motion in all directions. And my waistline had been decreased by more than three inches, without a weight loss, simply through improved muscle tone.

The Canadian medical observers were baffled by the whole affair, until the morning they took Stimul One and hooked it up to an oscilloscope so everyone could see the pattern of the shock wave it was emitting. They also hooked up a West German machine for comparison, a \$3,000 Siemens 627 to be exact. Where the Western machine gave off a regular pattern with the straight line broken by a whole series of rectangular shock waves, the Russian Stimul One gave off a series of sinusoidal curved waves with an overall pattern of extended rectangular shock patterns. In a technical sense the old machine was offering a straight faradic muscle stimulation, the new machine was giving out a galvanic muscle stimulation. The secret of the machine's ability to anesthetize the area it works on, according to Kots, lies with the intensity and frequency of the shock. His machine gives the nervous system a shock lasting only $50/1000$ of a second, followed by a rest period of $10/1000$ of a second. The rest periods could be the key to disabling the body's normal pain mechanisms for the duration of the treatment.

David Wise, who had done one of the Canadian research projects while he was at the University of Western Ontario, was all but contrite after viewing the test on the oscilloscope. "We never thought," he said, "never even imagined the possibility of our machines being out of date. You just take it for granted in North America that we have the latest and best electronic equipment available in our research. I feel humiliated, not that I didn't know about it, but that I never even thought about it."

Considering his academic credits and reputation, it would be a simple matter for Yakov Kots to let his own obvious abilities stand on their own as explanation for the Stimul One breakthrough. Instead he just laughs and admits it all came about by accident.

"Back in 1967," he says, "we were doing some postgraduate work, special theoretical work on electrical stimulation, studying special reflex responses, when I noticed one of my students sitting in the lab in his shorts using one of the machines on his leg. Anatoli told me he had been doing it for some time and even I could see that the muscle on his left leg was getting correspondingly thicker than the one on the right as a result of continual stimulation day after day. That got me to thinking of the possibilities, but it was still a matter of getting a research student to take on this subject for a dissertation, and then getting the Institute Board to accept it as a legitimate question for scientific research.

"That took a complete year because the Board was not particularly impressed to begin with. Fortunately, the student who finally accepted the project was Vadim Chvilon, a wrestler who had a tremendously high tolerance to pain. Vadim drafted several other wrestlers as his subjects and they went through agony in their research, since, after all, they were using the old-fashioned faradic-stimulation equipment that did not anesthetize as it went. Their statistical strength gain results were excellent, but we immediately decided that if this principle was going to be applied to other than wrestlers with high pain thresholds then we would have to invent a completely new machine. We started to work on that in 1969 and the full credit goes to Gana Andrianov, an amazing woman and the engineer who developed all the electrical circuitry."

After that it was a matter of convincing the Soviet coaches that a new medical weapon was indeed in their sports development arsenal.

"The coaches balked," says Dr. Kots, "until I took some of the wives of the gymnasts and trimmed all the extra pounds off their stomachs in a matter of three weeks. When the husbands saw this result it wasn't long before we were given the authorization to begin work with the gymnasts. The results were immediate and dramatic. Young males who didn't have the strength to hold a cross position with arms outstretched on the rings suddenly gained this ability in a few weeks after specific work on the muscles in the underarm area alongside the chest.

From there, the use of the machine spread quickly through most of the Soviet national teams, in spite of the fact that heading into 1978 there were still only five of the machines in existence, all directly under the control of Dr. Kots and the Central Sports Institute.

"Sometime within the next year we plan to go into full production of Stimul One for the mass medicine program," Kots says, "and most of the credit for this goes to my wife, Ella Demina. She is a doctor working in a clinic with children who have been hospitalized with severe spinal defects. She took the machine to work one day, and, in conjunction with doctors at her Institute, put it to work on thirty young children, severe scoliosis patients, with dramatic results. This is the research that led to my ability to work on your back here, and it is the research that led to the decision for mass production. Within a year this machine ought to be making its way into our hospitals and polyclinics."

And in the West?

"I don't know," he admits, "that is simply not my decision to make."

When asked for comments on some of his most interesting cases among the athletes, Dr. Kots was quick to turn to gymnasts and ice-hockey players.

"On the matter of training with healthy athletes," he says, "we have added an average of four inches in jumping ability to our entire national volleyball team. But that is a different matter from the treatment of injuries. Perhaps my favorite memento is a letter from Olga Korbut thanking me and the treatment for getting her to the Olympic Games. Although Olga has a tremendous personality that comes across beautifully in her performances, she is not a terribly warm person in her general personal relationships, and she is definitely not the type to spend much time writing letters to people. Her problems came from her bravery in training. She was always putting tremendous strain on her spine and as a result she had many back problems. But there were others as well—legs, ribs, ankles, she was always injuring something or other, and it was always difficult.

"Kharlamov was difficult, too, after a car accident in 1975 left him with broken ribs, broken ankles, and a host of internal injuries of the type that lead to long rehabilitation and great difficulties in restoring muscles to the tone of top-level fitness."

The Soviet national ice-hockey team always has Kots on hand in their training camps and World tournaments, and in 1977 in Vienna it was he who kept Sergei Kapustin and Vladimir Petrov playing when injuries. normally would have sidelined them both.

"Petrov has had a groin problem on and off for years," says Kots, "and although the groin is one of the areas where you have to be very careful in using this machine, we did use it in his case. It was possible, with twenty minutes of stimulation, to completely fatigue the muscle to the point where it was completely relaxed and could not respond at all for the duration of the game. It wasn't 100 percent, of course, because the other muscles in the leg had to compensate and fill in for the idle groin muscle, but he was able to play with just a little weakness and no real pain. This is much preferable, in my view, to attempting to freeze an injured area with Novocain. With Kapustin it was a shoulder, but we used much the same treatment—about twenty minutes of stimulation—and he was loose enough to play an entire hockey game without discomfort."

The Soviets even use Stimul One for major injuries.

"It is much more effective than ice," says Kots. "You apply ice for an hour or so, of course, but after an hour all the internal bleeding is finished and the time is then perfect for deep stimulation to help speed the rehabilitation process." This is the kind of news most trainers with North American pro and college teams will find fascinating, and just another reason why Soviet-styled electrical-stimulation machines will one day be regular fixtures in all training rooms. But by then Dr. Kots hopes to have moved on to more exciting developments.

"What we are working on now," he says, "is the development of a tiny transmitter, using the same theory as the heart pacemaker already in use, that can be installed alongside the spinal cord in a person's back. Once it's in place, in theory, you could hold a small activating device in your hand and dial your exercise once or twice a week just as easily as you would send a message on a telephone Pagette."

This is the possibility that apparently sprung NASA into action as soon as they heard about it. In the not-too-distant future it is entirely possible that man will be in space, working in a relatively small area, for long periods of time, perhaps even a matter of years, without an opportunity for a lot of exercise. Kots' "dial-a-workout" could be just the answer. So, although there was no great U.S. scientific interest in his ability to make a volleyball team jump four inches higher, it was a different matter when a possible application to the space program was realized. Money was immediately appropriated for the translation of his work into the English language. The bionic man might not be so far in the future as some people think.

"But the real value of my machine," says Dr. Kots, "will come with this machine's application for mass medicine, particularly in the cases of people who have a hard time getting their muscles back in shape after an accident. This is particularly true of older people who often are laid up for weeks after they slip, fall, and break a bone.

"Think of the handicapped, and the totally paralyzed. We can't offer them a cure, of course, but perhaps, particularly with transmitters, we can keep some tone in their muscles so they can at least manage some of the bodily functions on their own."

The most impressive thing about Dr. Kots' Montreal visit, however, was the results of the University of Montreal biopsies on the fifteen Concordia College students. Dr. Taylor of the University of Montreal lab was so startled by the first run-through that he spent the best part of a month having everything double-checked, and then had it all run through an independent computer one more time just to make triply sure.

"There is no doubt that there were changes in the muscle fibers in just ten days," he says. "There is just nothing in my experience in biochemistry that allows me to explain why that happened. To the best of my knowledge it shouldn't have happened. My problem is that I can't go any further in even attempting to find an explanation until Dr. Kots provides us with more information from his end on what really happens with his program. If anyone on this side of the ocean ever figures it out for himself, though, he's going to be in a position to make an awful lot of money in a big hurry. If, that is, he can get around the patent laws."

The one puzzle in all this, however, is the GDR claim that their machine does not have the anesthetizing effect on the muscle during stimulation.

"I have no idea what the GDR has been doing in the field," Kots admits. "I know that they were given the information right near the beginning of the program through an exchange agreement between our two countries. And I have heard that they have developed at least two new stimulation machines of their own. But we have never really gotten together to work it out. I really can't say if their machines are exactly the same as ours or not."

My own suspicion is they are not. Manfred Ewald's reaction when we spoke of stimulation during the 1978 World Bobsled championships in Lake Placid was that it wasn't a new development but was not too useful because of the element of pain. The same response Dr. Wuschech had given a year earlier. The GDR may still be using the West German faradic equipment.

But even that was a big help to Hans-Georg Aschenbach.

17

But Is It Sport?

When the President's Commission on Olympic Sports turned over its massive two-year study to a just-inaugurated President Carter in January, 1977, little attention was paid to the proposal on sports medicine, which, after a thorough study of existing programs, found:

Instructive and important as each of these programs is, none provide a truly national forum for research, clinical application, information, and education in sports medicine. Some are intentionally limited in their scope, or are regional in character. Others lack adequate funding to pursue their goals, or provide information too technical for the coach, athlete, or trainer to understand. Most operate independently, seldom in coordination with other efforts.

There is clearly a need to bring together findings in related fields and to improve the manner in which this knowledge is applied to sport. Equally apparent is the need to develop U.S. sports medicine by taking advantage of the work of approximately thirty sports medicine programs throughout the world, nearly all of which are much further along than are U.S. efforts in applying medical science to sport.

In short, what is needed is a national center for sports

medicine, established as a permanent committee of the Central Sports Organization. Specifically the committee should:
    —Promote research;
    —Provide, through clinics, workshops, textbooks and other literature, a continuing education program in sports medicine for physicians, coaches, trainers, and athletes;
    —Establish effective liaison with federal, state, and local government programs dealing with health and product safety.

If you think the Central Sports Organization sounds a little like the DTSB and the national center for sports medicine a little like the Leipzig Research Institute, you may go to the head of the class. But that isn't the question here. The question is, what will happen if and when the United States actually does create a sports medical research center of its own? For one thing, the U.S. will finally confront the moral dilemma that is already bedeviling every one of those "approximately thirty sports medicine programs throughout the world." Is sport to be a battle of athlete against athlete, or one of pharmacologist against pharmacologist?

The purist position on the role of drugs, or any kind of medicine, in sport is that their use contravenes a basic premise of competition—that it should test the comparative natural capabilities, skills, and strengths of athletes. Under the purist view, any violation of this principle is a violation of sporting morality. And yet, it is becoming increasingly evident that the purist position, in some ways admirable, is in fact irresponsible in its rejection of the guidance that medical knowledge can give—especially when one considers the high training levels introduced over the past two decades in the struggle to live up to the Olympic motto of *Citius, Altius, Fortius* (Faster, Higher, Stronger).

Today, once any elite sports training program starts to include blood tests, muscle biopsies, electrocardiograms, bone X rays and injections of enzymes, minerals and vitamins, it becomes harder and harder to know where to draw the line. The muscle biopsy is an excellent example. By sticking a needle into a muscle and pulling out a minuscule sample of tissue it is possible for a trained biochemist to tell much about an athlete's muscle fiber potential. Every human muscle is composed of fast-twitch fibers, which deal with quickness and speed, and slow-twitch fibers, which control the endurance capability of the muscle. Muscle-fiber varieties within the human species are very broad indeed. Finland's Lasse Viren, the Olympic champion in 5,000 and 10,000 meters at both the Munich and Montreal Games, is said to have more than 80 percent slow-twitch fiber preponderance in his muscles, a finding that helps explain his amazing distance-running capabilities. Most world-class sprinters, on the other hand, have at least 75 percent of their fibers in the fast-twitch category. Eric Heiden, the new superstar of U.S. speed skating, has tested out to a 60–40 ratio, fast-twitch predominating, which helps explain his remarkable ability to win both 500-meters sprints and distance races of 10,000 meters at the world level.

"But you can't always count on it," says Peter Schotting, U.S. national speed skating coach. "Sheila Young tested out at 53–47, which should have made her a great all-around skater and cyclist, but in fact she was almost purely a sprinter in both sports. Sheila never had the psychological desire to be a distance skater. Her case proves to me that the mental aspects are very important, too." And so GDR coaches do not base their athlete-selection decisions solely on physiological findings.

But many people in sport, particularly in countries following the British tradition, devoutly wish there was none of this application of science to sport. They say, quite frankly and vocally, that it is not sport. But the need for that application is increasingly obvious.

At the Montreal Olympics, Dr. Doug Clement of Simon Fraser University in British Columbia received a grant to take blood tests of a variety of Canadian athletes just a few days prior to their entering the most important competitions of their lives. All had been involved in months and even years of intensive training directed toward this one moment. Their state of physical health should have been superlative. And yet, Dr. Clement's eventual analysis proved, even to his own surprise, that the Canadian endurance athletes had nutritional levels that were below those for an average member of the non-sporting Canadian population. The Canadian Olympic endurance athletes were suffering, in a clinical sense, from marginal malnutrition. This is not to say that they were starving, but just to suggest that under 1976 Olympic training loads, the average North American diet of three square meals a day does not supply enough nutrients to offset what is burned up in daily exercise. To get that balance they have to have supplements. Is it "sport" to continue to refuse to study those needs?

Is it "sport" to allow an athlete to attempt a long-distance run—and this certainly applies to the thousands of joggers who go to the starting line in an annually increasing list of events such as the Boston marathon—when a blood profile might show deficiencies in one or more elements that might adversely affect the runner's health? Is it ethical to let a high school football player bash his head against the brick wall of an offensive line for years when bone X rays might indicate he shouldn't be involved in contact sports at all?

There was a perfect example of the latter risk in the Canadian Football League in the early 1970s. Bill Massey from the University of Hawaii was an excellent running back, but occasionally, when hit head on, his fingers became instantly rigid and the ball would pop loose. Finally a suspicious team doctor, Ted Percy, sent Massey to the Montreal Neurological Institute for a series of tests, tests that proved his spinal column had half the natural protection of the average spinal column. The experts at the Neuro came to the conclusion that it was exceedingly dangerous for Bill Massey ever to have played football. And yet he wanted to play football, even going so far as to say he would sign a release freeing the football club of all responsibility if he suffered an injury to his neck. To his thinking, he had made it all the way through high school and college football, and one year of professional football, so why stop now and end a lucrative career because of something that *might* happen. Dr. Percy finally settled the matter by writing a letter to the CFL commissioner to the effect that if Bill Massey played football he was playing it against professional medical advice. With that, the league decided that Massey's career was over.

In that instance, the action to be taken was clear. Yet much of the time in sports medicine the decisions are by no means so simple. It is one thing to analyze the percentages of fiber types within a human muscle, but another to attempt to use science to change those percentages. Given that it is morally wrong, and dangerous, to let athletes reach a state of malnutrition through overtraining and improper diet, how much dietary supplementing should be allowed? Enough to bring the athlete back to the average level for a nonathlete within society? Or is it all right to move beyond that and create a new metabolism?

A case in point is our understanding of the simple act of running. Anyone reading this book can go out and start to sprint as fast as possible. In short order you will be short of breath, and, if you battle on a bit past that point, your arms and legs will start to feel like lead weights as the muscles tighten up. In my running days we called it "tying up," and we didn't have the foggiest idea of what was really happening to the muscles. What we did know was simply that the more one trained, and the harder one trained, the longer one could run at high speed. Now, as a result of sports medical research, primarily in Sweden, we know that when an athlete "ties up" there has been a depletion of the glycogen in the muscles and a corresponding increase in the level of lactic acid. We also know now that quick spurts burn up a lot of glycogen, while a steady pace burns much less. This is why, for example, most horses can give one sustained burst of speed per race, a burst that carries between an eighth and a quarter of a mile, some horses can give two bursts, and an occasional world champion can manage three. And so it goes with humans. Some runners can continually alter a pace during a race. Most cannot.

No one argues against conducting basic research to learn more about the workings of the human body under stress. And no one, today, considers it immoral for an athlete to increase his natural glycogen capabilities through training. In the early decades of this century, however, even training was frowned on, with many international federations ruling that, for fair competition between athletes of natural strength, more than sixty days of practice a year was definitely excessive. Those were the days when sport was for gentlemen of leisure, and certainly not for the working class, who would have unfair advantage because of the rigors of their physical labor.

The modern Olympic founder, Baron Pierre de Coubertin, dis-associated himself from these early amateur rules, passed by a majority of his own International Olympic Committee over his strenuous objections. In 1934 he wrote: "The actual rules are wicked. Their terms are indefensible as much from the point of view of logic, which they offend, as that of human liberty, which they cheapen."

Today even the stoutest defender of the British ideal of sportsman-ship would agree that the development of muscle through training is both appropriate and acceptable. But when you start to discuss the transformation of the glycogen supply of a muscle through diet, you are going to get an argument.

The career of Dr. Bert Taylor of the University of Montreal closely parallels that of a number of sports medicine experts in the GDR. As an athlete he was an elite-level wrestler, which provided him with a practical sports background to go with his interest in research. Better yet, he did his graduate work in Sweden, certainly the most advanced country in the Western world in applying the study of human metabolism to sports. The problem with the work at this level, as the President's Commission report states, is that it is generally inaccessible to athletes, coaches, and trainers. Dr. Kots' work in the field of neurophysiology, for example, is far too abstruse in its particulars for a layman's understanding. In an attempt to simplify the question of glycogen level and its alteration through diet, I had the following discussion with Dr. Taylor.

Q. How does glycogen relate to diet?

A. Well, the glycogen is important because it has been shown that the more glycogen you have in a muscle to start a race the longer you can race at a higher speed. You build it up principally through training and diet. With training, most top athletes will build up glycogen to a similar level, but as soon as you manipulate the diet then you can increase the level of it even more. This has been going on since 1967 in Scandinavia and the East bloc countries.

Q. What do you do with the diet?

A. Well, normally what they have been doing goes something like this. Monday and Tuesday the athletes combine a balanced diet with good normal workouts, and on Wednesday eat a normal diet but work their butts off to a point of complete exhaustion. What they do is deplete all the glycogen in the muscle. So you have none. Well, on the Thursday, they go on a carbohydrate diet and you get a rebound effect. The muscle for some reason says, "I want carbohydrate, I want carbohydrate," which after all is what glycogen is, and it lays down exceedingly high levels of carbohydrate, perhaps three or four times normal levels. And then on Friday you have a light workout, you are ready to compete on Saturday, and you've got high glycogen levels. You are ready to go.

Q. Sounds like just the kind of thing for a 400-meter runner.

A. Oh sure, a 400-meter runner burns up a heck of a lot of glycogen. But, you know, most of the top track and field guys, most of the skiers, they are on the diet now. They use it. The wrestlers use it a fair amount.

Q. But when I spoke with Waldemar Cierpinski, the GDR marathon runner, he said he wasn't on the diet. Why not?

A. Because a marathon runner runs almost totally on fat. He has to have a certain amount of glycogen to sprint and get out of the pack at the first, and to break away in the middle, or to have a finishing kick at the end. But the other problem they have is that glycogen is inefficient in storage. Every molecule of glycogen you store takes three molecules of water to store it, so you put on weight. A marathon runner just keeps a moderate amount of glycogen, but has great fat reservoirs.

Q. But a marathon runner is not visibly fat.

A. No, not fat, but within the muscle and subcutaneous you have enough fat. Small amounts of fat have enough energy in them to get you a long distance.

Q. When I spoke with Frank Shorter, he said he didn't really agree with the diet either. He said it was a method of short-cutting training. He said if you are really trained for it, you don't need it. Do you agree?

A. Well, you know, when you get a group of guys who have all trained the same way, and they are all the same kind of athlete, then the edge is what's going to win. But in a race as long as a marathon, I don't think it would make that much difference.

Q. But what of the buildup of the lactic acid within the muscle. Is it true that as the glycogen depletes in the muscle, the lactic acid increases? Isn't that a prime factor, too?

A. No, that's a theory. It appears that when the muscle is becoming fatigued, it is very highly correlated with the glycogen level. On the same train, glycogen is converted to lactate, but lactate diffuses in the muscle very quickly and I know of no studies where people doing long-term endurance work have had a buildup of lactate in the muscle. That's a very old theory that some people still hold to, but it's fifty years old, and it has been reasonably well proven that it is not true in submaximal work. In maximal work, it may play a role because you have got a problem of circulation to the muscle, and at maximum levels you are working isometrically. Glycogen is broken down into lactic acid and it diffuses in the blood. So, what you might also get then is a higher plasma level of lactate in a runner who alternates his speed than in a runner who goes on at a set pace. But we don't really know what lactic acid does. We know what happens to it, but we don't know if it creates problems with the cell wall of the individual cells, or diffusion problems, or what. We just don't know."

One man who claims to have a lot of knowledge about lactic acid procedures is Dr. Alois Mader, who created a sensation in the sports medicine field when he defected from Kornelia Ender's Chemie Halle Club in 1974 and moved over to the Federal Republic Sports Institute in Cologne. Dr. Mader has had a mixed reception in the West. He did not come over like a political refugee denouncing GDR sports medicine, or painting pictures of a doctor fleeing a pack of mad scientists who were forcing him to change women into men. He came over to tell the rest of the world it had better get a move on if it wants to remain competitive in international sport.

Dr. Mader claims that by closely monitoring the lactic acid levels during the training of swimmers, rowers, skiers, paddlers and distance runners, it is possible to design training systems that provide optimum development under conditions of maximal safety for the athlete. In effect, while Dr. Wuschech was monitoring the Nordic combined ski champion, Ulrich Wehling, from 1972 to 1976, Dr. Mader was doing much the same thing with Kornelia Ender at Chemie Halle. The system is simple. A blood test before the workout, and then as many as five in succession in ten minutes, following a strenuous workout. The results are then computerized, and the computer can pinpoint the exact state of the metabolism under a specific training load. It can assure that the athlete is neither undertrained nor overtrained.

Dr. Mader has been to the U.S. to address the convention of the Amateur Athletic Union, and the head of the AAU medical committee, Florida's Dr. Bob Greenwell, has become a convert to lactic acid testing. So have several U.S. swim coaches who have been overwhelmed by the development of GDR women's swimming since 1973. But there are problems, not the least of which is the fact the cost of a lactic acid testing and computing program can easily run into the vicinity of $40,000, a figure far beyond the capability of most U.S. swim clubs and schools.

Other people, though, are quick to point out the fact that the GDR men's swim team, with all the same sports medical advantages as the women, trails far behind the U.S. men's team internationally. The U.S. men and women are trained in the same basic fashion, this argument goes, and thus if the coaches of the women are making basic mistakes in development, the men ought to be making the same mistakes in training, too. If they are, it sure doesn't show up in the results.

Dr. Irving Dardik, the head of the United States Olympic Committee's Sports Medicine Commission, is all in favor of continued research into lactic acid, but says he doesn't think any one development on its own is going to provide an overall answer in sports medicine. Under Dardik's direction, USOC sports medicine clinics are being established at Squaw Valley, Colorado Springs, and possibly, after the 1980 Olympics, in Lake Placid—three steps in the right direction toward a responsible American program in the field of sports medicine.

And yet the basic question still remains: Is it sport?

Many, and this list now includes International Olympic Committee President Lord Killanin, have come to the conclusion it is not. Lord Killanin feels the tendency is toward bionic man if the current trends continue with an emphasis on pharmacology as the key to Olympic success. He has even gone so far as to suggest, at an IOC executive board session in Uruguay in 1979, that it is now the biggest problem threatening the future of the Olympic Games.

Ah, how easy it is to long for the past, for the good old days when international athletes competed against each other with their own natural unadulterated bodies. The problem is that the past was never really like that at all. Strychnine used to be the big stimulant back in the 1920s and before, and occasionally it was a killer. Anabolic steroids have been in the Olympic Games since Rome in 1960 and possibly before; at that time they were taken openly and nobody really knew enough about them even to form an opinion on legality or illegality.

In the past the problem has always been swept under the rug. Now, with National Olympic Committees supporting major sports medical research operations in the name of *Citius, Altius, Fortius*, it is out in the open seeking sanction, demanding an affirmative answer to the question of "Is It Sport?" *if* the sports medical program is indeed a responsible one.

Responsibility. That's the real rub.

18

Anabolic Steroids and Doping Control

If responsible sports medical researchers all over the world are having a hard time deciding on guidelines for permissible metabolic change, the International Olympic Committee—never one to hesitate in areas where angels fear to tread—has shown no such qualms. The IOC firmly prohibits use of the anabolic steroid.

History may one day reveal this to be a hopeless and perhaps even irrelevant stand in the war against the misuse of drugs in sport, but, as of April 1975, the rule is there. Today all those who have been laboring to improve athletic performance through alterations in human hormone balances have been lumped in with those who for centuries have tried to stimulate performance with amphetamines, strychnine, cocaine, and the rest of the psychomotor stimulant family.

What is an anabolic steroid? A proponent might describe it simply as a catalyst that enables the body to retain more protein. There are three different types of steroids—estrogen, androgen, and cortico-steroids. The last belong to the cortisone family and are used medically to combat infections within the system that are unresponsive to normal treatment. The anabolic steroids belong to the androgen family—or the male hormone group—and are the reason little boys grow into muscular men after puberty.

Back in the early 1960s, few expressed any concern whatever when U.S. athletes interested in increasing their strength started to use anabolic steroids. Football players who graduated from college as 220-pound linemen were reporting to the pros just months later at 250 and 260 pounds. Shot putters who had struggled to throw sixty feet for years were moving relentlessly toward and then past seventy feet. College athletes everywhere started to speak of a drug called "Dianabol," and a few people, those with an ecological consciousness for the human body, started to get a little worried about side effects.

Anabolic steroids, after all, were not developed with athletes in mind. They were synthesized, in the United States, to help people suffering from severe malnutrition, cancer, and severe burns, to rebuild tissue when their bodies are incapable of rebuilding it naturally.

The problem for sports medicine is that since the drug companies never intended them for use by healthy athletes, no adequate manufacturer-related research information on possible side effects is available in the Western countries. What studies have been done, however, have led to serious alarms from some members of the medical community.

One of the most constant voices has been that of Professor Arnold Becket of the University of London's Chelsea College, a member of the IOC medical commission, and the driving force behind the new Olympic anabolic steroid tests. Dr. Becket is the founder and editor of the *Journal of Medicinal Chemistry* and the Chairman of the Board of Pharmaceutical Sciences for the Fédération Internationale Pharmaceutique. His credentials, in short, are impeccable. Writing in the IOC's official journal, the *IOC Review*, he says that:

> The side effects of anabolic steroids on sex organs in animals have been clearly established. In the rat they cause reduction in spermatogenesis and have marked effects on the testes and accessory sex organs (Kincl, et al., 1965); more recently, Rogozkin (1975) has also shown weight reduction of the prostate, testicles, and seminal vesicles in rats. The output of testosterone and gonadotrophins is reduced by large doses of anabolic steroids

in rats (Boris et al., 1969). It is to be expected that anabolic steroids will affect the sex organs in man; in two patients taking large doses of the anabolic steroids Oxymethalone and Methandrostenolone, Harkness et al. (1975) were able to show a reduction in testosterone and gonadotrophin output and some indication of reduction in spermatogenesis.

Anabolic steroids also cause effects on the liver. Orally active anabolic steroids show liver toxicity and can cause jaundice (Wynn, 1975). The long use of anabolic steroids may be associated with liver tumors, including cancer (Farrell, 1975).

There have been reports of jaundice, prostatism, hypertension, gastro-intestinal hemorrhage, decrease, but sometimes increase, of libido and oligospermia associated with the use of anabolic steroids (Freed and Banks, 1975). In studies using 13 highly trained athletes receiving 10 mg or 25 mg of Methandienone per day, Freed et al. (1975) showed a high incidence of side effects including headache, hypertension, urinary trouble, and raised levels of serum cholesterol and alanine transaminase. Also cholesterol levels were elevated, but this may be as a result of the diet rather than the drug effect.

Wynn (1975) has reported that orally active anabolic steroids produce a "host of unwanted effects and should really be regarded as highly dangerous compounds which should not be used except under careful medical supervision, and even then they have only a restricted place in therapy."

They cause disturbances in carbohydrate and lipid metabolism and such drugs can be expected to yield to an accelerated development of atherosclerosis, which leads to heart disease, strokes and peripheral vascular diseases. For instance, methandienone in ten healthy subjects gave a deterioration in glucose tolerance associated with a significant fall of the fasting blood sugar; circulating plasma levels of triglyceride were increased despite enhanced triglyceride removal in five female subjects. On the other hand the injectable anabolic steroids produced few side effects unless large amounts are used, which then produce virulization in women so that menstrual trouble, hirsutism, and deepening of the voice may occur.

The use of anabolic steroids in pre-pubertal children can lead to premature sealing of the epypheseal plates of long bones with resultant stopping of growth. Although muscle mass is increased by anabolic steroids' misuse under conditions of high protein diet, increase in tendon strength does not occur at a similar rate; thus torn tendons may result during vigorous exercise.

Why, one wonders on digesting all these warnings, would anyone be fool enough to take anabolic steroids for any reason whatever? But then again, some of us also wonder why anyone would ever be interested in smoking a cigarette after considering the confirmed health warnings of the links between smoking and lung cancer.

I do not smoke. But I did take three massive doses of steroids during 1977, when, on returning to Canada from the GDR, my strange kidney ailment receded to be replaced by a severe and unresponsive iritis infection in the left eye. Finally, after everything else failed, I was told I would be given 80 mg of steroids—of the corticosteroid family—per day for a period of three days. That is anywhere from four to eight times higher than the doses of anabolics that athletes take to become strong.

When the treatment was first suggested I was startled, and asked about possible side effects. I was told that they existed, which is why the treatment would only be continued for three days, but I was also told that the risks were minimal when compared to the almost certain loss of the eye if something couldn't be found to check the infection. As he gave me the first dose, the doctor warned about a possible "artificial high and sense of well-being" that might accompany the treatment.

"Be wary," he said, "because as well as you might feel tomorrow, you are not well, and when the treatment is stopped in three days time you might well go into a fairly deep depression."

The "high" was incredible. Within twenty-four hours of the first pill I was up and out of bed and pacing the Montreal General Hospital corridor feeling better than I could remember feeling at any time in the ten previous years. If it had been summer instead of winter I think I might have gone out and jogged around the park. If anabolic steroids do anything like this for athletes, I thought to myself, I can readily understand why they are reluctant to give them up, no matter what the warnings of the medical profession. Becket, in his article, mentions the effect on attitude in a final warning:

The reports of increased aggression caused by anabolic steroids may place other competitors at risk. It has been recorded by Payne (1975): "There are, undoubtedly, psychological effects resulting from steroid taking, and the ones who benefit most from these effects are the nervous poor competitors who suddenly find the confidence to lift themselves out of their mediocrity. They are the ones who would not like to come off the drugs if effective tests are brought in. The majority of athletes I have spoken to, however, would welcome the tests if they could ensure that no drug taker in the world can escape detection. The athletes themselves, on the whole, want to come off the steroids."

Yes, but how many alcoholics tell their doctors they want to give up drinking? How many smokers go around saying they want to give up smoking? It's not such a simple matter to take people at their word, particularly when they are saying one thing and doing the opposite. Often they even fool themselves. What I would be more inclined to say is that the athletes involved wish there were more research into the subject so they would really know more about the specific long-term effects of what they are doing. General apprehension just isn't enough. Millions of smokers know that their habit increases their chances for lung cancer. But they keep right on smoking.

It's an easy matter to test the human body for amphetamines and other drugs, because they are not normally part of the body chemistry. Testosterone and other hormones, however, are a part of the body chemistry; the testers must try to detect abnormally large quantities of it. It is a simple matter for an athlete to take steroids for months, increase his weight significantly, and then pass the urine test by stopping the drug a certain number of days before the competition. He doesn't lose the added weight, and he doesn't flunk the test.

The 1975 rule made a circus of the Olympic Village at Montreal, for, in contrast to the usual practice of conducting tests after an event, athletes could be selected for anabolic steroid testing at any time after they checked into the Olympic Village. Our two 1976 discus rivals, Wolfgang Schmidt of the GDR and Mac Wilkins of the United States, were almost 300 miles apart with Schmidt and most of the GDR track team working out at Laurentian University of Sudbury, Ontario, while Wilkins was lodged in a motel in Trois-Rivières,

Quebec, almost 100 miles northeast of Montreal. When the medical testers asked the Soviets for a test of super heavyweight weightlifting champ Vasily Alexeyev, they were simply told he was "out of town and unavailable." Were they all psyching themselves up far from the hustle and bustle of the Olympic Village, or were they off somewhere flushing their bodies with diuretics to hasten the elimination of everything that eventually must pass through the urinary tract?

Unfortunately, because of the official ban on steroids, no one will say anything publicly about the question of their obvious covert use. I have been privately told about apparent exact dosages of several shot putters, discus throwers, and hammer throwers in Canada, the United States, and Europe, but the information was given in the understanding it would not be made public. Within the GDR it was almost impossible to get anyone to talk on the subject, even privately, and, on the rare few times it did happen, it was off the record, and often hearsay as well.

While in the GDR I did learn, however, that every National Olympic Committee in the world was sent the raw data on the Montreal anabolic test, and by simply running a sample test through a laboratory, one learned that the cutoff day to pass the test was really just five calendar days and not twenty-one, as was generally assumed by Western athletes. The GDR source assumed everyone had that information since all NOCs had the test. Surely every country in serious competition at least ran a test.

As a matter of fact they didn't. The Canadian Olympic Association, I learned after some poking around in their Montreal headquarters, placed the test information in a filing cabinet after sending an FYI copy to the team doctors. Canada, at that time, did not have a lab facility for anabolics in existence, and would not have until just prior to the Games themselves.

"Besides," as one Canadian Olympic team doctor pointed out, "you couldn't run a test unless you had an athlete who would admit to taking the steroids and who wanted to be tested. I would assume most countries just placed their copy of the test in a filing cabinet."

"What we are looking at here," says Mac Wilkins, "are two basically different approaches to sports medicine. The East European research people look at the anabolic steroid as another tool to help the athlete advance his performance at the international level. The American sports officials look on it as something akin to heroin. Until we get that kind of thinking turned around there is no way we can ever have a serious American dialogue on sports medicine."

Knowing the Western attitude, East Germans don't care to discuss anabolic steroids. It's a subject that causes difficulty with friends, let alone with people who are suspicious of the motives of any Westerner who asks the question in the first place.

"Why," one asked in a moment of rare forthrightness on the topic, "do you people keep throwing these insinuations in our direction? You invented them and everyone uses them. What is the issue?"

When I told him that as far as I knew the North American female athletes—and at this moment I was thinking particularly of the swimmers—did not use them, he gave me a look of honest disbelief, followed by one of suspicion, and finally one of puzzlement.

"Why not?" he asked in amazement.

"Because," I replied, "they are females and they are frightened of fooling around with male hormones. They do not want deep voices, body hair, or greasy skin."

He blinked at me. "Is that what your girls think happens?" he asked. "Do they think such small changes in appearance are irreversible?"

"I'm sure they do," I said.

He shook his head, sat in silence for a while, and then changed the subject.

Confronted as they are with a continual barrage of snide comments about the femininity of GDR women athletes, everyone in GDR sport from Manfred Ewald on down has assumed a highly defensive posture.

"The instructions to our sports medical people and our athletes are clear," says Ewald. "They are not to violate the rules of the International Olympic Committee or the individual sports federations. The sports medical people themselves are well aware of these dictums and say they follow them completely. But some do add the rider that "what cannot be detected cannot be considered against the rules."

Which brings us back to the basic argument about the philosophy of sport. Is it Citius, Altius, Fortius whatever the means? Or is sport a hobby to be practiced by the leisure class in their spare time? Historical evidence would indicate that the driving force has often been the former rather than the latter, in spite of lip service for the latter.

Professor Becket thoroughly reviews the history of drug use in sports in a chapter on "The Work of the IOC Medical Commission" in *The Olympic Games*, a book edited by Lord Killanin, the IOC president, and John Rodda of the *Guardian* (MacMillan, Inc., N.Y., 1976). He writes:

> It is believed that athletes at the Olympic Games at the end of the third century B.C. tried to improve their performances by any means possible. In 1865 canal swimmers in Amsterdam were using drugs. Fourteen years later in the first six-day bike races, some riders were suspected of using doping agents, nitroglycerine, caffeine, ether, heroin, and cocaine were among them. In 1866 the first doping fatality in sport was reported. At the turn of the century football players and boxers were said to be using strychnine, alcohol, and cocaine.

As in so many things in society, it took some highly visible sports fatalities to bring the matter to the forefront of public concern. A Danish cyclist, Knut Enmark Jensen, collapsed and died during the 1960 Olympics in Rome. British cyclist Tommy Simpson died during the 1967 Tour de France. Those were widely reported, but in all it seems at least thirty athletes have died from drug abuse during competition.

One of the first to break the code of silence on the matter was the great French cyclist, Jacques Anquetil, who said, "Everyone in cycling dopes himself, and those who claim they don't are liars."

The most poignant testimony of all, however, came from U.S. Olympic hammer throw champion Hal Connolly, who went before the U.S. Senate Committee on the Judiciary in 1973 and said:

"I knew any number of athletes on the 1968 Olympic team who had so much scar tissue and so many puncture holes on their backsides that it was difficult to find a fresh spot to give a new shot. I relate these incidents to emphasize my contention that the overwhelming majority of international track and field athletes I know would take anything and do anything short of killing themselves to improve their athletic performance."

The international sports bodies have cracked down hard on the business of doping in sport in the 1970s, with somewhat mixed results. The use of the psychomotor stimulants, like amphetamines, has been virtually eliminated at the international level through thorough testing procedures, and no one, in any country, has been dismayed to see it happen. But there have been several unfortunate problems in the area of the sympathomimetic amines in that many of these drugs form the basic ingredients in common cold tablets and the drugs used to treat asthma and allergies. Everyone in the United States is well aware of Rick De Mont's unfortunate forfeit of a swimming medal in Munich because he'd taken an asthma drug. Canada's Joan Wenzel took a cold tablet in the middle of the night in the 1975 Pan-Am Games in Mexico City thinking she was taking a sleeping pill. Another medal had to be returned. A Soviet cross-country skier at Innsbruck, Galina Kulakova, woke up in the morning with a stuffy nose and unthinkingly sniffed her roommate's nasal spray. Poof went another Olympic medal.

And then there was a not-so-subtle confrontation in the 1976 Innsbruck Winter Games between the IOC and the Czechoslovakian ice-hockey team. A virus hit the team right in the middle of the competition, one stiff enough to put seven of the team's eighteen players in bed.

Knowing that two players would be drawn by lot for postgame testing, the Czech team management decided to treat the seven stricken players with pure codeine to break the virus. They knew full well they were playing a game of seven-come-eleven in the postgame test, but they took the chance.

And they lost. As soon as Frantisek Pospisil's name was pulled they went straight in and admitted that he would certainly test positive for codeine. As a result, the game against Poland was forfeited, and the IOC announced the suspension of the player and the team doctor, in spite of the explanation of why the drug was administered.

At that point, interestingly enough, both the Czechs and the International Ice Hockey Federation got their backs up. Knowing the IOC did not want to kick the Czechoslovakian team out of the Games and make a farce of the much-anticipated gold medal final between the Czechs and the Soviet Union, the team and the IIHF put the heat on. The Czechs insisted that they would continue to medically treat their sick players, and furthermore, they would bring in a replacement goalie from Prague since one of their goalies was sick and the other was injured. They told the IOC either to accept that state of affairs or cancel the hockey game. The IOC not only relented on those points, but also reinstated the team doctor. (Pospisil could not be, because he had flunked the test.) It makes you wonder if they'll ever get around to restoring Rick De Mont's swimming medal.

The Czech case, though, is likely to remain an exception. The problem with allowing Olympians drugs for illness, says the IOC Medical Commission, is that the IOC would then be faced with the possibility of team physicians making up nonexistent diseases to allow them to prescribe drugs containing Ephedrine or "speed" for athletes who were not sick at all.

The GDR, to the surprise of some, has long been a proponent of strong international doping control. No one speaks more forcefully than they do in federation or sports medicine committee meetings, and once the tests are put into practice no one gets caught less than they do either. The GDR had never been faced with a positive dope-testing result in international competition until Ilona Slupianek, who was the Düsseldorf World Cup shot put champion in 1977, tested positive for anabolic steroids in the European Cup final in Helsinki just prior to Düsseldorf. The GDR has appealed that finding, charging irregularities in the testing procedure.

"I knew absolutely nothing of doping when I first got involved in international sport in the early days," says Ewald. "The first time I came across it was in cycling when Tave Shur came to me one day and said his competitors were taking pills during the course of the race. He told me he would be going along feeling very confident about a race and then he would notice his competitors reach for pills, swallow them, wait awhile, and then pull away leaving him far in their wake. He told me that if we couldn't get such pills outlawed then we had better get him some of the pills."

Ewald claims the GDR's first introduction to anabolic steroids came in an Olympic Village when they noticed the Americans eating them in the dining room as a regular supplement with lunch. "Those were the days," he says, "when the U.S. shot putters were all a meter or two ahead of everyone in the world. We photographed those pills with long-range cameras and when we got back home our laboratory people told us what they were."

The GDR sports medical people, as one might expect, then began their own research into the field. As a result of this planned and supervised approach to the study of the metabolism, they have caught up and in many cases surpassed the United States in the strength events, while all of Eastern Europe has outdistanced the West in women's strength events.

Ewald agrees that the abuse of drugs in sport will never be fully controlled until everyone has some method of being completely sure that other countries are not taking advantage of the rules. "That's why I favor international doping control," he says, "but whenever I say that some people seem to be overlooking one very important word—'international.' What we have now, unfortunately, is national doping control for most events, even in the Olympic Games. At present it is not impossible for tests to be tampered with in the laboratories. I am not in any way saying this has been happening, but I am saying that it can happen."

Current international procedures call for a urine sample to be taken as soon as possible following the athlete's selection for testing following an event. The sample is then divided in two parts, both of which are sealed and coded with a number to prevent anyone from knowing whose sample it is, and then the samples are taken to the lab for testing. In case of a positive, the federation is informed, and representatives of federation and athlete are invited to observe the second test, which, of course, must match the first.

In the mind of Ewald there are just too many opportunities for monkey business in a laboratory under national auspices. "For example, you can take a sample from a North American and a sample from a European, code them completely and send them to a modern laboratory. If they wish, it is no great matter for the lab technicians to decide which specimen comes from North America and which one comes from the Europeans. Because of long-term dietary habits there will be different chemical compositions. Since that's the case, how can one side fully trust the coding techniques of the other?"

This argument might sound a little self-serving until one imagines the public reaction in the United States if several U.S. athletes were disqualified in the Moscow Games over charges they took drugs that the athletes themselves deny having taken. Would the United States be quick to challenge the accuracy of the Moscow lab? That question doesn't even require an answer.

"Exactly," says Ewald. "Which is why at some date in the near future, doping control will have to be truly international. We will have to set up a laboratory just for this purpose, or perhaps even a series of laboratories with half the sample sent to one and half to another. Testers from several countries will have to be trained for the work and assigned to work in the international labs. When samples are tested they will have to be handled by technicians from a variety of countries working together. Only then, in my opinion, can we all have full faith and confidence in the validity of the result."

But the cost? "It will be expensive," he admits, "but I don't think it is entirely beyond the abilities of the major countries to share in the cost of such a project. International sport, after all, is one of the rising social forces at work in the world today. If we are going to police it properly we must work toward that goal in a proper international fashion.

"Then we can start to discuss the broader issues, such as which substances might be permitted and which must be banned. I for one am not in agreement that substances used to balance metabolisms should in any way be considered in the same vein as psychomotor doping substances."

On the last point the IOC might seem at least partly to concur, for it has not prohibited the use of estrogen as it has anabolic steroids. But if the use of anabolics is immoral, not to mention dangerous, and so must be banned, what about the morality of using the birth control pill, another "substance used to balance metabolisms?"

The Federal Republic's Eva Wilms came from almost nowhere in 1977 to set a world record in the women's pentathlon, a track and field event that involves competition in five events: hurdling, shot put, long jump, high jump and the 800-meter run. In the wake of the new record, her trainer, Christine Gerhmann, admitted that birth control pills, diet, and exercise had created virtually the same changes that can be managed with anabolic steroids without the danger of breaking the rules or coming back with a positive in the tests.

Perhaps the GDR swim coaches have been completely truthful when they deny all use of anabolic steroids on their young and talented female swimmers. Perhaps they have been changing the metabolisms with birth control pills all along. Or perhaps they have been using something else entirely.

What there can be no doubt of—and this does not in any way face up to the unsolved problem of legality and illegality—is that a lot of scientific work has been done in the field of altered metabolisms, so much so that by the 1984 Olympics, if indeed this is not already the case, no female with a natural metabolism anywhere in the world will likely be able to reach the Olympic qualifying standard in a strength event by means of her own natural development. Come 1981, when the International Olympic Committee, National Olympic Committees, and International Sports Federations gather in Baden-Baden, West Germany, for only the second Olympic Congress to be held since 1930 (Avery Brundage, as IOC president, didn't believe in such massive tributes to Olympic democracy), the question of science and sport is going to be paramount. What is needed is an agreement that will enhance honesty in sport, disseminate sports medical information in such a way as to create equal opportunity for all nations, and to protect the health of all athletes. That's a very tall order, but the research that has already gone on in Leipzig, Moscow, Stockholm, Cologne, and to a lesser extent the rest of Europe and North America, has set the groundwork for a fascinating, if contentious, future.

19

Sport and Politics

It is a widely held Western opinion that the institution of sport must, of necessity, be kept separate from politics. It is a noble idea, but hardly realistic. Sport and poltiics have, in fact, never really been separate in the past. In the future we can expect more of the same. Nothing that can create the kind of passion international sport is capable of creating is ever going to be free of political turmoil. Nothing in the world that people are really interested in is free of political turmoil.

Nationalism, of course, is the villain, the lynch pin of international affairs and also of international sport. It is routine, in North American sport, to play the national anthem at the beginning of the game. But, in hockey's 1979 Challenge Series in New York between the Soviet Union and the National Hockey League, players came skating out onto the ice to dimmed houselights and the theme song from *Star Wars*. Then the lights switched to the flags, fluttering wind-blown by indoor fans, while singers with booming operatic voices came onto the ice to sing the Soviet anthem, the Canadian anthem, and the American anthem. As the television cameras panned the crowd, the hockey players looked entranced, awestruck at the psychological enormity of their own anthem and flag in such a setting. It was the same look that terrified the world when it appeared on the faces of young German

soldiers in Leni Riefenstahl's film *Triumph of the Will* in the Hitler
era. Same technique, same artificial hype, one for the purpose of
politics, the other for the purpose of sport. And the nationalism of
sport is too easily transferred to the political arena for international
sport ever to have political exemption.

People of all nationalities constantly convince themselves that
"their" teams and sportsmen are striving for honor and fair play at all
costs in the face of a furious onslaught of corrupt practices by the rest
of the world. The same thing happens at every level of competition in
every country. Just take a seat in the stands, or perhaps in front of your
television set, say for a game of baseball or basketball, and put your
personal backing behind one of the two teams. You will soon notice
you are favoring that side in at least three calls out of four.

At the international level the bias problem invariably escalates in
proportion to the importance of the match for the opposing countries.
That was certainly true in the June 1978 World Cup Soccer final in
Buenos Aires, Argentina, a game that matched the traditionally
temperate and responsible Dutch against host Argentina, a team
certain to attack with fanatical fervor, with the final played at home in
their own River Plate stadium.

Just imagine the mental state of the Italian referee in the midst of
the greatest assignment of his life. He wants to keep the game under
control with the full knowledge that an estimated 1.2 billion people
are watching around the world on television, fortunes in advertising
endorsements are on the line, and players' tempers are on razor's
edge. So he calls it tight. When the Dutch attempt to tackle hard and
physically knock the feistiness out of the constantly attacking Argenti-
nians, he whistles them down consistently. A man and not a
computer, he probably makes some errors along the way.

Argentina wins it 3–1 in overtime. The home side and its fans think
the referee called an "adequate" game. Dutch soccer fans back home
in The Netherlands have different ideas and they express themselves
in a rather political fashion by taking to the streets and stoning the
windows of both the Argentine and Italian legations.

Sure, the rest of the world can shake its head and say, "Hey, you
guys, it's only a game!" But how many Americans were saying that
back in Munich in 1972 when the Soviet Union won the basketball
gold medal by getting the last three seconds of the game replayed three
times over until the Russians finally sank the winning basket? Did any

U.S. fan present or watching that night really want to know why Robert Jones, the German-based president of the World Basketball Federation, had left his seat in the stands to go to the officials to order those replays? Did they want the whole dreary tale about how one referee called a time-out for the Russians while his partner was putting the ball into play allowing the clock to tick off two seconds? About how Jones, seeing that time-out called, rushed from his seat fearing the game would be protested by the Soviets? About how they set the clock back to three seconds, but forgot to reset the game-ending buzzer as well, so that on the second try it went off with two seconds still left on the clock? How that necessitated a *third* replay?

No American official, player, coach, or fan watching that night wanted to hear about any of that. What's more, the next day, after all appeals had been exhausted, the U.S. basketball team refused to show up and receive the silver medals as the first U.S. basketball team to win less than gold in Olympic history. They are convinced to this day they were given an unholy shafting by all the sinister political forces of the world. If the situation had been completely reversed the chances are the Soviets would have felt exactly the same way—in spite of the fact everyone knows it was only a game.

Sure, we can try to keep politics out of sports—and if everyone in the world could accept the fact these things really are "only games" we would probably succeed. But then, since no one but the players would really care, no one would come to watch, televise, or write about their efforts, which might lead to a situation where competitive sport would atrophy at the very least and quite possibly fade away altogether.

Theoretically it would be possible to remove all vestiges of nationalism from the modern Olympic Games. No more team uniforms, symbols, flags, and anthems. Every performance could be the performance of an individual on his own representing only himself and the purity of sport. But who would pay for his trip to the Games? His government that he was no longer representing? A school that he wouldn't represent? The fact is, he would almost certainly have to pay his own way to and from the Games. Sport would once again, just as in the beginning, become the exclusive preserve of the privileged classes.

That just wouldn't do either. Nationalism, and politics, with all the evil influences they admittedly bring, are almost certain to be the cornerstones of sport in the foreseeable future. The sports world, if it is to become civilized, must deal with the misuse of sport for the sake of politics, a phenomenon that became a trend and a problem during the Hitler Olympics in Berlin in 1936.

Those Games, almost every Olympic historian seems to agree, were both the best and the worst in Olympic history—the best in terms of organization and innovation. The Berlin Games brought the first torch relay with the flame ignited at Olympia and run all the way through to Berlin itself. The first Olympic television coverage took place there, and the first attempt to provide the athletes with a really first-class Olympic Village.

Jesse Owens, the hero of those '36 Games and quite possibly the greatest athlete in Olympic history, still describes the Village of Döberitz as "the best I ever saw."

But when it comes to the political misuse of sport, there is a history behind that Olympic Village that even Jesse Owens didn't know about. I myself stumbled onto it partly by accident and partly through reportorial persistence. In my six-year coverage of all things Olympic for the Montreal *Gazette* prior to the 1976 Games, I'd been researching, among much else, details about various Olympic Villages. The Village itself is the biggest headache facing any Games organizing committee today.

I knew about the depression-age housing put up in Los Angeles in 1932; the London barracks of '48, the first of the postwar Games; the Helsinki apartments of '52; the Melbourne housing development of 1956; the scandals that imprisoned the Village planners of Rome in 1960; the U.S. airbase near Tokyo in 1964; the low-income Mexican apartments of 1968; and the Munich extravaganza of high-income apartments in 1972.

And, I knew that the Döberitz Village had been in a beautiful wooded setting some thirteen kilometers (about eight miles) from the Olympic Stadium, with lakes, woods, pathways, and two-story structures that had everything, including saunas where the athletes could work up a sweat before diving straight into the water behind the housing unit.

With the 1972 Games in Munich, what better opportunity for a one-day expense-account visit to Berlin? The problem arose with the discovery that the 1936 Village at Döberitz was not located within the city limits of West Berlin, as was Albert Speer's impressive 110,000-

seat stadium, or of East Berlin, but just beyond the East Berlin city limits by a couple of miles or so. Anything less and there would have been no problem, for Westerners can get a one-day visitor's tourist pass for East Berlin any day they wish. Anything beyond that into the GDR, however, requires a formal visa.

Realizing this, I wrote a letter to the GDR foreign office explaining my needs and my purpose, and seeking some kind of an accommodation for a one-hour visit and quick tour of the 1936 Games Village. The letter went unanswered. Writing to the Foreign Office, in case you ever want to visit the GDR, is not the quickest way to gain access to the country.

A year later in 1973, Takac, the Yugoslavian technical director of the Montreal Games, offered to help give it another go round since we were both going to the Olympic Congress in Varna, Bulgaria, and since he had good friends in the higher echelons of GDR sport. He told me to write a letter to the GDR National Olympic Committee and said he would write one, too. This time, both letters went unanswered.

But finally, on the second night of the Varna Congress, I literally bumped into Gunther Heinze of the GDR National Olympic Committee while both of us were milling around at a cocktail party. I knew him only because his name tag was right in front of my nose as we crossed paths in the crowd. We couldn't have been closer if we had been standing in a New York subway at rush-hour. I asked him if he remembered my letter. He stared at my name tag for a few seconds, and then finally his eyes lit up in recognition. "Yes," he said, "you wrote a letter and Artur Takac wrote a letter. When did you want to come to the GDR?"

"How about right after this Congress?" I asked.

"I'll see if it's possible," he promised, before gently drifting away to another conversation.

The following morning at breakfast Takac winked conspiratorially. "You are going to the GDR," he said. "Gunther called and told me how busy he was and wanted to know if I considered it a big personal favor for him to grant your request. I told him I considered it a big personal favor."

Hal Connolly must have been happier back in 1957 in Belgrade after Takac managed to pull enough strings to convince the government of Czechoslovakia to grant him a visa that eventually led to his marriage to Olympic discus champion Olga Fikotova, but he wasn't much happier.

Later that day Wolfgang Gitter, the press chief of the GDR Olympic Committee, stopped by to discuss an itinerary, gather the necessary passport information, and assure me that a visa would be waiting in Berlin on my arrival from Sofia. What followed were the four busiest days of my journalistic career, as first Gitter, and then the Olympic Committee secretary, Dieter Rehahn, would scoop me up for 6:30 A.M. departures for Leipzig, to mass sports clubs, to classes where volunteer coaches were working on certification programs, and to interviews with DTSB leaders. Although none of us realized it at the time, we were actually laying the groundwork for this book.

What I did not see, however, was the 1936 Olympic Village in Döberitz!

"But the Games were held in West Berlin," said a puzzled Rehahn when I first asked about it.

"Sure," I agreed, "but the Village was in Döberitz."

His amazement was complete and honest. He said that if this was true he wanted to see it himself, and if I could excuse him for a moment he would make immediate inquiries. Fifteen minutes later he was back looking apologetic.

"You were right," he said, "but it was bombed during the War and there is nothing left to see."

That was that until the next day when Dr. Hans Georg Hermann, the deputy rector of the Leipzig Institute, wondered whether I was getting to see everything I wanted to see in my quick trip around the country. When I told him of my disappointment about Döberitz and the Village he reacted in surprise and told us Döberitz was indeed alive and well. On the way back to Berlin, Rehahn said he would get to the bottom of this once and for all. And yet, the next morning, there was yet another explanation.

"It's true that the Village wasn't completely destroyed in the War," he said, "but they were all old temporary buildings that have been replaced with newer structures, so there is no point in going there because nothing from 1936 remains in its place."

I never gave the matter another thought until the spring of 1975 sitting in a Montreal bar with Huhn, sports editor of *Neues Deutschland*. As I told him the story of my hunt for Döberitz he kept giving me sideways looks while trying not to break out into open laughter. Finally he could restrain himself no longer.

"As a foreign journalist," he said, "you have been pushing your luck. The one place you keep pressing to see happens to be a Soviet military center for the entire region. Nobody goes there."

Klaus knew these facts because he had been one of the exceptions to the rule—for the purpose of his own Olympic research into the facets of the Nazi Games. He had not only been to Döberitz, but also to Potsdam to check the records of the Third Reich's 23rd Infantry Unit, home base of Major General Ernst Busch, the man in charge of the construction of the 1936 Village.

"From the beginning," says Huhn, "The Olympics was a cover for secret military preparations. It was perfect because it was well back from public view. The Village was basically completed well before the Games and was filled up with civilians working on projects unknown even to the regular residents of Döberitz. All the townspeople knew was that the Olympic Village was in their midst in 1935, a village known in the political pamphlets as the Village of Peace. When it came time for the athletes to arrive for the Games, the civilians were ready to depart. When a bus full of athletes would pull up at a curb in front of a unit, the civilians would be waiting at the curb ready to depart.

"No one guessed where they were going. Actually, though, it turns out they were going to a ship in the Hamburg harbor, berthed by chance right alongside the U.S. ship that had brought the American Olympic team to Germany. The German ship, the *Usaramo*, had the cover of a ship leased to a tourist company. But the truth is, it contained a cargo of disassembled Stuka dive-bombers.

"As the Olympic torch was literally being run into Berlin some days later for the opening of the 1936 Games, those Village of Peace "civilians" were dive-bombing Spain to open the German intervention in the Spanish Civil War. Döberitz was the pre-Games training camp for the Condor Legion! But even the townspeople had no idea of this until the pilots returned to Germany and were awarded the Spanish Cross by Hitler personally."

Meanwhile, back in Döberitz, Jesse Owens and the rest of the world's top athletes were loving the woodland setting, taking their saunas, diving into the man-made lake. How were they to know that the lake doubled as a secret submarine training center? No wonder the

Soviets are there today. If it had been located in West Germany when the War ended, Döberitz would probably now be an American military installation!

While it is possible to give Hitler credit for having some purpose for his Olympic Village, in contrast to some of the recent Games host cities, the use he made of it certainly stands as one of the most cynical political contraventions of the Olympic ideal ever unearthed. Even so, lest we get too sanctimonious about who did what to whom in the '36 Games, let's make certain everyone knows the Germans were not the only ones who played political games with the Berlin Olympics. Such literary efforts about the Olympics as Richard R. Mandell's well-documented *Nazi Olympics* (Macmillan & Co., N.Y., 1971) and *All That Glitters Is Not Gold* by William O. Johnson, Jr. (G. P. Putnam's Sons, N.Y., 1972), may have missed the story of the Condor Legion, lacking access either to Döberitz or to the Soviet-controlled records of the Potsdam 23rd, but they sure did focus in on the strange politically motivated doings of the U.S. track team.

Anyone who has ever studied the Olympics is aware by now of Hitler's negative reaction to Owens and other U.S. "Black Auxiliaries," who wrote so much of the 1936 Games history.

But how many know that the U.S. Olympic team scratched its only two Jewish track and field athletes, Marty Glickman and Sam Stoller, from the finals of the 400-meter relay on the very eve of the race itself? Although this race would have been Glickman and Stoller's only chance to compete in the Games, and the only chance for Jewish athletes from any country to win medals in Berlin track and field, the USOC coaches chose to switch their relay alignment to a makeup of Owens, Ralph Metcalfe, and the University of Southern California pair of Frank Wykoff and Foy Draper. Head Coach Dean Cromwell, also of Southern Cal, said he was making the change "to make sure of the gold medal," a medal any combination of the six U.S. sprinters in Berlin should have been able to win by margins now associated with U.S. America's Cup yachting triumphs.

How many remember that these were times when Gen. Charles H. Sherrill, the then-International Olympic Committee member in the United States, could say in answer to protests against the U.S. participating in the Berlin Games at all:

"It does not concern me one bit the way Jews in Germany are being treated, any more than lynchings in the South of our own country."

It was a time when U.S. Olympic Committee president Avery Brundage, and track coach Cromwell, were both members of the German-sympathizing American First Committee.

No one will ever know for sure whether Dean Cromwell wanted a couple of his own Southern Cal athletes on the winning relay team, or wanted to keep a couple of Jewish boys off it, but it is known that both Owens and Metcalfe offered to withdraw and were refused.

On the other hand, no one could blame Hitler for walking away from the Games with the feeling his brand of anti-Semitism wasn't without at least a modicum of support from elements of the U.S. establishment. Owens and the Black Auxiliaries were a blow to Germany's Aryan propaganda image, it's true, but then again blacks were not the internal political scapegoats of 1936 Germany.

It's probably unfair to hold people's prewar quotes and actions over their heads so many years after the fact, but sometimes it is an effective way to show just how far we can go in our own self-delusions.

One U.S. Olympic Committee official, in testimony before the U.S. President's Commission hearings in 1976, said he could think of not one single instance in its entire history when the USOC had permitted politics to enter into its decisions.

"I can think of one," snapped Ralph Metcalfe, then a U.S. congressman from Chicago, and a member of the President's Commission.

And how about Philip Agee, who, in his exposé on what it was like to work as a CIA agent, mentioned his work in Mexico City in 1968 as the official attaché to the U.S. team? Agee, in a *Playboy* magazine interview, described this assignment as the silliest he had ever received, but added the tidbit that the job was routinely filled by a CIA man if for no other reason than we knew the Russian attaché was a KGB man.

And finally, at the Montreal Games in 1976, when the political shit hit the fan over Canada's last-minute refusal to admit athletes from Taiwan unless they called themselves Taiwan rather than the Republic of China, everyone looked to the U.S. Olympic Committee for a response.

And what did the USOC, which never mixes politics with sports, do? Why, it told reporters that it was awaiting word from the White House before deciding what to do next. There was no way the U.S. Olympic team was going to pull out of the 1976 Montreal Olympic

Games without full consultation with the U.S. State Department.

The International Olympic Committee finally offered Taiwan a compromise. It could stay if it called itself Taiwan rather than the Republic of China, didn't play the ROC anthem, or show the ROC flag. Taiwan's Olympic delegation refused that compromise . . . after it too had spent time consulting with its own government . . . and went home. The U.S. grumbled and fussed about yet another "intolerable" intrusion of politics into sport, but stayed at the Games. Two years later the U.S. Government withdrew its recognition of Taiwan and recognized the People's Republic of China in Peking. Within days of that decision the first political and diplomatic steps were taken within the IOC to bring China back into the international Olympic community.

When it comes to sport, everyone, at one time or another, is going to give in to the temptation to play a little politics.

20

Visa, Visa, Who's Got the Visa?

My own baptism into the world of sport and politics—German style—came in November 1973, during my initial visit to the GDR.

"Why," I had innocently asked Dieter Rehahn, "did GDR athletes not accept invitations to major sports events in Canada and the United States?"

He looked at me as if I were quite daft. "You know why," he said, with the condescending tone of a man answering a question about why the Yankees don't play baseball in New York in the middle of winter.

"Why?" I repeated.

"Because your government won't give us the visas," he replied. "The United States wouldn't let us go to the World Ice Hockey championships when they were held in Colorado Springs some years back, you wouldn't let our officials into California for the Squaw Valley Olympics in 1960, and Avery Brundage once had to threaten to resign as president of the International Olympic Committee unless the U.S. State Department stopped interfering with an application by our people trying to get to San Francisco to see him on Olympic business."

I told him I didn't believe it. In the 1950s that might have been true, particularly when John Foster Dulles was running the ship of state. Even in the early sixties, immediately after the creation of the Berlin Wall, it might have been true, but in 1973, when U.S.–Soviet competitions in track and field, basketball, and gymnastics were as routine in many U.S. cities as the annual visits of our own Ice Capades and the Barnum and Bailey Circus?

"You get us the invitations," said Rehahn, "and I am sure they will be favorably received if they fit into the overall training plans of our individual federations and athletes."

It was as good as done. One phone call to Ken Twigg in Toronto set in motion an invitation to the Toronto *Star* Indoor Games, one of the major track meets on the North American circuit. Telegrams were sent and received and preliminary arrangements made to send four GDR athletes to Toronto in the second week of February. The Canadian Department of External Affairs told Twigg, director of the meet, to tell the GDR to get their passports and visa applications to the Canadian Embassy in Vienna at least twenty-one days prior to the date of departure.

Twigg sent a telegram to Berlin with all that information. Then he started churning out the publicity in Toronto heralding the first-ever appearance of GDR athletes in a Canadian track meet.

Then, a few days before the scheduled arrival he received another telegram from Germany to the effect they still had no word on the visas. That brought a worried call to the government in Ottawa, who assured him that the GDR visas were ready and waiting to be picked up in Vienna. But External Affairs did add the ominous warning that this sort of thing had happened before between the GDR and other countries, and, well, sometimes the GDR people just never do show up. He suggested that if they didn't appear, a protest to the International Amateur Athletic Federation offices in London might well be in order.

The athletes, who included Olympic sprint champion Renate Stecher and Olympic hurdle champion Annelie Ehrhardt, both world record holders; veteran distance runner and Olympic medalist Gunhild Hoffmeister, and world-ranked hurdler Thomas Munkelt, did not show up. No explanation, no final telegram, nothing.

I heard all about it from a thoroughly disgruntled Ken Twigg. Something didn't ring quite true about it all, of course, and that was the fact that there had been, just as Rehahn predicted, a visa problem. Thankfully, Dieter had left me his office card and a phone number in Berlin. I phoned and he answered.

"Those visas were simply never issued in Vienna," he said. "As a matter of fact we just received the passports back here in Berlin this morning [this was the Monday after the Friday-night track meet] and there never was a visa stamp placed in them."

"Could you," I asked, "send me a signed telex to that effect with all the pertinent information?" It arrived from Berlin within the half hour.

The following morning the full story, including the telex, appeared in the Montreal *Gazette*, one of two English-language daily newspapers that circulate every morning in Ottawa, the national capital. There had, of course, been calls to Ottawa the day before to seek an explanation for the foul-up, calls that brought forth the initial promise that, of course, they would check on it. A second call admitted the error and added the explanation that there seemed to have been a mix-up in the Vienna Embassy. All that information had been in the initial story.

By 7:30 in the morning of the day the story appeared, the phone rang at my home, with the Canadian Ambassador to Austria, no less, on the other end. He was curious to know, for starters, how I or anyone else outside the Vienna Embassy had come to know anything about this case.

"We have checked everywhere," he admitted, "and we cannot find any evidence of a GDR complaint on this case. They have not written about it in their newspapers, they have not broadcast it on radio or television, they have not protested to the IAAF, and they have not protested through their New York UN Legation."

When I explained that I had found out by picking up a phone in Montreal and calling the GDR National Olympic Committee office in Berlin, there was a moment of silence at the other end of the line.

"Do you mean," he said, "that when a Canadian reporter picks up a phone and calls an East Berlin government-controlled office you get an answer, just like that?" When I said that I guess you do if you have the right phone number, there was another pause, and then a chuckle. His work, at least, was done.

"The only complaint I have," he finally said, "was with the part about there being some kind of a mix-up in the Vienna Embassy. Anything that happened here—and I want you to know I am not admitting that anything did happen here—was on orders from Ottawa."

On orders from Ottawa? Now wasn't that an interesting piece of news. Another call to Twigg in Toronto brought forth the name of the contact he dealt with at External Affairs, but a call to External Affairs asking for this man by name brought the startling information from the girl on the switchboard that no one by that name was listed in the employ of External Affairs. The mystery was deepening. A call to Montreal Olympic Organizing Committee offices brought forth the private phone number of the man in Ottawa, who, this time, answered his own phone on the first ring.

"Damn," he muttered on hearing my name, "how did you get hold of this number? Look, I am just a little guy who sits here at a desk in the government and does what he is told to do. I have nothing to say about the GDR athletes' case at all." And he hung up the phone.

By this time the public relations boss of the External Affairs Department had intervened somewhat above my head with an old personal friend, the editor of my newspaper. The result of that call was an editorial suggesting that any country that came to the aid of the Soviet Union to suppress the Czechoslovakian uprising of 1968 deserved what it got in return on the diplomatic front. That and a private off-the-record briefing for me from an External Affairs officer.

The gist of that briefing was that in Canada's opinion the GDR was using its athletes as pawns to try to break down Canada's requirement that visa applications be filed twenty-one days in advance of a proposed trip. The need for twenty-one days, I was told, was to allow a full security check on the person seeking to come in since the countries have virtually no trade relations and it is exceptional for citizens of the GDR to travel to the West before they are past the retirement age sixty-five—unless they work for the government or are in high favor with the Communist Party. Since Canada does not have its own security information on the GDR, the applications have to be processed by West German intelligence, United States intelligence, and the military authorities in control of West Berlin. It really does take, I am assured, twenty-one days.

I was told that when top government people were traveling there was never any problem, but when world champion athletes were involved the applications tended to arrive perhaps eighteen days before departure. Sometimes, when it came to Olympic business, it would be as few as twelve days before. When we approve one on such short notice, so the argument goes, they use it against us in future negotiations, asking why Canada cannot do this for everyone.

"We are not the ones playing politics with sport in this case," said my External Affairs spokesman. "They are. Whenever they want to get those athletes over here, all they have to do is get the passports in on time. Actually I suppose the athletes do get them in on time in Berlin. It's just that their foreign office is never in a hurry to get them over to our embassy in Vienna."

All of that may sound plausible enough at first. But the Russians routinely get visas in less than a week, and usually in three days' time. And there is an obvious difference in security risk between a GDR official making an application on his own to travel through Canada, and a GDR citizen, athlete or whatever, who is invited to come for a specific purpose under the auspices of a Canadian organization.

"We aren't worried about the athletes," was the official answer to that one, "but what about the team manager and coach that usually travel with these teams? Who is going to vouch for them?" What a soap opera!

And consider the reverse of this situation: although at first I got no answer at all to my request to visit the GDR, all it took was a phone call to have a visa issued and waiting at the border when I finally was invited.

Shortly after all the fuss about the GDR athletes' visas was made public in the papers, there were some subtle changes in policy. A delegation of GDR swimmers that were due in Vancouver, just two weeks after the Toronto track meet, received their visas after a strenuous intervention from the Canadian Amateur Swimming Association. The Montreal Olympic Organizing Committee moved quickly and diplomatically to make sure there were no such incidents in any future Games-related competition. If it had anything to do with the Olympics, the government agreed, visas would be issued immediately upon the request of the Organizing Committee with no questions asked.

Competitive exchanges started to flourish. The Canadian women's track team had a 1974 three-way meet with the GDR and Romania in

Bucharest. The GDR women returned for a dual meet with Canada in Sudbury, Ontario, in the fall of 1975. Canadian swimmers competed in Berlin for the first time. The GDR track stars who had not made it to Toronto in 1974 were invited back and did show up in 1975. A few have been back since. In the post-Olympic year of 1977, sprinting star Eugene Ray, and Rosemarie Ackermann, World record holder in the high jump, hit Toronto, Cleveland and Montreal, all in one weekend. The U.S.–GDR dual meet in Concord, California, was the big swim meet of 1974, and there was a return engagement in Berlin in the summer of 1977. And yet, in the winter of 1976, just six months before the Montreal Games, the Ottawa bureaucrats almost forgot themselves and did it again.

This time it was the Pointe Claire swim club in suburban Montreal, who had invited four of the top GDR swimmers, Kornelia Ender, Birgit Treiber, Ulrike Tauber and Roger Pyttel, to come over for their annual January invitational meet. By publicizing the fact the GDR stars would be attending, Pointe Claire suddenly had a flood of entries from leading U.S. swimmers as well.

Then, just a day before New Year's Eve, Pointe Claire program director George Gate came out with the news that Ottawa had called and told him there could be a problem with the visas—the same old problem, it turned out, in that the visa applications had come in just eighteen days before the departure date.

"We have been told that we had to honor late applications for Olympic-related events," said a spokesman for the Manpower and Immigration Department, which has the final say on the issuing of a visa. "But this meet is not technically an Olympic event. One must, after all, draw the line somewhere."

This time the stories in the paper brought an instant reaction from the ministerial level in Ottawa. "The Ottawa Government offices open at 8:30 in the morning," said Julian Carroll, the executive director of the Canadian Amateur Swim Association, "and by 8:40 I had a call telling me Manpower and Immigration had decided to grant the visas and was at that moment drafting a message to the Canadian Embassy in Warsaw."

Just to make sure of everything, Carroll immediately fired off telegrams to Berlin and Warsaw on his own to make doubly sure that everyone knew exactly what was going on. This time, thankfully, there were no problems. The Germans arrived and put on a great

show against the Canadians and Americans. The supposedly suspicious role of "team manager," by the way, was filled by Dr. Helga
Pfeiffer, one of the leading sports medical experts in the GDR. She
was accompanied by Treiber's coach, Ewe Neuman.

With luck, this visa problem will soon be a thing of the past.
Although it may provide fun and games for the bureaucrats on both
sides, it is absolute hell on the athletes involved. What can be worse
than training for an expected trip overseas, getting all the plans in
order to the point of turning in one's passport at a foreign embassy,
and then not being allowed to go at the last minute? In a sense it's
even worse than that, because Europeans can go nowhere without
their passports, which means anyone planning to come to North
America has to stay on the home front for three full weeks before
departing.

Frustrating is a mild word for that kind of treatment.

21

The Battle of Turin

How sport is used as a political weapon depends on the political climate of the time. Witness the success of the Black African bloc in forcing first South Africa and then Rhodesia out of the Olympic community through relentless political pressure. Politics encroached upon the realm of sport, which in turn influenced the political picture as the two racist governments further lost credibility, because of the IOC action.

On the other hand, the Black Africans' last-minute boycott of the Montreal Olympics in 1976, in protest over a change in New Zealand's attitudes toward South African sports exchanges, proved little beyond the ability of the Supreme Council of Sport in Africa and the Organization of African Unity to carry out a boycott in spite of internal discontent from athletes and team managers, who would have preferred to compete in the Games. Yes, the Africans proved their threats were not idle. But, when the question was New Zealand rather than South Africa or Rhodesia, they could not force the IOC to back their stand and oust the offender. A principle was defended, but African athletes, some of whom in being kept from Montreal may have missed their one chance at Olympic immortality, were the biggest losers. All the training, all the preparation . . . for nothing.

A changed political atmosphere explains Canada's refusal, under heavy Chinese Communist diplomatic pressure, to allow Taiwan to compete under its Olympic-approved name of the Republic of China Olympic Committee. The origins of the conflict are mixed up in the murky IOC politics of 1949 to 1952 when the headquarters of the Chinese Olympic Committee were transferred from Nanking to Taipei, Formosa, under the strangest of circumstances. No formal action was ever taken on this by the IOC, there was no correspondence between the IOC and Taipei, and, indeed, there was no such address as the one initially listed with the IOC as the Committee headquarters in Taipei. There obviously were grounds for the Communist insistence that the Chinese Olympic Committee, so surreptitiously set up in nationalist Taiwan, not be recognized.

That the transaction was made at all can be explained by the fact the IOC's thinking was dominated by the West with its sympathy for the Chinese Nationalists on Formosa. The arch-conservatism of the just-developing McCarthy era in the United States was, of course, influential. Those were the days when accused atom spies Julius and Ethel Rosenberg were convicted and executed for, among other things, giving away the secrets that permitted "the loss of China."

By the time of the 1976 Olympics in Montreal, the Canadian Government had made its peace with Communist China, severed its direct diplomatic ties with Taiwan, and, although a healthy trade relationship between Canada and Taiwan continued unabated, the great desire for future relationships and expanded trade lay with mainland China. Months before the Games themselves, the Canadian Department of External Affairs let it be known to the IOC that Canada would have a hard time living up to the Olympic rule that says all host countries must accommodate everyone the IOC chooses to invite as part of the Olympic Family under IOC designation. IOC president Lord Killanin was told that Taiwanese cannot enter Canada if they claim to be representatives of the Republic of China.

Killanin later said he assumed, after that briefing, that the Canadian Government understood the importance of the IOC rule of keeping the Games clear of political interference. Canada's Department of External Affairs says it thought the IOC understood the government would not back down on this issue. That lack of clarity in communication nearly derailed the Montreal Olympics in the final seventy-two hours prior to the Opening Ceremony. In the final analysis, it was the IOC that had to retreat and work out a compromise. And today, now that the United States has recognized Communist China, Taiwan's future status in the Games is more uncertain than ever.

To understand how sport was used by the two Germanies as a political weapon, one has to go back to the time of the Soviet attempts to gain control of all of Berlin and the ensuing Berlin airlift. At the end of the War in 1945, almost every surviving German longed for national reunification and the withdrawal of all foreign armies as soon as possible. At first the Communists imagined that a quick election held in the midst of the uncleared rubble might bring them to power throughout the entire country. The Marshall Plan's pouring of money into the Western Zone soon put an end to that.

In 1949 the Soviet-controlled territory was consolidated into the German Democratic Republic, independence was declared, German reunification was denounced as a Western plot that would bring Fascists back into power throughout the land, and the political battle lines were drawn. A new country had been created, even if it was only recognized by the Soviet Union and its satellite states.

From that day, in October of 1949, the main political goal of the GDR Government has been to establish its legitimacy around the world: the battle to get formal recognition from outside countries; the battle to get a seat in the United Nations and other world forums; the battle to break open trade markets so that high-quality GDR-crafted goods could enter world markets against high-quality West German goods that are invariably much more expensive thanks to the much higher cost of Western labor. Sport, of course, has been caught up in the middle of it. The GDR has battled to gain recognition from international sports federations, and battled for more than fifteen years to win the right to their own National Olympic Committee and a place for GDR athletes in the Olympic Games, a struggle that wasn't completely won until the 1972 Games in Sapporo and Munich.

A strong case can be built for the contention that sport was the main weapon in the GDR arsenal for gaining political acceptance in the 1950s and the 1960s. The GDR has always maintained an immediate and total link between politics and sport and has had no compunction whatever about using the latter to help the aims of the former. The country got little sympathy in the West on economic matters, and none on political matters. But, in sport, ironically, they could count on sympathy from those who (unlike themselves) felt that sport and politics shouldn't be mixed. In West Germany, it is true, some who abhorred everything Communism stood for did still favor continued sports relationships with the East as a possible means of political change. But, then as now, many in the world of sport felt it must remain above all political considerations. Witness those today, for instance, who oppose sanctions against South Africa in international competition, their feelings about apartheid notwithstanding.

This division in Western thought undoubtedly gave the GDR the political advantage right from the beginning. The GDR had the tactical advantage of knowing exactly what it wanted and was able to fight for it in a persistent and relentless fashion. The West always found itself fighting one brush fire or another in trying to keep sport above political questions. It has always been easier to be "for" something you really believe in rather than adamantly against something somebody else believes in. Easier to be for the U.S. civil rights movement in the 1960s than against it. Easier to be for women's liberation than against it. And, easier to be for fair play for the GDR in sport than against it.

Today, in the late 1970s, the battle seems all but over. The problems aren't solved, of course, any more than the "progress" of the 1960s "solved" the civil rights problem in the U.S. But the GDR is in the United Nations. Erich Honecker worked out a détente with Willy Brandt, and it continues on today with Brandt's successor, Helmut Schmidt. The two Germanies now "get along" in ways that would have been out of the question ten years ago. Sport certainly didn't cause all this to happen, but it did hasten it along.

Alfred Heil, in his role as the DTSB vice-president for international affairs in the Fifties and Sixties, was responsible for some of the most damning political broadsides ever vented against the leadership of the *Deutscher Sports Bund* across the Wall in the Federal Republic. After the Games of Munich in 1972, Heil was promoted to head of Panorama, the GDR Government agency directly responsible for foreign press relations and international public relations. In that role he was instrumental in inviting many of those he used to denounce to attend the 1977 GDR Sports Festival in Leipzig. Most of them came.

"It was quite a feeling," he recalled, "to stand at a party with a drink in your hand and trade stories of the old times with people you once considered arch enemies. Now we can both look back at things we did and said in those days and smile about it."

Klaus Huhn's favorite "I was there" anecdote goes back to the 1954 European swimming championships in Turin, Italy, in the very early days, when the international federations were just beginning to accept the GDR into independent membership. Membership was one thing, it turned out, getting the team to the championships in Turin quite another.

There was the same problem of the travel visa. "For some strange reason," the journalist recalls, "I was issued a visa for the championships as a journalist while our team and team officials were denied visas to participate. My first thought was not to go, but then Ewald told me that he thought maybe I should go a few days ahead of the competition to try to lobby from within the swimming federation in hopes of freeing the visas.

"The first contact was with the members of the federation from the socialist countries, who immediately promised to help in any way they could. Next came a meeting with the general secretary of FINA, the international swimming federation, a Swede as it happened. He was very polite, heard me out, and wished me much success. But when I left him I still didn't really have much hope. The possibility of launching a formal protest had been placed on the agenda of the FINA meeting, but only in thirty-seventh place under the heading 'miscellaneous.'

"The congress would open on Monday morning and if we were to be in the competition, our first swimmer would be in the water on Tuesday morning according to the timetable. But then some friends, and primarily the British delegate, intervened within the Congress and managed to get an immediate discussion started on the GDR visa problem. The British delegate begged the Congress to help us get the visas.

"I ran to the nearest phone to call this good news back to Berlin only to be told that there was no possibility of a phone connection between Turin, Italy, and the GDR. Next I tried to call the Italian Consulate in West Berlin, in hopes that someone from the GDR swimming federation would be sitting there waiting for any possible news of the visa. By chance the man who answered the phone was the angry consul himself, the man who had mistakenly granted me a journalist's visa to go to Turin in the first place. He called my friend to the phone, however, and arrangements were immediately made to charter a plane to fly our swimmers to Turin on a moment's notice.

"I was left to handle all the details at the Turin end of the operation. First, a bus had to be brought to the airport to take the team into town. But the man who rented buses was demanding a high rent for night work, much more money than I had in my pocket.

"As I turned to leave his office, wondering what to do next, a man who had been standing nearby came over, looked me right in the eye and asked me if I was a Communist. I wasn't sure what to say because, after all, I was in Italy, and I wasn't sure whether the answer would bring friendship or a fist fight. When I admitted what I was he asked me to come with him and have a cup of coffee.

"He made a phone call and soon another man came up to us in the coffee shop with a huge smile and a single word of greeting: 'Communist!' He said there would be no question of money at all for his bus, all he wanted was the time and the place to show up with it.

"Just when everything seemed to be finally settled, though, a new problem arose. Planes were not allowed to land at the small Turin airport at night, except under very special circumstances. Only the airport chief himself could allow such a thing. So, wondering if the whole effort would fail because of this problem at the very last minute, I phoned the Turin airport chief. Fortunately for our team, it turned out he had been a partisan officer fighting against the Fascists in Italy all through the War. With a voice full of enthusiasm he told me that only an event such as an earthquake would prevent the GDR swim team from landing at his Turin airport in the middle of the night.

"And, indeed, promptly at three o'clock in the morning, the plane from Berlin touched down on the Turin runway, which had to be lit up just minutes before their arrival. They didn't have even the faintest notion of what I had gone through trying to make these arrangements.

"That morning we had only one swimmer in the qualifying races, a girl named Jutta Langenau, who would swim in a relatively new event for women, the 100-meter butterfly. Since everyone else was exhausted by the trip, the last minute rush of it all, and the late night, I offered to use the last money in my pocket and take Jutta to the swimming pool by taxi.

"It was the first race of the morning in the qualifying heats, a race where you usually don't expect all that much to happen, particularly with a girl who has been up most of the night before traveling to Italy. But, when Jutta stepped out of the pool at the conclusion of her heat, the scoreboard flashed the time and the words "Record Mondiale" beside her victory. The GDR had just set its first ever World swimming record!

"After all the planning that had gone toward such a moment, it had happened first thing in the morning with no one from our country present except for myself. It didn't really matter, though, as we were both flushed with emotion as we stood embracing each other by the side of the swimming pool. What must they have thought back in Berlin when they heard the news?"

One wonders if anyone then suspected that in less than two decades the GDR women swimmers would come on to "own" the swimming pools of the world with Kornelia Ender, et al. Or, if Ender, and other GDR champions of the 1970s, realized what their predecessors in the 1950s really went through.

"Oh, I am sure they didn't," says Huhn. "Inge Utecht, one of our women's track coaches, told me just such a story. Inge, back in 1953, had run in a 400-meter race in the Berlin park of Cantianstrasse and had covered the distance in 59.3, well behind the winner, a girl named Ulla Donath, who won the race in 55.7, three tenths of a second faster than the listed world 'best' time of 56.0 for Valentina Pomogayewa of the Soviet Union. While it's true 400 meters was not a recognized World record event in 1953, it was still run often enough for the world's best times to be officially recorded in the International Amateur Athletics Federation statistics. But Ulla's time could not be recognized because the GDR was not a member country of the IAAF. Then in 1954 Inge Utecht and several of her teammates were invited to the Cross de l'Humanité meet in Paris, only to be told when they arrived that they could not formally compete, again because of the lack of formal IAAF membership. Inge and her friends ran in unofficial races against worker sportsmen clubs instead.

"In 1972 Inge went to Paris again, but this time as a coach of the GDR track team. This time her bus was accompanied by the president's motorcycle escorts, who led the bus with sirens and flashing lights to the stadium at Colombes. This was just a month before the Munich Olympic Games and Inge was coaching a young schoolgirl, the champion of the 1970 Spartakiad competitions, Monika Zehrt. That afternoon in Paris, Monika covered the 400 meters in a time of 51.0, a World record.

"Later that night, at the post-meet athletes' banquet, Inge told Monika all about her own experiences in Paris and that day back in

Berlin in 1953 when Ulla Donath had run the 55.7. Monika just pinched an eye skeptically. 'Could it really be true?'"

Oh how quickly the younger generations forget!

"I can remember," says cycling World champion Tave Shur, the first great World hero of GDR sport in the Fifties, "getting up one morning and riding my racing bike all the way from Mecklenburg to West Berlin and back, a distance of about two hundred and fifty miles.

"The purpose was to buy a new set of lightweight handlebars that were only available in the West. I had to change my money (and oh, how I had saved for this moment) at an unfavorable 4–1 exchange rate on the black market just to get the funds to buy the equipment. And then I had to ride all the way back home to be ready for work the next day.

"This year my son's club gave him a new bike for his competition in the Spartakiad, a bike that was twice the bike I ever dreamed of owning when I was his age, and he just takes it for granted. As a matter of fact, I think he feels they owe him a free bike as his birthright. Are we getting that old, my generation? Surely the Fifties and the Fifties' values aren't all that far in the past?"

It's a funny feeling, to be in far-off Leipzig, and hear a father make the same plea that fathers make at home when they compare the material benefits of the current generation with their own.

It's also a good feeling.

22

Perks, Promotion, and Politics

Who can remember the Munich Olympic pole vault of 1972? For track and field fans, the question is really, who can forget it? Bob Seagren of USC, then-World record holder and defending gold medalist from the Mexico City Games; Wolfgang Nordwig from the small, but powerful, Motor Jena track club in the GDR; and a newly marketed vaulting pole with what, in retrospect, can only be viewed as the unfortunate name of "Catapole."

In war, governments start disputes; generals plan battles; and soldiers end up fighting them. In top-level international sport it sometimes isn't all that different. Nationalism—in the definition of "our country is the best there is"—sets the tone. Sport federations create the training plan and put the team together. The athletes then get to fight it out. As silly as it may seem, whenever two athletes representing countries in political disagreement meet in sport, any controversy coming out of that competition will be magnified.

In the Montreal Olympics, to cite an example, there was a bitter protest in the women's discus when Faina Melnik of the Soviet Union was judged to have made two starts on her final throw (only one is allowed) with the result that what would have been a medal-winning throw was disallowed. The dispute was between the Soviet Union and the GDR. No one saw it as political in nature. Had this been between an American girl and a Soviet it would have undoubtedly been seen quite differently. A story that wound up as a paragraph in most papers would have been a headline. Similarly, if the Munich pole vault controversy had been between two Americans battling for the same gold medal, or between an American and a Canadian, it too might only have brought a passing mention. But it wasn't. It was between vaulters from the GDR and the United States; and between the International Amateur Athletic Federation, ruling body of track and field, and an American equipment manufacturer. Everyone got sucked into a debate of sport, politics, economic opportunism, and the Olympic ideal.

For years I have poked about in hopes of finding out what really happened behind the scenes in a dispute that saw Seagren's pole declared illegal, legal, and then illegal again on the very eve of competition, forcing the American champion to vault with a borrowed pole, finishing with a silver medal to Nordwig's 5 meters, 50 centimeters (18' ½"), which won the gold.

When it was done, well into the gathering darkness of a Bavarian summer evening, the official Olympic film, *Visions of Eight,* captured one passing moment beautifully as Seagren went out of his way to present the borrowed pole to Adrian Paulen, the senior jury official and now president of the International Amateur Athletic Federation, an act performed with a dignity and sense of irony worthy of a Shakespearean drama.

The more you look into this involved story, the more confused you become. There's the U.S. side of it, the GDR side, the manufacturer's side, the IAAF side, and about as many fringe plots as you'll find in the major political assassinations of this century.

The story uncovers much that is wrong with modern-day international sport and the Olympic Games. But it also reveals the personalities of two of the most attractive and talented athletes to grace the world stage in the 1960s and the 1970s, two men whose single-minded desire to win an Olympic gold medal put them and, for the media, their countries as well, into a head-on conflict on the afternoon of September 2, 1972.

First, let's take a look at the story from the American side of the fence, a story that must begin with a look at the IAAF rules, or rather one rule in particular, which says that no implement can be used in the Games unless it has been on the market and available to all the athletes in the competition for at least one year prior to the Games. "The point of the rule," says Artur Takac, who was directly in charge of the technical phase of the Munich track and field competition, "is to make as sure as humanly possible that the Olympic Games are between athletes and not implement manufacturers."

That is a very laudable IAAF sports federation ideal, but one can't say it's upheld very stringently at the Olympic level in light of what has gone under Games sanction in the skiing events. There is no limitation on the development of last-minute technological break-through in skiing. In the final months and weeks before the Games, the top stars are all whisked away to the training hills of the manufacturers whose equipment they have contracted to use. Rumors abound. Within forty-eight hours of the downhill in Innsbruck's Games of 1976 the papers were full of "exclusive" pictures of a new, supposedly faster, Fischer ski with a hole in the front tip to let air through and cut wind resistance, thus picking up fractions of a second. Very interesting. But the top skiers didn't use them, other than for the psychological advantage Fischer skiers might have gained over Fischer opponents.

Track and field seems to have a sensible rule in trying to eliminate unfair technical advantage, but when it comes to enforcement, alas, it is easier said than done. Equipment manufacturers, it goes without saying, like to have their products "winning" Olympic medals, too. How far does a pole vault company have to go to make sure its products are available to all the athletes of the world? Does it have to put them on sale in a store? Take out advertisements in sports publications all over the world? Send free pole vault poles to everyone in the world who has cleared 17 feet?

The manufacturer, in this case, insisted that the pole was invented and in operation more than a year prior to the Olympics and they would have certainly had no objections to anyone of World Class caliber making use of their poles at any time. But that is the position the GDR track and field federation chose to challenge.

Sitting down after work one day in Jena in January of 1977, Wolfgang Nordwig took a deep breath and gave me his side of the story.

"I am convinced," he says, "that the pole the Americans brought to Munich hadn't been in competition more than a couple of months. The performances in the U.S. championships in June were indicative of a major breakthrough in technology.

"While it is true we had been hearing of this amazing 'Catapole' for about a year, it is also true that we had not been able to get them until shortly before the Games, and the ones I did try were not the proper weight for me. I wasn't really too angry about it at the time, because I knew we had the rule on our side and should win if we protested at the Games.

"It was not just myself, either. France's François Tracanelli did not have access to the new pole, and neither did Chris Papanikolaou of Greece, both of whom were leading contenders for a medal in the Games. From the information we had, only the Americans and the Swedes had access to the poles."

And there you have the basic plot. The Americans claim the poles were available and should have been legal, and if Nordwig or any other World Class vaulter didn't have a Catapole it was because he didn't want one. They feel the protests in Munich were laid by the GDR because a last minute change of equipment would be upsetting to Seagren, the gold medal favorite.

And what does a "neutral" vaulter have to say about it all?

"I am not sure what to say," says Bruce Simpson, who went on to finish fifth in the final while vaulting for Canada. "We all knew well ahead of time that the pole was being protested and might not be allowed in the Games. With that in mind, I took along new poles and old poles, just to make sure I had everything I needed in case the new ones were banned. Why wasn't Seagren better prepared?"

"Don't get into that," warned another of the American vaulters who competed in Munich in 1972.

But we have to get into "that" in order to understand fully what goes on behind the scenes at the Games, or at least what went on in Mexico and Munich since there were some signs of it being toned down a little in Montreal.

"That" is under-the-table money from equipment manufacturers. It's the same kind of endorsement money that is paid over-the-table if the sport is a professional one like golf or tennis, motor racing, football, baseball, hockey, basketball or whatever.

There's an interesting story that makes the rounds every time the

Tommie Smith–John Carlos black-power protest at Mexico comes up for discussion. When it happened, the officials of the U.S. team in Mexico were predictably furious. So furious, in fact, that some of them buttonholed a few of the favorite reporters that night and told them not to miss a special press conference that would be held the following morning. Smith and Carlos, so the rumors went, not only would be thrown off the U.S. Olympic team, but out of the Games Village and the country as well. The rumor spread like wildfire, through the U.S. team quarters as well. Remember, this was in 1968, when protests against the Vietnam war, the draft and racism were at fever pitch in the United States. These were the days of the 1968 Democratic Convention in Chicago, and the death of hundreds of student protesters on the streets of Mexico City just days before the opening of the Games themselves.

Late that night one member of the U.S. track team, acting as a spokesman for others, dropped in on the higher-ups with the news that if they moved against Carlos and Smith there just might be another press conference held by the athletes to reveal which athletes had professionalized themselves by accepting what money from which equipment manufacturers. He asked them to consider how they were going to explain the need for the U.S. team to return many of its track and field medals.

Some reporters were surprised to find that there had been a sudden change of heart overnight. Although the Carlos–Smith incident had been most certainly regrettable, there would be no press conference to discuss further disciplinary measures.

And how do the top athletes justify this tactic of accepting under-the-table monies, which in the case of a top pole vaulter might run to around $16,000 a year?

They do it without any twinge of conscience whatever, first merely because it is being offered—there are few among us who would not be flattered and tempted by such insistent offers. Secondly, it is because they are so conditioned to accepting "expense" payments from U.S. indoor and European outdoor meet promoters, payments so considerable that the best amateurs couldn't possibly consider turning pro in 1973–76, when the ITA tour was trying to make a go of things. And thirdly, because the top U.S. amateur track stars feel so utterly abandoned by their own country when it comes to financial support that they see these payments as the one thing that evens the balance a little, the one thing that gives them a chance to compete on even terms with the best commercially supported athletes of Western Europe and the state-supported athletes of Eastern Europe.

If we don't get into "that" in a discussion like this, we miss out on a major element of what is going on behind the scenes. Equipment manufacturers—and it doesn't matter if it's a maker of U.S. pole vault poles, Austrian downhill skis, or German or Japanese track shoes—like to win Olympic gold medals, too.

Some track people doubt whether Seagren's Catapole was any better than other poles in the competition at all. Takac tends to be in this category.

"I think," he says, "that it had a rather unfortunate name. The name brings forth the vision of a catapult, an implement that simply throws the competitor higher, just like a catapult might be used to attack a castle in the Middle Ages. The domestic advertising in the U.S. did seem to hint that there was something very special about this new product."

In a sense there was something special. It contained carbon fiber, which created an interesting sidelight to the entire case. It was against U.S. law in 1972 for any company to export carbon fiber, then a brand-new item on the market, to any East European country. It is possible that the company did indeed attempt to send poles to Nordwig at his club in Jena, only to have the poles impounded by the U.S. Government as an illegal export to a Communist country.

Another rumor—although GDR sources insist it is not a rumor at all—had one of the shoe manufacturers offering to get new carbon fiber poles smuggled to Nordwig in the GDR in return for the right to use Nordwig, who uses their shoes, in a promotion poster. Although the DTSB lets its athletes use of a lot of Western equipment, they have never permitted any advertising as a part of the deal.

Perhaps the closest anyone ever came to putting this story into a human perspective was shortly after the event in Munich when one reporter made a point of asking both athletes, what, in light of all the bitterness and bad feeling, the gold medal really meant to them. The answers say a lot about the athletes as people, the countries they live in, and the systems they operate under.

Seagren, with visions of Hollywood dancing in his head, said that if all went well after the Games he was hoping to take up on a few offers he had received from the film industry. And why not? After all, didn't

Johnny Weismuller parlay an Olympic swimming career into a legendary film career playing the role of Tarzan? Didn't Lee Majors parlay a college football career right into TV superstardom with "The Six Million Dollar Man"? O.J. Simpson does all right in the movies, and so does Jimmy Brown. Why not Bob Seagren?

There is absolutely no reason why not. One must get the proper door opened at the proper time, though, and what better way to do that than to win back-to-back gold medals in the pole vault in the Olympic Games? It has to be in the Olympic Games. The American public, after all, remembers what Jesse Owens did in Berlin in 1936, not what he did in Ann Arbor in 1935 when he broke four World records in a single afternoon in the Big Ten championships. They remember Mark Spitz from the Olympics, not from the NCAAs. Jean Claude Killy is remembered for Grenoble, not the World Cup. It's not surprising that Bob Seagren wanted that Munich Olympic gold medal very badly.

And so did Wolfgang Nordwig, who got a bit of a chuckle out of hearing about Seagren's lifetime ambition when the reporter came around to his digs in Munich. Nordwig is not going to be a movie star, although, when it comes to basic good looks, both he and Seagren would have little trouble qualifying.

"No," said Nordwig, "I do not have that problem. For me the gold medal is a very fine thing, and an excellent way to finish my career in sport. I have been at it for many years and a gold medal in the Olympic Games is the dream of everyone. There could not be a better finish.

"But when it comes to my work, I am finishing my studies for a postgraduate degree in laser beam physics, and, unfortunately for me, the laser beams do not care whether or not I win a gold medal. My career will be the same, win or lose. Perhaps this is an advantage for our sportsmen in the GDR. Our future jobs after sports do not depend on winning the gold medal."

As far as his career being the same, in a way that is true, and in a way it isn't. My own feeling, after a couple of months of observing the athletes of the GDR, is that Wolfgang Nordwig would get as many perks from winning the gold as Seagren would get back in the United States, perhaps more. Not in the job area, it is true. When I saw Wolfgang in 1977, he was the head of a department of research for the Carl Zeiss firm in Jena, doing no doubt exactly the same work he would have been doing had he been the silver medal winner in the Olympic Games. He would probably have had the same apartment and same government-issue car, win or lose, and pretty much the same life-style.

But there are other advantages. When it came time to light the torch to open the World Youth Festival in Berlin in 1973, it was Wolfgang Nordwig who was given the honor. There will almost certainly be opportunities wihin the Party, opportunities to travel and represent Motor Jena and the DTSB at sports functions all around the world. The GDR does not forget its gold medal winners and world champions, particularly those who come along and take the title in the pole vault away from the United States.

Wolfgang's victory in Munich was a very big political victory for the GDR as well. First they forced the Americans to back down in the IAAF committee rooms, and then they beat them on the field as well, with a new Olympic record to boot. One almost wonders why he didn't attempt to go on a little further.

"That was just about my maximum performance, that 5.50 in Munich," says Wolfgang. "I was twenty-seven years old at the time, and even then I wasn't quite so fast as I was at twenty-five. You could see that the future of the event was rising very quickly. Soon we knew you would have to clear heights close to 5.70 to be at the top and I wouldn't have been capable of that. and, besides, I was ready to start my professional career. I was very fortunate while doing my graduate studies in that I was allowed to slow the progress of the study to allow for the training in sport. I found it a very relaxing thing to be able to get away from the physics for a few hours a day and work with the pole vault. Sometimes I think it helped me retain my mental stability. Sport, I think, is very good that way."

But, I wondered, don't some people in the GDR resent the favors that go to international sports champions, the trips to Cuba for vacations and to other countries in the West where they are not allowed to travel? The cars, the apartments, the Party assignments?

Nordwig thought about that one for half a minute and then, justifying himself just as easily as any Western athlete justifies his financial perks from the system, said:

"I do not think I have taken any more out of our system than I have put into it."

And he is right. He hasn't. When it comes time to push a public appeal for a campaign like running a mile for your health, there will be Nordwig up front, running with the public, signing autographs, making speeches to school kids, working hour upon hour for the promotion of sport within the system. Nordwig has an image within the system and he puts a lot of time into maintaining it. He is a happy man.

"Sometimes," he adds with a smile, "I still even try my hand at the pole vault. I am still comfortable at around the 4.70 level (15'3"), but now that I am thirty-three I just haven't got the speed for more than that."

And Bob Seagren?

Well, first there was the pro track circuit, and then a lot of success in the Superstars competition, an all-around event that matches the skills of the stars of several sports, an event that is all but a setup for a top pole vaulter. No one pole vaults beyond the 18 foot mark these days without a lot of speed and a lot of upper body strength, the two talents that will always pay off in Superstars.

But he has also never given up on acting. When last seen in 1978, he was making an appearance in ABC television's sitcom "Soap," playing the part of a homosexual football player. He played it well, and one would like to think the director and producer, not unlike Wolfgang Nordwig's laser beams, weren't concerned whether or not he ever won an Olympic gold medal.

23

Politics and the IOC

The International Olympic Committee, bastion of the theory of separation of sport and politics on the one hand, and, on the other, one of the most politically-minded bodies in the world under the iconoclastic leadership of Chicago's Avery Brundage, may have been singularly ill-equipped to deal evenhandedly amidst the political intrigue of German sport in the 1950s and the 1960s.

Avery Brundage's sympathy to the Germans in the middle Thirties, and his role as head of the U.S. Olympic Committee in assuring that the 1936 Olympics would be staged in Berlin, is a matter of record. It is also a matter of record that even today, on the eve of the 1980s, the IOC has never elected a Jew to its membership. Or a woman.

Just the same, the IOC has never claimed to be a democratic institution. Its members are not considered to be members "from" certain countries; they are considered to be IOC members "in" those lands—an important distinction. If you are "from" the United States in an international organization you represent the United States in that organization. If you are a member of an international organization "in" a country you represent the organization, not the country. The IOC views itself as a sports aristocracy, men of a like mind from around the world coming together to defend a principle: the Olympic idea and the purity of amateur sport. Avery Brundage believed in this, body and soul, and, when the Soviet authorities tossed Dr. Karl Ritter von Halt, one of his Olympic compatriots, into jail at the conclusion of World War II, he was outraged. The Brundage files, now stored at the University of Illinois, show that Avery was quick to write letters and do whatever else he could to alleviate his friend's suffering and get him back into the IOC. In October of 1950 Brundage wrote to defend von Halt, citing their long friendship and stating that von Halt was never in politics and never a Nazi. Perhaps, then, he was going to a costume party late in the War when he was photographed in an SS officer's uniform? Artur Takac has another instance.

"In 1944," he recalls, "I was a Yugoslavian prisoner interned in Lausanne, Switzerland, having escaped from an Italian prison camp. For work I was allowed to offer my service to the IOC headquarters by day, returning to our internment camp at night. Since 1944 would have been an Olympic year, we sent out a call to all members who could get to Lausanne in neutral Switzerland to come for a commemorative meeting. We even staged a little 'Games' with prisoner-athletes from the camps, all representing their own countries. We even let the Italians compete, by a vote of 3–2. I know. I voted.

"But everyone was astonished and furious when von Halt showed up in Lausanne. This was in the final year of the War. There was no way Germans could travel abroad unless they were working for the government. No one would even sit to eat with him at the dining table. It was embarrassing for us, and I'm sure, for him, too."

"And in the final weeks of the War," says Klaus Huhn, "when everyone else was trying to throw away their uniform and take on a new identity, von Halt was still going for a promotion to become the Nazi Government's sports minister."

And yet, von Halt was able to bounce right back into his Olympic role when his jail term was over and became Brundage's closest confidant on the politics of the German question, despite his wartime loyalties. Letters to Brundage reveal not only the ongoing friendship of the two men, but also the fact that policy on the form of postwar Germany's IOC representation was not always the product of due consideration by the Executive Board, but was often made independently by the president—a man who listened to his friends.

In November of 1953, von Halt, concerned about a permanent East–West separation, wrote to Brundage to note East German propaganda favoring IOC recognition of a separate Eastern Zone Olympic Committee, and to state his opposition. He cited the IOC rule that each country can have only one committee, and also protested that the Eastern Zone officials were paid Party men, not honorary sports officials.

A late von Halt letter deals with the 1959 battle to restrict access of GDR sports officials to the Games. The GDR was fighting to prevent it by urging that two sets of administrators be created for the combined German team, one for East, one for West. By this time the GDR did have its own Olympic committee, a big improvement over 1953, but West Germany still had control of the management of the combined team and was conducting all correspondence with the IOC on behalf of both German NOCs. Von Halt warned Brundage of the ulterior political motives of the GDR Olympic officials, and thereby revealed his own, insisting that only one National Olympic Committee could correspond with the IOC, and that the Communists certainly could not correspond for both East and West. Again, he emphasized his opinion that sport, to the East Germans, was a political tool.

In a letter to Brundage from Otto Meyer, the IOC Chancellor and manager of the Swiss office, in December, 1959, the implication is clear that the final decision on separate administrative units is Brundage's alone to make, though Meyer put in a word for the sensibility of separation, despite von Halt's feelings.

Sure enough, two weeks later, von Halt wrote to express his gratitude to Brundage for finally favoring the West German solution—and a personal friendship going back to 1912.

Karl Ritter von Halt saw Brundage in Squaw Valley for the 1960 Olympic Games, but all GDR sports officials, coaches, and media were barred from entry by the United States Government, a government that publicly goes out of its way to separate politics from sport.

Avery Brundage went to his grave convinced the IOC was better equipped to handle the problem of the reunification of the two Germanies than any forum in the world. He considered the combined East–West team, which accepted Olympic medals together from 1956 to 1964 under an IOC-designed flag to the tune of Beethoven's *Ode to Joy*, as his crowning personal diplomatic achievement. He had single-handedly shown the whole world a viable solution to the German problem, at a time when the United States, the Soviet Union, the

Germans themselves, and even the United Nations, were failing miserably.

It was a delusion, but it was a kind of delusion that the West (Europeans form a majority of the membership in the approximately seventy-five-member IOC) could be comfortable with in the midst of the Cold War decades. In their minds, the East German athletes were not being excluded from the Games, which eased their consciences, and all options were being left open for the eventual reunification of Germany into a single political unit.

Again, in defense of the IOC, there were many people on both sides of the German frontier who sincerely wanted reunification. But with the advantage of hindsight, one can see that a reunified Germany was nothing but a dream. Both sides, even when they didn't realize it, were using the combined team to soften up the other side for a takeover, with the result that neither got the final advantage.

In its founding declarations, on October 1, 1948, the brand-new (East) German Sports Committee proclaimed that "the only German championships satisfactory to us are those which determine the best athletes from all provinces and all zones." Arguing that "The Democratic Sports Movement is fighting against the intrigues of the U.S.A. imperialists and their lackeys to separate Germans from Germans," the Committee was given the task of furthering sporting relationships as much as possible, and to this end they declared that they favored the promotion of sports conferences, joint German championships and common discussions by representatives of both sides on "unity and freedom in German sport."

It was pretty hard for anyone of any political persuasion to disagree with those sentiments. What, one wonders, were the new leaders of the soon-to-be-created GDR really up to in light of the fact they had already decided to go their own way as a Soviet-backed independent state?

Party leader Walter Ulbricht cleared that up on January 15, 1951, when he addressed a Congress of the Sports Committee and said: "We must use each relationship with the West German sportsmen to influence them to resist remilitarization. Each individual sportsman and each individual association in West Germany has to be told that we have to struggle together for peace."

The young GDR of 1951 had great fears (after all, this was just six years after the end of the War) of a rearmed German military machine in the West setting about to reclaim its lost territories in the East. The GDR obviously saw sport as a wedge that could be driven between possible militarists in the Bonn Government and the West Germans themselves to help assure the status quo in the German balance. In pragmatic terms, their young country, just two years old in 1951, needed time to develop, and if a move toward combined sports relations would help them buy it, then of course sport would be used as a political weapon in the ideological battle.

Representatives of the two German sports movements met in the winter resort of Oberhof in February of 1951, and the GDR emphasized its view of the importance of the meeting by sending Ulbricht himself to head their delegation.

The meetings, of course, had no chance of accomplishing anything meaningful. How could they meet as equals when the West represented a country of more than sixty million and the East a country of fewer than twenty million? If the proposed alliance were put on a one-man-one-vote footing, then West Germany would have taken control of East German sport. The GDR denounced this and stressed the need for sport to come together throughout Germany for the purpose of waging war against imperialism. They might as well have been speaking two different languages.

Two months later, in April of 1951, the GDR announced the creation of its own National Olympic Committee, a move that officially brought the IOC into the brouhaha. The IOC had been keeping its eye on the scene for some time in hopes that all of Germany could be represented at the upcoming 1952 Games in Helsinki.

Two weeks later, at the IOC's 45th Congress in Vienna, the membership bids of the Soviet Union and the Federal Republic of Germany were accepted, with the Soviets getting in only after a stiff battle from some who feared the creation of an East–West Olympic split. The GDR bid was turned down because of the IOC rule that only one National Olympic Committee can be recognized for any country or territory. The IOC also noted that the GDR was publicly working toward the unification of German sport and urged it to continue its work in that direction.

The GDR was thus hoisted on its own political petard. While it is possible for the IOC to recognize an NOC from a territory that is obviously not a recognized independent country (such as the recognition of Puerto Rico as separate from the United States), this is only possible when the country responsible for the territory agrees to have it done this way. The Federal Republic was not about to agree to an independent GDR Olympic team in 1952.

Representatives of both German committees met in Hannover on May 17, and then again at the IOC headquarters in Lausanne, Switzerland, on May 22 where a tentative agreement was reached to develop a combined team under the complete management of the Western Federal Republic Committee for the Helsinki Games. That "agreement" immediately fell apart, however, when the GDR delegation returned home and had their efforts overturned by Ulbricht, who stated that the GDR would only go to Helsinki with its own committee and its own team. And that was that in spite of a continuing series of meetings and negotiations by the IOC president at the time, Sigfried Edstrom of Sweden.

The GDR then opened another debate by demanding that separate sporting arrangements be created between West Berlin and the GDR. They did this by refusing to accept the Western position that West Berlin was in any way an integral part of the Federal Republic. This issue was kept alive until the 1970s, and even blocked a preliminary proposal that the 1972 Olympics be held in West Berlin rather than Munich, before finally being dropped as a bargaining point by the GDR.

The upshot of it all was that there were no GDR athletes in the Helsinki Olympics of 1952. But immediately after, when Avery Brundage took the helm of the IOC as its president, the dream of the combined team was once again dusted off for political action. At the IOC meeting in Paris in June of 1955, the GDR National Olympic Committee was recognized by a vote of 27 to 7, with the rider that it could only compete in the Melbourne Games as part of a combined German team. The IOC also added an additional stick to this carrot-and-stick approach with a provision that if a joint German team was not formed for Melbourne, then the recognition of the GDR National Olympic Committee would lapse.

The GDR didn't like the arrangement, but they had no choice but to accept it. By 1955 they were starting to develop some fine athletic talent. The school in Leipzig was four years old and the first graduates were entering the field. The IOC acceptance would open the door to membership in more and more international sports federations. This was not 1951: if the GDR turned its back on the IOC this time they would risk a continuing escalation in the rate of defection of athletes and coaches to the West, a rate that was already unacceptably high. So they agreed. And Avery Brundage started to tell the world of how the spirit of the Olympics had solved the political problem of Germany. The problem of fielding a combined team was left for others to deal with.

What problems there were! Forget the little ones, such as anthem, nonpolitical uniforms, and the flag. The major problem concerned a fair selection of athletes and coaches, team managers and top officials. The solution was that within each sport, the side that qualified the most athletes would get to name the coaches and managers. It was a fair system, but it left the GDR again on the outside looking in. They qualified eighteen athletes against fifty-eight for the Federal Republic on the 1956 Winter Games team for Cortina, Italy, and just thirty-seven against one hundred thirty-eight from the West for the Melbourne Summer Games.

But they did hit for a gold medal when Wolfgang Behrendt came home a winner in boxing. The country was seven years old and it had an Olympic champion. Not bad.

On the personal side, there were problems and frustrations. Tave Shur, the two-time World cycling champion and first great GDR postwar sports star, spoke of the problems of the road cycling team in Melbourne.

"It simply didn't work out in a sport where teamwork is of prime importance," he said. "We had three from our republic on the road team, and one, Pommer, from the Federal Republic, but since the overall cycling team was predominantly West German, they controlled the team management as well. Under this system there was little communication and little cooperation—in a sport where all four members of the team must work together if there is to be a real success.

"As the race moved into its latter stages, the Italians, led by Ercole Baldini, broke ahead of the field working as a unit of four. When he saw the break, Pommer, the westerner on our team, broke after them on his own without giving any indication to us what he was up to. It proved to be a completely fruitless move, however, and he soon fell back out of contention taking with him our team chances for a possible silver or bronze medal.

"But there was still the individual phase, and when I broke to regain contention I was followed alertly by my teammate Tuller and an Englishman named Jackson, the three of us suddenly racing as a unit toward a possible individual bronze medal.

"The strategy here has to be for the teammates to share the lead, off and on, to allow the second rider to take advantage of the wind break and get a breather. But when I asked Tuller to take over from me he begged offf saying he had a cramp in his leg and could not manage it.

"Finally, late in the race when I was tiring from setting all the pace, Jackson pulled out and made his move, a driving finish that brought him the bronze medal, while Tuller, who suddenly didn't have a cramp at all, shot by me into 4th place to be the first German cyclist to finish. Some teammate he turned out to be, and then, to top it all off, a few months later he defected to the West.

"This is the fiasco of our joint Olympic team. There were simply too many tensions, too much distrust. It was not a good solution."

Tave Shur, who is now a member of the GDR Parliament and one of the leading party activists in the sports field, says he was not a political person at all in his early cycling days.

"I don't think many young athletes are political people to begin with," he said. "For me the politicizing came with the personal experience. The more aware you became of what was going on the more thoughtful you became about what you were doing yourself.

"There were a lot of chances to go over to the West in the 1950s, and there were a lot of inducements to our best athletes to defect. I felt I was approached on three separate occasions with the possibility of offers to go West for a professional career, but it was done so subtly that one could never be sure.

"The approach would usually be made at a party following a race or a track competition. Nobody ever came right out and asked whether you were interested in switching sides, they would simply start up a mild political conversation by asking what you thought about some happening or another. If they had any hint that you might be unhappy, or having personal problems, or in disagreement with the government, then you might get an invitation, usually from a girl, to head off to an apartment for a further meeting. That's the way the contacts were made in West Berlin. Like I said, it happened to me three times, I think, although I could never be sure because I never followed up on the hints.

"With the passing of time I became more and more convinced that the GDR approach to sport was the correct one, and the commercial approach was the less healthy one. That was when I started to get more and more involved in the management of sport within the DTSB. That was when I started to become politically aware."

Many others made the opposite choice, as was to be expected in a world where people were being asked to choose between collective responsibility and personal well-being. The defections were more than annoying to the GDR government and its sports hierarchy. They were downright embarrassing. But early attempts to try to control the problem by making sure of the politics of athletes traveling abroad almost certainly added to the problem instead of curtailing it. No one in any country appreciates the overt tactics of the police state.

The upsurge in the GDR economy in the 1970s helped slow sports defections to a trickle, in spite of the fact GDR athletes are now traveling around the world to all major competitions virtually without restrictions. The reason is simple: life is getting much better in the GDR these days. For the first time since the War, it is arguable that an athlete in the GDR has a better life-style, both in material gain and in athletic opportunity, than his counterpart in the Federal Republic.

But it was a long time in coming. If the trip to North America for the 40-gold-medal 1976 Games in Montreal was the high point of GDR sports history to date, the trip to Squaw Valley for the 1960 Winter Games had to be a low point.

The U.S. State Department was willing to allow the GDR athletes on the combined team to make the trip to California, but that was where they drew the line. There would be no accompanying sports officials, no government officials, and no journalists. Not even Manfred Ewald, who usually managed to go just about everywhere during this period, in one capacity or another. In one photo from the Rome Summer Games of 1960, Ewald is seen working as a trainer for the German road cycling team, passing off the sponges to Tave Shur.

But at least he was there. He was not present for the Winter Games in Squaw Valley, for what turned out to be a pretty good trip for the GDR contingent. Helmut Recknagel won the first of his two Olympic ski jump titles. But the sympathetic heroine, as a result of the lockout of officials, coaches and journalists, was young Helga Haase, today the coach of the Dynamo Berlin speed skaters, but then an aspiring young skater herself.

A skater without her coach: thank heavens for the telephone. Strategies were planned via long distance. Pep talks were given via long distance. And then Helga Haase went out on the ice and won a gold medal, carried herself off on her own shoulders, and called Berlin to conduct her own press conference with reporters waiting back home.

"It was an impossible journalistic situation," says Klaus Huhn. "Thankfully some of our friends from other countries put together a pool of their own stories so we would have something to put in the paper. It is a situation we would never like to see repeated in the future."

Most American sports officials either don't know that all this happened, or simply don't remember it. The Lake Placid and Los Angeles Olympic delegations, in seeking the bids for the 1980 and 1984 Winter and Summer host roles, both were startled when asked by GDR representatives if there would be any repeat of these problems when the Games return to the United States.

Through it all, the relationships between the two German sports governing bodies did not improve much, if at all. In 1961 when it became apparent that the GDR and the FRG would meet in the ice-hockey World championships, the West Germans withdrew rather than risk a situation where they might have to stand at attention and honor the GDR anthem and flag in the postgame ceremony if they lost the game.

And then the GDR built the Berlin Wall, throwing the entire world into yet another German crisis. The West broke off all sporting relationships with the East, a move that caught the entire GDR jumping team, including Olympic champion Recknagel, literally on top of the jump at Oberstdorf. They were already up the hill and ready for competition when a West German Government official came running to the scene insisting it was illegal for them to compete and they must climb down the steps from the top of the hill. The jumpers explained that this was not possible since an ageless superstition among all jumpers says that once you have climbed to the top you only come down by jumping, never by climbing back down again. The police on the scene nodded their approval of the jumpers' complaint, since they were all locals and well aware of jumping traditions.

Down at the bottom of the hill, the crowd was beginning to wonder why the start of the competition had been delayed. The nervous bureaucrat then went to a nearby phone to call for reinforcements. The call was never completed. As soon as his back was turned, the four GDR jumpers shot down the jump together in tandem, all four at once, to a tremendous ovation from the waiting thousands, who had never seen anything quite like this.

The IOC, of course, paid no attention and blandly started to prepare for yet another combined team for the 1964 Games. The GDR was quick to accept the IOC proposal in March of 1962, since this act would force the West to reopen the relationship that had been canceled because of the Wall. The Federal Republic was not happy, and counterattacked with a demand that West Berlin be designated as a host city for combined German team trials and a further demand that athletes who had defected from the GDR be allowed to participate in the trials without fear of retribution. The IOC agreed to these requests and reaffirmed that in their opinion the West Berlin sports associations were within the territory of the Federal Republic. Now it was the GDR's turn to be unhappy.

But really, as the sports rivalry between East and West continued to develop, neither side was very happy with what was happening. "The situation was not a just one," says Ewald. "We were obviously two completely separate entities, and in some sports we were developing two very strong teams. Rowing is an excellent example of this. Their Ratzeburg teams were the best in the world in the late 1950s and into the 1960s. But our team was the second best. In the trials we were losing to them by the narrowest of margins, and then their boats were going on to the Olympic Games and winning gold medals with open boat lengths to spare. Those would have been silver medals for us in rowing if we had been eligible to enter our own team in the Games.

"A lot of people have looked at our medal production in Mexico in 1968 as being the starting point for the development for GDR sport internationally, but those figures are misleading because we had our own team in Mexico. In actual fact, we would have won many more medals in Rome and Tokyo if we had had the same situation."

For his part, Willi Daume, the man who was Ewald's counterpart in West Germany's *Deutscher Sport Bund* (German Sports Union), and also the man who would do such a magnificent organizational job with the 1972 Munich Games before moving up the ladder to a vice-presidency within the IOC, could also see the writing on the wall. Daume knew all about the progress in coaching in Leipzig, about the improvements in the application of science to sport in the GDR, and about the fast-improving level of GDR sport.

Willi Daume knew, as perhaps many in the Bonn Government did not, that if the GDR did not soon get its own Olympic team then the GDR would soon come to dominate the combined team with athletes, coaches and officials.

The problem was more political than practical. If the Federal Republic offered a compromise the GDR would rebuff it out of hand. If the GDR offered one, the West would likewise feel obliged to reject it. A third party was needed, and who better than Albert Mayer, the respected IOC member in Switzerland.

After a private meeting with Daume, Albert Mayer suggested the following compromise:

1. West Germany and East Germany will, subject to IOC rules and regulations, send their own teams to the 1964 Olympic Games in Tokyo and Innsbruck.
2. As in 1960, the teams will appear under one and the same symbol and Olympic flag (with the IOC rings on it) and the same anthem (Beethoven's *Ode to Joy*).

On paper it was a master stroke for both sides. The GDR would finally get its own team, coaches, and officials to the Games, while the Federal Republic would still not be officially recognizing the legitimacy of the GDR as an independent country. At an Executive Board meeting in Uruguay, the IOC, interestingly enough, dusted off exactly the same compromise in April of 1979 as a possible compromise solution to the Communist China–Taiwan impasse. The big disadvantage to both sides would be the continuing loss of national expression. Neither side would have its own flag, or its own anthem. For the GDR, though, another political victory would have been won on the road to independence.

Both sides were given until January 13 of 1963 to approve or disapprove. The GDR sent its agreement on December 20, 1962. The Federal Republic turned it down on January 12, 1963, one day before the deadline. Willi Daume could not deliver his own government's approval.

The two Germanies were back to trying to field a combined team for the 1964 Olympic Games. It was incredibly difficult. The effort required fifteen National Olympic Committee conferences and ninety-six formal meetings between the various sports associations of the two sides. Again the GDR was demanding separate status for West Berlin, and within the IOC, the Soviet member, Konstantin Andrianov, sought to have the officially recognized West German NOC title changed from 1951's National Olympic Committee for Germany, to a much more specific National Olympic Committee of the Federal Republic of Germany.

Once again the status quo and the combined teams survived, but just barely. When the IOC gathered for its annual congress in Barcelona on October 8, 1965, the GDR Olympic Committee won full acceptance of the right to field an independent team for Mexico in 1968, but, still in hopes of German reunification down the road, the IOC still refused to allow the national anthems and the national flags. Both teams in 1968 still had Beethoven for the anthem and the Olympic rings superimposed on a German flag for the emblem.

Barcelona's vote was a great political victory for GDR sport, but behind the scenes the harassments went on, all the way down to the pettiest of levels, some of which look pretty humorous in retrospect. *Neues Deutschland*'s Huhn still gets a kick out of the doings in the press center in Grenoble at the 1968 Winter Games.

"We put a sticker on the door of the ADN" (the official wire service news agency of the GDR) "identifying the office as the headquarters of the GDR press office," he says, "and the other side complained that this was against the rules. But the manager of the press center saw it our way. He said it was reasonable to put up such a sign so visitors could know whether they were dealing with the GDR or the Federal Republic, and he pointed out that the office was not in view of the general public anyway since none but accredited journalists had access to the building. They said the sign could stay.

"Overnight, however, it disappeared. Someone had scraped it off the door. So we put up another, exactly twice the size of the first small sign. That night it, too, disappeared, and the same thing was repeated the third night with an even bigger sign. After that there wasn't any trouble, which was too bad in a way because our final door sticker would have been large enough to cover the entire door."

And then there was the battle of the anthems in Mexico City in the Summer Games. Once again, Beethoven was the thing, supposedly, but at the Federal Republic's Olympic Village flag-raising ceremony, someone switched the music on the band and out came the stirring strains of "Deutschland Über Alles," the Federal Republic's anthem, instead of Beethoven. The Mexican Organizing Committee was embarrassed by the diplomatic goof, and immediately offered to play the GDR anthem at their flag-raising ceremony. But Manfred Ewald refused, saying that his side would stick by the IOC rules.

The Mexicans decided to bide their time and wait for the closing ceremonies, specifically the moment when the anthem of the next host country is played while their flag is run up the pole. Since the 1972 host was to be Munich, this marked the first time since World War II that it was within Olympic protocol to raise the German flag and play "Deutschland Über Alles."

The band, of course, played Beethoven instead.

That, however, was just about the end of all that sort of nonsense. At the Mexico IOC session held the week prior to the 1968 Games, the members voted that all restrictions were off for the 1972 Games and both German teams would compete as complete members with anthems, flags, their own uniforms, and the rest of it.

That made 2 P.M., January 24, 1972, a very big moment in GDR sports, a moment recorded in detail for their history. Two o'clock was the exact moment when Kumi Takso, a First Class Sergeant in the Emperor's Japanese Army, gave the orders to Sergeant Oonishi and Captain Itoka to raise the flag of the GDR in Sapporo. At 2:02 P.M., it fluttered on the mast in the middle of the Winter Olympic Games Village. Seven months later, it was on the mast in the Munich Olympic Village as well, a full twenty-three years after the GDR's unilateral declaration of independence from the rest of the Germany of old.

Diplomatically, the battle was over. In the field of sport, however, it was just beginning. In hopes of avoiding a humiliation in Munich in 1972, private industry and the Bonn Government sprung into action pouring hundreds of millions of dollars into upgrading the Federal Republic teams. If Leipzig would have the DHfK, then Cologne would have a fine sports university, too, and today it is one of the best research centers in the world. If the East would have government aid, then the West would have "Sporthilfe," a private industry "Sport Aid" program for athletes to provide the basic needs of top Games contenders. Olympic dressage star Josef Neckermann, the wealthy industrialist, headed it up. The government role came in improved physical-education systems, new gymnasiums, and advanced coaching programs.

How much of that would have been spent if the GDR hadn't made sport such a cornerstone of its political policy two-and-a-half decades earlier? It's impossible to say for sure, but none would be a pretty good even-money bet.

24

The Athlete and the System

One of the more sentimental moments of the 1976 Summer Olympic Games came during the victory ceremony for the women's 1,500-meter run, when the Soviet Union's Tatiana Kazankina strode to the podium for her second gold medal of the Games, flanked by GDR teammates Gunhild Hoffmeister and Ulrike Klapezynski, winners of the silver and bronze respectively.

Hoffmeister, veteran of a decade of top-flight international competition and a double medalist in Munich, was carrying a small stuffed animal in her hand—the kind of thing one expects to see in the hands of teenage Olympic gymnasts and swimmers, but not carried by thirty-two-year-old schoolteachers. After the medals had been draped around their necks, but prior to the playing of the national anthem, Gunhild reached over with a big smile and presented the animal to the gold-medal-winning Tatiana.

"It's something I had to do," Hoffmeister later explained. "That animal was a last-minute gift from my nine-year-old daughter, Kerstin, who had made it herself and given it to me as a good-luck charm for the Games. She said if I didn't win the gold medal she wanted me to give it to the woman who did win. She said she'd be watching back home on television to make sure that I did."

Kerstin Hoffmeister means a lot to Gunhild, who chose to have the baby just when her running career was starting to blossom before the 1968 Mexico City Olympics, and in spite of the fact she was not married at the time and has not married since.

There was an easy out, for the GDR guarantees women the right to abortion on demand, and she was, after all, just getting her track career off the ground after first coming to the sport as a late-blooming nineteen year old.

"I never thought of that," she says, nine years after the fact. "Kerstin's father was a marathon runner in the Cottbus club, and although he and I were very fond of each other we were not ready for marriage at that time. It would have been a mistake. But I definitely wanted to have the baby. Kerstin's terrific fun, and she's a good runner, too, already the best in her school and in the district Spartakiad."

There are not many countries in the so-called Western world where a young unmarried mother could possibly find the time to train herself to the level of international competition in any sport, and there are probably even fewer where that same unmarried mother could aspire to a career as a politician.

Oh yes, that's the other thing. Gunhild Hoffmeister is a member of the People's Chamber, the national legislative assembly of the GDR. Or at least she was until 1977 when she grew too old to represent the Free German Youth Party at the national level. Why would the sports system of Manfred Ewald slate an unmarried mother as a national politician? "Because," says Ewald matter-of-factly, "she was the smartest one available. There can be no other consideration."

Tell that to swimmer Donna de Varona, track and field star Willye White, skier Suzy Chaffee, or any of the other women who have made it to the top in American amateur sport and then tried to find a way to have their voices heard in sport's political board rooms.

Or even on the nation's TV screens. Donna de Varona, one of the more distinguished members of the President's Commission on Olympic Sports, was a swimming regular on ABC until she made some pointed comments during the Montreal Games.

There's a lot of Donna de Varona in Gunnie Hoffmeister, and a little of Suzy Chaffee and Willye White, too. There's even a little of the talent for politics one sees in U.S. Olympic diving champion Micki King.

All that became obvious one afternoon in the summer of '77 when we spent an afternoon getting familiar with the town of Cottbus, a city of 100,000 on the eastern side of the GDR near the Polish border, and the smallish sports club where she has been competing for the last twelve years.

"We've got a small club," she explains, "with just two hundred and fifty athletes in four sports (track and field, boxing, cycling and gymnastics) and 75 percent of those are in the children and youth age groups."

The sports club, to hear the locals talk, is just about the biggest thing in town. When Gunnie and Olympic high jump gold medalist Rosie Ackermann led the Cottbus contingent of six home from Montreal, 10,000 showed up in the town square for the welcoming party.

"Everyone knows us here in Cottbus," she says, "and I don't think it can quite be that way in a city of a million people like Berlin. Here we are a much more intimate group. At the club there would be one hundred twenty-five to one hundred thirty children in the boarding school with the gymnasts as young as ten years old and the track and field athletes quite a bit older. Rosie, for instance, was fifteen when she came here from her village of Losha, which is right here in the district, but I was nineteen before I started to run seriously. We have only seventeen coaches in the club and four full-time administrators. It is not large."

And yet the development system is continuous. Since Hoffmeister was in Cottbus, and is looked up to, others make a try at matching her feats. Olympic bronze medalist Klapezynski was developed as a local girl. The same for Ackermann. At this moment, the second-best high jumper in the GDR is a young schoolgirl named Christine Nitschke, who was clearing six feet two inches as an eighteen year old. Christine was the 1977 Spartakiad pentathlon champion, too.

The Olympic medals and the political work have brought their privileges, surely enough, as Gunhild makes her way around town in her Wartburg (in the Volkswagen class) and lives in a modern apartment block not unlike something you would find in a comfortable middle-class American suburb.

As we looked at all this, I told Gunhild about a social counterpart of hers on the Canadian Olympic track team, a Vancouver girl named Marjorie Bailey, who was the best sprinter in Canada, the anchor relayer on a relay team that finished 4th and missed a medal by a tenth of a second.

Bailey, who has a child and is divorced, lives in the Catch 22 world of North American amateur athletics. Because of her exceptional talents, she gets invited to major track meets on the weekends. Indeed, in order to receive financial backing from the Canadian Olympic Development Program she must compete in these meets and in training camps as well.

The other side of the coin is that because she needs weekends off she lost her job as a qualified nurse in the Vancouver hospital service and wound up accepting part-time work as a checkout clerk in a supermarket. And the government says she can't use her grant money to pay for the baby sitter, either. The Canadian Government is very helpful with Marjorie Bailey's competition expenses and training needs, but it is totally disinterested in her social situation. They don't really want to know about the son she is trying to support, and, as a result, Marjorie Bailey is a bitter athlete, who silently protests by wearing a plain white shirt in most competition rather than anything with "Canada" written on it.

All of this seems unbelievable to someone like Gunhild Hoffmeister, who has always had her needs taken care of by government social welfare programs. As we sat and chatted, she took the time to outline some of them.

"In this country," she explained, "your apartment is assigned by the authorities and the rent is controlled at a small percentage [usually around 5 percent] of the salaries of the working adults living in the unit.

"When a young couple decides to get married, the government offers an incentive plan with an immediate 5,000 marks (about $2,750) loan to get the marriage started with money for furniture and other necessities. This is an interest-free loan that you don't have to begin repaying for five years. If you have one child in that time, you only owe back 4,000 marks. If you have two children in five years, you owe 3,000 marks, and if you have more than two, you don't owe anything."

But this, too, has turned out to be a social Catch 22 situation since most GDR apartments are small one- and two-bedroom units and most couples, just on the basis of available space alone, do not want more than one child, or two at the most.

Beyond that, since marriages are not based on economic necessity or religious conviction, the GDR divorce rate is one of the highest in the world. No one gives you a figure, but everyone agrees it is very high indeed. What's more, almost everyone seems to have relatives or neighbors who are in Gunhild's unmarried-mother category, cutting away the social stigma of that situation.'

"If you are an unmarried mother," she explains, "or as soon as a woman gets divorced, she becomes eligible for child-support benefits. The woman will receive an increase in her pay, get a permit allowing her 50 percent reductions on all transportation systems, and receive an immediate reduction in housing costs. Children are not a problem because of the almost universal system of day-care centers set up throughout the entire country."

Day care in the GDR is one of the most remarkable systems any visitor will come across. Since all adults of working age are needed to make the economy function (unemployment is unheard of, indeed, an employee cannot be fired until the employer has lined him up three other potential jobs to choose from), women are allowed three months' pregnancy leave to have their babies, get them started, and then get back to work.

The system calls for the mother to drop the infant off at a crèche (a nursery for babies from three months to three years of age) in the morning and pick it up again on the way home from work. Since most worksites have crèches on the grounds or nearby, it is also possible in many cases for the mother to drop by in the lunch period. For the following three years, the child will be in a kindergarten under much the same situation. About the only exception to this system seems to be in the case of families where the grandmother is living with the children. This appears to be about the only time GDR women get to be mothers rather than workers. The system works, but it is tough on the women if a couple of private discussions I have had with them are an indication of general discontent.

"What happens," one woman explained, "is that the wife gets up at about 5:30 or 6. A.M. to get breakfast for the family, and the child prepared for the crèche. She drops the baby off at 7:00 A.M., goes to work, picks the baby up at 4 or 4:30, rushes home to get the baby fed and ready for bed, makes dinner for the husband, and then sets about doing all the cleaning and laundry while he takes it easy and watches television.

"German men are not very diligent domestics, and a lot of them are very resentful of all the rights women have received from our government. It's not surprising to me that, after the novelty of marriage wears off, a lot of women come to the conclusion the only thing the husband means is a greater workload. One of these days the government is going to have to deal with this and give women an easier load to bear. I think one way to do it would be to give women who have children the right to work just half a day instead of a full day. Then we'd have time to do the work around the house, spend more time with our young children, and have a happier family life as well."

On the other hand, families one sees out on weekend shopping excursions in cities like Leipzig and Berlin seem to have a much happier and more relaxed atmosphere about them than do most North American families in similar situations. You seldom, for instance, see parents and children trading angry outbursts in public places. What's more, the level of teaching and care that is made available in the crèches and kindergartens is excellent.

Gunhild teaches physical education in Cottbus while working on an advanced degree that will qualify her to work as an official in municipal recreation planning. Toward that end, her political work has been most beneficial.

"My political involvement is at two levels," she explains. "Within our sports club we have a board of twelve members, three of whom are active athletes. Over the last two years we have been very active planning a new sports complex for the city and the nine nonathletic members of the board have been very considerate in relying on the active athletes for technical expertise on what is really needed in the sports construction.

"As far as my work in the People's Chamber is concerned, you have to understand the makeup of our government. The majority party is the SED [Socialist Unity Party], and it controls 38 percent of the seats in the Chamber. Other interest groups like the unions, the youth, the women, the cultural associations, and the Christian Democrats, who represent religious thought, have their percentage of seats. Since I was a member of the FDJ youth party, my time was spent in committee work on a new youth bill. Members who represent the farmers work on agricultural problems, while those who represent the unions work on their specific areas.

"I had to qualify to be slated through a series of district meetings. My district involves the town of Cottbus, the surrounding county, and the towns of Carlau, Finsterwald and my own hometown of Forst. I had to attend a series of fifteen meetings in these areas to answer questions from representatives of all groups within the communities. Before you are elected, you have to explain what you hope to accomplish, and after you are elected you have to go back periodically to appear before the same committees and report on what you have actually done. If you are going to have an opponent, this is the time when the opposition can be presented and then the committees can decide who will be slated for the election.

"At times it was difficult to combine politics with sport because there are always occasions when an important committee meeting would conflict with a chance to travel to a major track meet, and then I would have to decide. If you are serious about your work with the government, you can't miss the meetings and, in that sense, I am sure my athletics suffered a bit.

"On the other hand, my experience in sport has made some of my duty very easy and enjoyable. Occasionally we have problems in different areas of the country without sports programs. In one recent case, there just seemed to be a total lack of stimulus for the local people. Part of the problem turned out to be with the administration, but part of it was outside that area completely. I was able to go in there, with my reputation as an athlete, relate my own personal experience to the sports administrators of that town and get them encouraged again. Now things are running quite well there again. I think that is the kind of activity that would bring satisfaction to any athlete, the ability to use your own experiences to help other people."

Gunhild first went into politics as an FDJ member in 1971 and finished up in October of 1976 by mistake.

"I just forgot about her age," admits Ewald, "and when it was brought to my attention she was too old to serve another term in the Youth Party, it was too late to do anything about it. If I had become involved sooner, I probably could have had Gunhild considered for a position with the Women's Party or even with the Socialist Unity Party itself, but the slating was being done at the time we were in Montreal for the Olympics. The slates were filled when we got back home. It's a situation I hope to be able to correct at the time of the next election."

Meanwhile, Gunhild's political talents have not been getting rusty. In 1977 Gunhild became the GDR delegate to the Havana festival planning committee, as Cuba held its first World Youth Festival in the summer of 1978.

Her running career concluded on the victory stand in Montreal, but the political one is just beginning. What remains of the track and field career are trophies, medals, and four big scrapbooks on the coffee table in the apartment.

Every international trip has a section of its own with newspaper clippings, press photos, airport postcards, and personal snapshots taken along the way. There was a warm personal letter from Walter Ulbricht going back to the earlier days, and a nasty one with a Munich dateline sent to her home shortly before the 1972 Olympic Games.

"You Goddamn Communist . . . we know all about you," that letter began, "and if you dare to come to Munich for the Olympic Games your life will be over." This not-so-delightful piece of hate mail was, of course, unsigned.

"But it was frightening," says Gunhild, "because whoever sent it knew my home address in Cottbus. I took it straight to the authorities but they said not to pay any attention to it because the same letter had been sent to many of the members of our team. We tried to take their advice but a lot of us were still nervous about it when we were in Munich. Something like that can really have a bad effect on your training and the last minute buildup of total concentration you need to do well in a major race."

In 1974 Gunnie was right at the top of the pile in middle-distance running with a 1:58.8 in the 800 meters and a European championship time of 4:02.3 in the 1,500, but she missed most of 1975 with an ankle operation that had her on the brink of quitting.

"There were lots of times in 1975 when I thought of quitting," she says, "but I actually got my spirits back when I went into the hospital for the operation. In the space of fourteen days I had sixty-three visitors, many of whom I didn't know at all. Some were actors, some were artists, and one entire family named Lehman, who were just track fans, came by to encourage me not to give up competition."

So she didn't, and in spite of two thirds of a year off in the pre-

Olympic year, she came back to win the silver medal in the 1,500 meters. When it was obvious she was going to manage that in the final strides, her smile gave it all away. Gunhild Hoffmeister was the happiest silver medal winner in Montreal.

Tatiana Kazankina has Kerstin's stuffed animal to remember it by. Keep your eye on that little Kerstin, by the way. By about 1981 she'll be eligible for her first national Spartakiad as a middle-distance runner. By about 1988 or 1992 she might just make it to the Olympic Games.

She has about as much chance of doing that as her unmarried mother has of someday winning a spot in the Central Committee of the Socialist Unity Party. If you are a betting person you can list those odds at about 50–50.

25

Festival of Sport

When we left the GDR Sport Festival of 1977 back in Chapter 1, the torch had been ignited on a solemn Sunday morning at the crematorium of the Buchenwald concentration camp, marched to the gates by Olympic pentathlon champion Siegrun Siegl, run on a ceremonial lap around the grounds of the National Memorial, and dispatched still ablaze to Leipzig on the back of an open truck to await the official opening ceremonies of the Festival on Monday night. Margitta Gummel, shot put champion of the Mexico Olympics and silver medalist in Munich four years later, would run the torch a little more than 400 meters, from the Sports Institute to the opening-ceremony podium behind the stadium, and Olympic luge champion Hans Rinn would handle the actual lighting of the torch. As twilight slowly turned to darkness, both were as tight as finely tuned violin strings. To understand why you would have had to be there on the night of July 25, 1977.

The feeling is almost impossible to describe. You know something of it if you have sat in or near the pit area in the hour before the start of the Indianapolis 500 on Memorial Day. You might have felt some of it sitting in the crowd minutes before the teams run on the field at the start of a Notre Dame football game. There's the excitement that runs through an Olympic stadium just before the opening ceremonies, or when they play "My Old Kentucky Home" in Louisville on the first Saturday in May. They are all hard to describe.

And so it was in Leipzig at this Sport Festival, this drawing together of an entire sports system—five years in the planning and two years in the rehearsing—with every component from elite to mass, volunteer to DTSB professional, working together in a common cause. By the time Margitta Gummel and Hans Rinn were having their butterflies, more than 70,000 Festival participants had been billeted in private homes in Leipzig, a city of just 600,000 all told.

The day had begun in an inauspicious fashion with intermittent showers sending everyone off to department stores in search of rain capes and umbrellas at the last minute. But shortly after the supper hour the drizzle finally eased and there were, at long last, the first hopeful signs of clearing.

The Leipzig "Sport Forum" is a huge open area of ground between the back wall of the 100,000-seat Leipzig Stadium and the Sports Institute itself. It's an area more than 400 meters in length and perhaps 250 to 300 meters wide, or four football fields by three football fields, if you will, bounded by rolling hillside all the way around. There is a mounted platform at the base of the Werner Seelenbinder bell tower at the back of the stadium, featuring a dais for the national and festival flags, a speaker's podium, a seating area for a choir of 2,000 who will sing music composed just for this festival, an area on both sides for hundreds of fanfare trumpeters, and, of course, the container for the torch, which will be ignited simultaneously with the torch permanently positioned on the top of the bell tower.

The first few rows of seating down in front of the colorful display are reserved for government officials and foreign guests, who are seated according to protocol. All of the world's National Olympic Committees have been invited, as have representatives of all of the governing bodies for international sports, and, in all, fifty-six countries will be represented as observers at the Festival.

There is no admission charge for the opening ceremony, since the Forum is not enclosed, which also means there is no way of truly estimating the crowd. The official estimate the day after was 160,000 people, including the 70,000 Festival participants who filled the Forum at ground level and the curious onlookers who packed the hillsides.

Tens of thousands came early, just as they do at Indy and the

Olympics, and the announcers on the public-address system wasted no time going to work on building their enthusiasm by reverting to slogans used in the prewar Thirties by the trade union workers' sport clubs against the more established sport clubs reserved for those of power and financial privilege. The slogans were interspersed with the music of the marching bands bringing their Festival performers to their positions on the field.

Whenever there would be a lull, the announcer would come on with a bellow of *"Schporrrt,"* in a voice that would roll across the gathering, stilling all attempts at idle conversation. After a pause of a second or two the crowd, in what almost seemed like a single voice, would roar back with their own cry of *"Frei!"* They repeated it three times over, this arresting chant of "Sport" and its liturgical response of "Free," between a half hour and an hour before the formal ceremonies were to begin.

Then, as more and more people started to arrive, the announcer began to change his approach somewhat, starting it off with a question such as "Who's here from Magdeburg, Schwerin, and Rostock?" questions that would immediately be followed by huge roars of recognition from those from the named areas. The announcer would then roar out his own encouragement of them before leading the whole group into yet another round of Sport-Free, Sport-Free, Sport-Free. Then he'd go on to Berlin and Pottsdam and Frankfort-on-Oder, to Halle and Cottbus and Leipzig. When the loudspeaker fell silent, the drum and bugle bands broke into a noisy competition of their own.

Standing in the midst of all this, I couldn't help but feel it was a good thing Canada's official delegates, the federal government's Assistant Deputy Minister for Sport, Peter Lesaux, and Canadian Football League Commissioner Jake Gaudaur, were not arriving until the following day. One hundred and sixty thousand people all demanding "Free" Sport at the same time might be enough to drive a jet-lagged professional sports commissioner into a state of depression.

It was chilling enough for the few North Americans who were present, a group that included Dr. Ed Enos and an eighty-four-delegate group sponsored by Concordia University in Montreal, to study comparative approaches to sport; Canada's Fred Oberlander, representing the International Wrestling Federation; swimming's past international president Dr. Harold Henning of Chicago, who had come straight from West Berlin where he had been making arrangements for the 1978 World Swimming championships; and the London-based film crew working for Mike Wallace's bit on the "60 Minutes" documentary.

My mind was drawn back to a sociology class in 1960 when a professor who had been a Mormon missionary in Germany in the 1930s tried to describe the feelings he had while attending Hitler's Nuremberg rallies. He said he really couldn't describe it properly aside from assuring us it had been the most frightening moment of his life.

To non-German-speaking North Americans, the chant of "Sport-Free," brought to a fever pitch by the public address system, sounded an awful lot like "Sieg-Heil." No matter what the actual message, it's not surprising they would find that chant, performed on cue by such a mass of people, more than a little reminiscent of a terrible, frightening past.

Their feelings were reinforced over the next ninety minutes. The national and festival flags were marched solemnly in by synchronized drill teams of Olympic athletes. Margitta Gummel ran the torch, a tiny beacon winding its way through the sudden darkness of descending nightfall, and the huge crowd, in hushed expectancy, strained to hear as the Seelenbinder Memorial bell pealed in its tower. The choir's special cantata followed, then the music of the National People's Army Band, and the inevitable speeches, first by Manfred Ewald and then by the nation's head of state Erich Honecker.

The GDR sports officials, for their part, are extremely puzzled by the Western response to the event, very insulted that anyone could compare their sports aims in the 1970s with those of the Hitler Youth movement and the buildup of Nazi Fascism in the 1930s. Their purpose, they insist, is the absolute antithesis of Nazism.

"Does anyone seriously think," they ask, "that Erich Honecker, who spent twelve years in a concentration camp, would come before 160,000 people and try to emulate something that happened under the Nazis?"

Indeed, to give them their due, the events of the following week, although incredibly disciplined in concept and execution, did carry a message totally the opposite of the once-familiar cry of German nationalism.

The total presentation in this eleven-million-dollar (but perhaps twice that much when all ancillary costs are taken into consideration) event included:

1. The Spartakiad, a national junior Olympics with 10,000 youngsters involved in final competitions in most Olympic disciplines, in three separate age groupings, with the whole program completed in one week rather than the usual two.
2. Top-flight international competition every night in a track meet, a GDR–USSR soccer match, cycling contests and displays of competitive gymnastics.
3. Three performances of the Mass Gymnastics Sportshow, a two-hour spectacular in the 100,000-seat stadium with 14,700 on-field participants. There were three performances of this Festival centerpiece rather than one because, in order somewhat to satisfy ticket demand, the public is allowed in for the "dress rehearsal" and the "encore" as well as the scheduled show itself.
4. A parade in the style of East Europe's May Day, with more than 60,000 Festival participants marching through the downtown streets on Friday night past the assembled Central Committee and international guests.
5. A week-long festival of mass sport activities in Leipzig's Clara Zeitkin Park, which is the size of New York's Central Park.
6. And, finally, a two-hour closing ceremony that became a festival of flickering light, a drama that aroused feelings far surpassing those of an Olympic closing ceremony.

Throughout it all there wasn't a single appeal to the militant German nationalism of the Thirties. When 1,100 kindergartners raced onto the field for the opening act of the sportshow, armed only with teddy bears, hoops, and balloons and ready for a ten-minute routine without a single adult in sight, the message was that "all the children of the world should be here," accompanied by music much in the vein of the Disney tune "It's a Small World After All."

Instead of "*Deutschland Über Alles*" it was "Friendship *Über Alles*," and some Canadians who were in Zeitkin Park on the final morning for the mass 1977-meter Festival Mile run—jogging along with Gunhild Hoffmeister, who ran Festival Mile after Festival Mile with group after group, pausing only long enough to autograph participation badges before starting off again—told me they will never forget the feeling of friendship they got from these people with whom they couldn't communicate except through the use of an interpreter.

These feelings were there at the opening ceremony, too, particularly within the group of Canadian students of comparative physical education, some of whom wound up accepting offers to trade T-shirts with Germans in the crowd, right in the middle of the political speeches. While Erich Honecker is forcefully reminding everyone of the importance of the moment, people in the crowd are trading T-shirts. One wonders if that happened at Nuremberg in the Thirties.

What does it feel like to be a participant right in the middle of it all? What does it feel like to be Margitta Gummel running through the middle of that throng carrying the torch arm's length, at shoulder height? How does one deal with the sense of the moment?

We had a chance to speak of it after the fact.

"My one concern while running with that torch," she admitted, "was simply not to fall down. It had been raining and the footing was so slippery that from the moment we started out from the school I noticed almost nothing except where I was putting my feet as I ran across that field. Can you imagine what it would feel like to slip and fall and have the torch go out? I was so nervous!

"But it was a proud moment, to put on my national uniform after five years and stand there before all those people. It wasn't quite the same feeling back when I won the gold medal in Mexico in 1968, because those were still the days when they could not play my country's anthem on the victory podium. We still had the Beethoven then. Back in 1968, I felt I missed something that all other Olympic champions realize, and in 1972 in Munich when they would have played our anthem, I had won only the silver medal."

Margitta has had an interesting life since retiring from shot putting. She's living in Leipzig, is married to a surgeon, has a child, and has been using her training in sociology to make a study for the Leipzig Research Institute on the effects of special sports boarding schools on the lives and needs of young children.

"But I can't tell you about it just yet," she says, "because it has just been completed and turned in to the sports officials for consideration.

They may well decide to accept some of the recommendations while rejecting others. But it was very interesting work."

What would the result of the study have been, I asked, if you had simply been a trained sociologist and not a high-performance World class athlete as well?

"It would have been completely different," she said. "It was my experience as an international athlete that brought the new thinking to the study. If I hadn't been an athlete at that level there is simply no way I would have understood the real need of high-performance sportsmen."

Quite a woman, this Margitta, shot putter *extraordinaire*, mother, professional sociologist, and torchbearer at the Festival's opening ceremony.

Back at the Forum, as the immense rally wound to a close, with fireworks, military searchlights strobing through the sky and then focusing on the flame at the top of the tower, a new chant was being heard, one that becomes the official chant of the Spartakiad and the Festival. The massive crowd was counting off, "*Eight, Nine, Ten,*" followed by a pause of not more than a second, then the word "*Klasse,*" which is drawn out across a span of three seconds.

The rough translation of the meaning is "First Class" and it is repeated whenever anything goes off without a hitch or whenever athletes go to the medal podium and receive victory flowers in the Spartakiad competitions. Sort of a Germanic version of the three cheers of British tradition.

As I walked away from the Forum after the opening ceremonies, I left a tape recorder running while we were making our way through the crowd; most were walking back to the center of town, since public transportation was jammed far beyond capacity.

Later, listening to a playback of the tape, it was fascinating to hear the excited buzzing of the voices in the crowd. Hearing perhaps a hundred little children in the seven-to-ten age group counting and shouting "*Klasse!*" at the passing horde from the police-sponsored Sports Club Dynamo, only to have the Dynamo bunch drown out the youngsters with their own organized chanting of "*Dee-NAM-O, Dee-NAM-O, Dee-NAM-O!*"

Back in Montreal a month or so later, I was playing that tape for the purpose of compiling notes when a couple of fellow workers started staring in amazement and wondered what on earth it was. When I told them they looked dubious indeed. You had to be there to get the real feeling, and even then one had to wonder about it all.

The discussion in the bar at the hotel, where Festival organizers were housing the handful of international press, most of them from the Federal Republic, went on into the wee hours of the morning. Some admitted they were concerned and frightened by what they had seen in the Forum. They think that it is naive to assume that this amazing GDR sports machine, with its 40 Montreal Olympic gold medals produced by a less-than-affluent population of seventeen million, does not have nationalistic implications for the future.

If it does, they have not shown up so far. GDR athletes do not beat their breasts in victory, nor heap criticism on their opponents in defeat. Nor do their officials. Their athletes do not run around stadiums waving flags and pointing "We're Number 1" fingers to the sky. It is our Western athletes who do that. What the fears do show is that old German prejudices, fueled by two World Wars within this century, are going to be with us for some time to come. The combination of friendship, sport, and all the Disney-styled pizzazz in the world are not going to break that down overnight.

Foreboding or not, the GDR's grassroots nationalism is a feeling to be reckoned with by its totalitarian Communist neighbor to the east. To my surprise, in the course of the Festival week, I came across an elephant joke I had already heard back in Canada—the same joke in a different country with a different punch line—which coincidentally makes the point. In this story every country in the world is ordered to write a book about elephants. The Americans write theirs on the subject of the creation of bigger and better elephants. The Japanese write one about creating a cheaper and more efficient version of the American elephant. The tale can wind on and on in shaggy-dog joke fashion for as long as you want to take it, but in Canada's federal bureaucracy, where I first heard it, the Canadian book title was "Elephants, Is It a Federal or a Provincial Question?" In Leipzig, the GDR storytellers got a big kick out of the fact that the GDR was the only country in the world that had to write two books, one on elephants and the other on the good relations between the German elephants and the Soviet elephants.

It's a good story because it puts the finger squarely on the major problems that face the two countries, the federal-provincial problem in Canada, and the all-encompassing presence of the Soviet Union and the Soviet military machine, operating with the total political support of the GDR Government, which almost certainly never would have reached or maintained political power without it.

Underneath it all, quite apart from the continual slogans promoting the theme of GDR–Soviet solidarity, the average Russian and the average German don't like each other very much. The War and its memories are still much too recent. Soviet Army soldiers never mingle with the GDR populace, and aren't even allowed to enter a German restaurant.

On the other side of the coin, while in six years of watching Soviet star Valeri Kharlamov play hockey in North America I have never seen him reveal a trace of violence; against the West Germans in the Innsbruck Olympics he leveled a German player with one of the most purposeful cross-check blows I have ever seen. Kharlamov is a child of the Spanish Civil War, the son of a Russian father and a Spanish mother who fled to the Soviet Union following Franco's victory, a victory that probably would not have been possible without Nazi aid. For Valery, that blow helped even an old score even if it was thirty years after the fact and absolutely unrelated.

When the GDR and Soviet soccer teams met on the Wednesday night of Festival week, it marked their first meeting since 1973, not counting the Olympic matchup of 1976, and the Leipzig reception of the Soviet team was indeed something to behold. The Germans booed (with the traditional European whistles of derision) when the Soviet team took the field for the warmup, continued right through the playing of the Soviet national anthem and on into the game itself. The Festival organizers were embarrassed as they rushed around making profuse apologies to the visiting foreign delegations.

"If we had been thinking," one was to admit later, "we would have invited a British club team over to play one of our own club teams rather than trying to stage an international with the Soviets."

But Jake Gaudaur, the Canadian pro football commissioner, felt right at home and enjoyed every minute of the game, thinking no more of the crowd goings-on than he would have of a similar response at a Michigan–Ohio State game. But Jake does not live in a country that feels it has to write two books about everything. None of us in the West live like that. When 100,000 GDR soccer fans sit in the stands and pour out their feelngs in a manner they'd never dare attempt against the Soviet Army, are they just being soccer fans or are they making a nationalistic political statement?

Whatever it is, it's enough to make their own leaders shudder visibly and wonder if thirty years of continual political education is getting through to the seventeen million minds they are trying to turn around. As Manfred Ewald said, it isn't so much a matter of cleaning up the rubble in the streets as one of cleaning up the rubble in the mind. Some of that rubble yet remains, behind the healthy aspects of national pride, in lingering resentments—which is why so many international observers can quite legitimately be chilled, as well as astonished, amazed and delighted, by the absolutely incredible sports doings in Leipzig in the summer of '77.

26

The Sportshow

Can you imagine yourself trying to explain the intricacies of Florida's Disney World to an Eastern European who has never heard about Mickey Mouse? If you can't, then perhaps you'll have sympathy for the problems the few North Americans who attended the GDR's 1977 Gymnastics and Sports Festival have been having explaining that one-of-a-kind phenomenon back home.

If you saw the segment Mike Wallace and the CBS "60 Minutes" show put together in November of '77, you have some idea what it is all about.

To start with, imagine yourself sitting in an open stadium at the mass gymnastics *Sportschau* oohing and ahhing for two solid hours, while all around you 100,000 others are doing the same thing in appreciation of the performances of 14,100 people on the field, and 12,500 more seated in the stands in what must be the world's most intricate card section. Two hours broken only by gymnastic and musical presentations streaming on and off the field while you applaud and wave back with the colored scarf that came with your ticket, a scarf that blends in with more than 90,000 other scarfs to light up the entire stadium with color at every ovation.

All the while not one hawker comes by to ask if you want to buy a hot dog, or a cola or an ice cream. To have done so would have seemed sacrilegious to the moment.

Have you ever done anything like that? Would you ever want to do anything like that?

"Why," I had asked Manfred Ewald months before I had seen the show, "would anyone plan for five years and rehearse for as much as two to create a spectacular that would live for two hours three times in one week?"

He looked a little startled by the question.

"The show isn't what it's all about," he replied. "The real value comes in creating the organization to put it together, an organization that demands total cooperation from every phase and facet of our sports organization. You could never hold something like this every year, or even every two years [indeed the last one was held in 1969 and the dates for the next one have yet to be announced more than a year after the fact], but when we do have a Festival, the long-term value to our sports system cannot be overestimated.

"Everyone has a role to play in the Festival. The DTSB, the sports clubs, the schools, the elite athletes, and physical-education students who are training to be teachers, the factory sports clubs, the coaches and officials and volunteers by the tens of thousands, and those who are involved in sport only as recreation. There is even a role for the cultural people in the fields of music and art, and the students of those fields. The Festival brings them together in a spirit of cooperation. It's the one thing that keeps them all from getting isolated into their own little sectors, one apart from the other.

"In life it is normal that some people will have trouble getting along with others. Many people within enterprises do not cooperate all the time and sometimes they work actively against one another. The Festival helps break that down. When coworkers have to get together and work on a routine once a week for a year they have to cooperate. The same for those who work together in the planning. The Festival helps make the entire sports system function by giving everyone a role to play."

"Cooperation" is probably an understatement. The task of organizing one of the world's most massive sports undertakings in a city of 600,000, indeed in a country of seventeen million, is almost beyond comprehension to any resident of an individualistic Western society.

You can start with the needs of the 10,000 athletes in the Spartakiad, all of whom have to be brought to Leipzig from their home counties, housed, fed, and prepared for what to them must be the most important competition of their lives. The athletes are all billeted in private homes. Same thing for the thousands of coaches, managers and sports officials needed to organize an entire Olympic program three times over in three age groupings. They all must be taken care of. And so must the 14,100 who will appear on the field in the Sportshow. The 1,100 kindergartners in the opening act are local, it's true, but most of the rest of the cast are not, and have to be in town a week ahead of time to prepare for all the final rehearsals.

Then there are the needs of all the enterprise sports teams from the factories, the schools, and the rural areas, including collective farms, who will compete in the mass recreational sport competitions in Clara Zeitkin Park. There are 1,000 players in the table tennis tournament, thirty-six volleyball courts going continuously and simultaneously, plus bowling, and much more. In all, more than 60,000 must be housed and fed, a far larger number than Leipzig normally could accommodate. The problem of food is solved by creating huge tented outdoor dining facilities to serve up food trucked in nightly from all over the country—a system that has every county provide enough food for all of its Festival participants.

The problems of logistical support are simply staggering. To walk away from the stadium after the closing ceremonies at week's end was to have the feeling every bus in the country must have been pressed into service to get the thousands of Festival participants back to their hometown before dawn Monday morning. At one corner police held back traffic while I counted seventeen of the world's largest and most modern European buses accelerating away from the grounds in Indian-file, each filled with seven to ten year olds being swept away from the mob scene within thirty minutes of closing. Some were still smiling and waving, others had already fallen asleep.

Neither the United States Government nor the U.S. Olympic Committee were represented at the 1977 Festival, but Canada had professional football Commissioner Jake Gaudaur, and Peter Lesaux, the Assistant Deputy Minister in Canada's new federal sports ministry.

Gaudaur was there because his league had given the half-time show of the Grey Cup game (Canadian football's Super Bowl) over to amateur sport for a mini-Festival, and he wanted some ideas; Lesaux was there because his cabinet minister, Iona Campagnolo, had been unable to find the time to attend.

Gaudaur has always had a fascination with amateur sport. His father of the same given name, who was sixty-one years old when the future football commissioner was born, was one of history's great single scullers, the world champion at the turn of the century when thousands lined riverbanks, and newspapers held the presses for the results of the great challenge races. Rowing, before team sports in the 1880s and 1890s, rivaled heavyweight boxing in popularity.

Peter Lesaux, on the other hand, is a government man, a pragmatic bureaucrat of planning, policies and budgets, a realist who gets to quarterback the planning behind the spending of much of Canada's thirty-one-million-dollar-a-year budget for fitness and sports.

Even Gaudaur was first to admit it was a bit odd for a professional sport commissioner to be in Leipzig right in the middle of his league's football season.

"It's a funny thing," he mused over coffee soon after arriving in town, "but I have been writing letters and making presentations of my ideas on amateur sport for about twenty years, ever since the Canadian Government first got involved, with that first five-million-dollar grant. The Campagnolo ministry is the first ever to answer back in response to my presentations. In a way, I guess you could say I am here because my bluff is being called."

That and the fact that just like everyone else he was curious to find out more about a country that won 40 gold medals in the Montreal Olympics.

So there they were, Jake and Pete, in the VIP section of the massive stadium on a sun-blessed July afternoon, sitting like a couple of kids at a first-ever circus, trying to make notes on how one goes about organizing a sports festival, even a mini-festival, for half-time of a football game.

"For a while," chuckles Lesaux, "Jake was trying to keep track of how many people were on the field, but that effort ended in fairly hopeless confusion with variances of several thousand in our assorted estimates. I was just sitting there most of the time with my heart thumping watching it all. When I came to Leipzig, I suppose I had set opinions on what we would be seeing in the mass sportshow. I expected to see a West Point presentation with all sorts of musicians and athletes marching around the field directed by people in military uniforms laden with medals down the left side. Instead, when they unveiled that first act, with the five- and six-year-old kindergartners out on the field with their hoops and teddy bears for nine or ten minutes, more than a thousand of them without a single adult in sight, I just came apart emotionally. I wasn't ready for that at all. And yet when I came back to Ottawa and tried to explain it to my senior staff, I could see that the message wasn't getting through at all. At least the drama of the moment wasn't getting through."

How do you tell people about the little ones, who are followed by more than 1,000 seven to ten year olds, matched sets of boys and girls carrying springboards and lightweight aluminum folding parallel bars that are set up for perfectly synchronized and balanced gymnastics displays? How do you explain the moment at the end of that ten-minute segment when a handful of the more talented children tried to exit the length of the stadium with a continual series of back flips? Or the ovation that last one received when he got all the way down to the equivalent of the ten-yard line before pooping out? That feat seemed totally impromptu, which means it probably wasn't, as the jammed stadium rose as one with a huge scarf waving tribute, and the roar—"Eight, Nine, Ten—*Klasse!*"

They were followed by the ten to sixteen year olds, who, using nothing but human bodies as boundaries, set up handball and volleyball drills all over the field. Then the women, more than 2,000 of them from the mass sports clubs, all in blue leotards with square yellow boxes and ribbons as props. Then the amazing drills, first of the athletes of the Army sports clubs, and then by their counterparts in the police-supported Dynamo clubs—tremendous routines with bodies balancing in pyramids, twisting, turning and occasionally flying through the air like rag dolls, only to be caught in the gentle grip of teammates.

And the music—marching band after marching band until the entire field was filled with thousands of young musicians. Try to imagine about six of the largest U.S. college football bands on the field at once. And then imagine someone playing "Amazing Grace" as a trumpet solo in the midst of it all. That youngster just may have gotten the biggest spontaneous ovation of the entire afternoon. A

Christian hymn, played as a trumpet solo at that, in the middle of a Communist Sports Festival! One wondered if the government realized the significance?

"Well, I'll tell you," one of the Festival hosts admitted over a drink in a downtown hotel later that night. "At the last Festival back in 1969 that particular piece of music would have never been permitted. Things are changing here."

And then there was the card section—"The Eastern Tribune," as it is called in Leipzig. If you have seen the card sections at U.S. college football games, then imagine that expanded until 12,500 seats are included, or every prime seat, goal line to goal line, down one side of the field.

In America it would be economically impossible to take perhaps half of the very best seats in the stadium and turn them over for non-revenue card section use. If we ever had such a thing as this, it would have to be placed in the end zone, and it wouldn't be half so effective.

What an amazing job they do, these teenagers in the Tribune, close to eighty stunts in all counting the afternoon show and the closing ceremonies. And in order to qualify for doing it they have to be members of the DTSB and run at least one 1,977-meter Festival Mile for fitness. But the real job here is more in the planning than the doing. The game plan for every youngster appears on a chart on the back of the individual seated directly in front of him. When a display is planned, the 12,500 teenagers look to the scoreboard on the top of the other side of the stadium, get the number of the card trick that is shown there, look to the back of the person seated in front for their own personal instruction, get the proper flag, and then flash it up under their noses when they get the countdown command, again from the scoreboard.

Many of the stunts are extremely complicated with motion, color changes, winking eyes on fairy-tale animals, and a Moscow skyline in the tribute to the 1980 Games that rolls up from top to bottom and then changes color twice before it is finished. For every stunt, some volunteer has to plan and then draw up 12,500 individual cards. No wonder the planning can take five years! And the rehearsing as much as two!

When I was in the GDR in January of '77, I visited a Leipzig kindergarten where an entire class of youngsters were hard at work learning the fundamentals of their routine. They had been at it for one hour each week ever since school had started in September. By this stage of the proceedings, they already had their hoops and their bears, their personal partner, and a copy of the music that would be used in the show itself. At this point in time they were still working as twosomes, the boy with the hoop and the girl with the bear, learning where to sit and how to coordinate the entire effort with the music. The teacher patiently went from one to the other for more than half an hour, and then tried to bring them all together for the last half hour. In January, it was still a struggle getting it together but there was no sign of frustration on any part. The teachers moved patiently from one pair to another, occasionally chiding gently, occasionally praising a job well done, and smiling and laughing time and time again.

And how did they feel, six months later, out on the field in front of 100,000? For the answer to that, all you had to do was look at the faces as they ran off the field waving at the end of it. They were simply super, and so was the combination of music and card stunts so perfectly planned as an accompaniment.

That was the moment when I was prompted to turn to a GDR Festival interpreter, seated alongside me in the press section, and give an animated, but futile explanation of the utter enchantment of the "It's a Small World" Disney exhibit. I even wound up humming a few bars of the music. I drew a blank!

Peter Lesaux wanted to know how much it cost. A very good question, and a very difficult one in terms of Western comparison. The basic budget, based on the value of 1977 Deutschmarks vis à vis the dollar, was eleven million dollars for the entire week's activities. That eleven million dollars, by the way, was not provided by the GDR Government. The entire sum was raised by the DTSB fund-raising activities. What the government did provide was all the necessary support services such as transportation, use of the military, cost of the facility usage, and more. If those costs are taken in, it might be more accurate to peg the cost of the Festival at closer to twenty-five million dollars.

To duplicate the effort in the West, however, would probably cost 100 million dollars and more, maybe much more. This is simply because our travel costs would be much higher, unions would prevent the massive outpouring of volunteer labor (even such things as stadium-cleaning and dish-washing were done by sports-club volunteers in Leipzig) and things simply cost much more in the West than they do in the GDR. How many of us would be willing to rehearse something for two years without remuneration? And beyond that, what Western sports organization could possibly raise eleven million dollars without turning to the government or hitting up even one major corporate sponsor?

In the GDR, this is not a big problem. Although the U.S. Olympic Committee creates the image that it is perhaps the only National Olympic Committee left in the world that raises its own money to send the U.S. athletes to the Games, it is fooling itself if it really believes that. The GDR Olympic Committee has a fund-raising arm known as the Society to Promote the Olympic Ideal and it raised more than two million dollars to send the 1976 GDR Olympic team to Innsbruck and Montreal without any recourse to direct government funding.

The key to their Olympic fund-raising is the slogan "My Heart for Sport," and Madison Avenue would have been proud of the little cartoon figure of a smiling valentine-shaped heart with spindly little arms and legs bounding around from one activity to the next. It's the perfect tie-in between the mass recreation program and the elite program. The "heart" gets into everything. It appears on beer glasses autographed by Olympic champions, on T-shirts, on shopping bags, and on a magnificent pair of hardcover photo books put together for each set of winter and summer Olympic Games. Rather than give a grant to the NOCs, the government gets involved in printing the books, which would sell for at least fifty dollars a copy in the West, and brings them out at a third of that price. They are not sold; orders must be placed before the Games are held, with the money paid in advance and the book to be delivered later, on the understanding that every cent of the money paid for the book goes to help send the athletes to the Olympic Games. Most of the 2.7 million members of the DTSB contribute in one way or another, and thus have the feeling that it is they who are supporting the Olympic program.

And so it is with the Sports Festival. The biggest single fund-raising effort comes about through the DTSB in cooperation with all the employers in the country. The request is that members of the sports organizations agree to work one day of overtime during the Festival year, with the wages earned going straight to the Festival organizing committee on a corporate check-off system. They raised seven million dollars in one day! Every pfennig of it came from the little guy in society. If they had agreed to work two days, they could have paid for the whole show in two weekends.

"But we wouldn't want it all from one source," says Ewald. "It's much better for the system if it comes from a variety of sources. More people get involved in contributing to the Festival, whether it's by working overtime, buying souvenirs [they have unique and very popular sets of postcards of the Olympic medal winners] or contributing their time. When people give time or money they are getting involved and will remain involved, even if it's only staying home and watching the events on television when the Festival is on. If the government did it all, we wouldn't have that sense of commitment at all."

Sometimes Manfred Ewald sounds like a California Republican!

27

Spartakiad: Looking to the Future

Fourteen-year-old Innes Schimmel was sitting with her coach in Leipzig's Friendship Stadium, a modest track and field facility with an aging, crushed brick surface rather than a modern American tartan one, looking for all the world like Lewis Carroll's little Alice moments after she fell down the rabbit hole into Wonderland.

Twenty-four hours earlier Innes had won the GDR Spartakiad championship in the 400-meter run (fourteen-year-old girls' category) with an age-group record clocking of 55.97. And just half an hour earlier, in an attempt to duplicate the stunning Olympic track and field 400-meter–800-meter double gold medal Cuba's Alberto Juantorena pulled off in Montreal, she had run the 800 meters in 2:10.6 to qualify for yet another final.

But now she was sitting with her coach from the Dynamo Berlin Sports Club, being interviewed by two Swedish and one Canadian journalist, all of whom seemed bent on asking the silliest Alice-in-Wonderland questions. Questions like: What did her parents think when the State, in the form of the talent scouts from Dynamo, came and snatched her away from her small-town environment in the

Thuringian Forest and trundled her off as a budding twelve year old to the special sports school attached to the world's largest sports club?

"They were very pleased."

And how did she feel about it all?

"I was very pleased, of course."

I had the thought at about this point that if I went back in time less than two decades, a similarly aged young Canadian hockey player named Bobby Orr would have given the same answers to foreign reporters wondering how it felt to be snatched from parents and home in Parry Sound, Ontario, and whisked off for his Boston Bruins apprenticeship in the Toronto suburb of Oshawa. Bobby Orr was undoubtedly pleased, just as any young American athlete when he first hears word that the college scouts are taking a close look at him in a high school game.

Innes Schimmel, it turns out, grew up as a bit of an oddity in her little village, where most sport expectations turn to ski jumping and tobogganing, the prime sports of the Thuringian snow belt. Innes just loved to run. Through the village, to school and back, anywhere. She didn't care a fig about skiing and sledding.

That kind of interest, in a country that now boasts more than 8,000 professional coaches, cannot go long unnoticed. When the coaches heard of this little girl who loved to run on the village roads by herself, they put her through some basic testing for size, aptitude, cardiovascular capabilities, and attitude, and quickly came to the decision she was a "keeper," a definite prospect for elite training toward the prospect of international competition in time for the 1984 Los Angeles Olympic Games.

If she had been a sprinter, she'd probably have gone to the Motor Jena sports club to be with Horst-Dieter Hille, the coach behind first, Munich double gold medalist Renate Stecher, and now, Renate's successor as world-record holder, the amazing nineteen-year-old Marlies Oelsner-Grohe. But, as a middle-distance runner, it was Dynamo Berlin where Innes could develop in the shadow of Olympic silver medalist Christina Brehmer, who was only nineteen herself when she chased Poland's gold medalist Irena Szewinska home in the Montreal Games.

For Innes, who spends one long four-day weekend a month at home and the rest of the time studying and training at Dynamo Berlin where her small classes at the special sports school (between four and ten students to a teacher) are structured around her training, the Leipzig Spartakiad victory was a very big moment. For her coaches it was just another step along the way, and another measure of their own program progression.

"That's why," one of them explained, "we do the entire Olympic program in three different age groupings. In track and field there is a fourteen-year-olds' group, a fifteen group, and sixteen and seventeen groups. Other sports like swimming and gymnastics have much younger groupings because in those sports athletes can be at the international level when they are fourteen and fifteen. Still other sports might want to look at older athletes."

Innes Schimmel is typical, though, of the entire modus operandi. She's a very early find, in track and field terms, and she is in serious training at the elite level. Her coaches knew how fast she would run in the Spartakiad, and thus were neither surprised, pleased, nor displeased with the result. The truth is, they were really there to look at others. Starting with the local school level, perhaps 500,000 youngsters had filed entries in the first round of Spartakiad competition. The district, regional, and national eliminations had pared them down to 10,000 for the finals in all Olympic disciplines in which the GDR competes. More than 9,000 of those finalists were not students in special sports schools.

"In Innes' 800-meter final," said her coach, checking the list of the just-completed semifinal, "there are only three girls from the elite program. That means five have not had the benefit of Innes' training. Those are the girls we will really be looking at most closely tomorrow. Who knows, the next Olympic champion could be a girl who finishes 6th or 7th tomorrow off a background of minimal training. After we have finished analyzing the result [including possible televised videotape replays if they need them], we might invite one or two more into the special school program."

That is also the reason for the three age groups: first they find Innes and her friends, then they take two more looks over the next two to four years (Spartakiads are held at the national level every two years and at the district level every year) like fishermen continually casting their nets in hopes of finding the late bloomers, the ones they missed in earlier competitions. Christina Brehmer was one such herself, not coming to Dynamo until she was seventeen, just two years before her

Olympic silver medal. And, as we saw a couple of chapters back, Gunhild Hoffmeister was nineteen.

And yet, there still is that problem of taking kids away from their homes and halfway across the country at a very early age to sport schools. How many parents want to give up their sons and daughters for all but four days a month when they are just entering their teens, or even younger in the case of gymnasts? In the GDR, the incentives to do so are strong, since success in any of the special school programs, whether it be music, art, language, science or sport, virtually assures one of a better life in generally difficult economic circumstances. The parents have the knowledge that the education will be excellent, food and health care the best the country has to offer, and the coaching superlative. There will almost certainly be a good job later on.

But those who strive to reach world-class excellence in any endeavor these days do not live what most people would consider a normal life. Oddly enough, some of the parents who might hesitate the most are those who have already been to the top of the mountain, parents like Wolfgang Behrendt, the GDR's first-ever gold medalist back in 1956, in boxing. When he is not working at his job as one of the country's top sports photographers with *Neues Deutschland*, or pursuing his hobby of playing the trumpet in a jazz band, he's at home in Berlin playing father to a teenage Spartakiad-eligible son. Wolfgang Behrendt is not at all sure he wants Mario to follow in his footsteps as a boxer. He smiles at the recollections of his own beginnings.

"I was eleven years old," he remembers, "and I had enough talent in music that I was taking violin courses in a special school setting. On the side, along with other youngsters my own age, I was taking boxing lessons and doing well at that, too. Well enough, at eleven, to have my picture in the paper one day. The next time I showed up for violin practice my teacher called me aside and asked if I was the Wolfgang Behrendt whose picture she had just seen in the paper in a boxing match. When I said yes I was strongly advised to give it up. So strongly, in fact, I was told I would have to pick one or the other before I came back to the next lesson. To the teacher's chagrin I picked boxing.

"For me it worked out, but, if I had any idea, back in those days when I was boxing with such abandon, that I would one day be a professional photographer, with a hobby in music (trumpet), I would almost certainly have given up the boxing. My teacher had been concerned about what boxing might do to the fingers. Well, if you are going to be a photographer you had better worry about the eyes as well. If you are going to play the trumpet you had better protect your lips. I still look back at the fact I had more than 140 fights without suffering permanent damage to either eyes or mouth as a stroke more of good luck than great skill. Certainly, I was as delighted as any father when my son showed an interest in sport, but I dreaded the thought he might want to follow behind me and be a fighter."

Wolfgang dreaded it so much, in fact, that at first he wouldn't hear of boxing for Mario. He told his boy to be a football player. Mario didn't care for football. So, he channeled him into track and field to train for the 800 meters and the 1,500 meters. Mario hated it. All he wanted to do was to be a fighter like his father.

"I kind of figured if he couldn't make it to the top in football or as a runner, there was a pretty good chance he couldn't make it to the top as a boxer either," says Wolfgang, "so I decided to let him have his chance, but only on my terms. If he was going to box he would only do it after learning from the man who taught me how to box. That proved to be a bit of an imposition since my coach of the 1950s is now a man in his eighties, who is long past his active coaching days. But, after I went over and had a long talk with him he agreed to do it for old times' sake."

And here it was, less than a year later, with young Behrendt finally finding the sport he could excel in, moving quickly up through the ranks of the Spartakiad on his way to the finals in Leipzig. Wolfgang was both proud and horrified—secretly delighted that his boy might go on to become one of the best young boxers in the country, but very worried that he might get seriously hurt before he managed to win anything at all. To counter this possibility, Wolfgang decided he would go out of the way to make sure no one outside a handful of close friends knew Mario was his son.

"What I am afraid of," says Wolfgang, "is his age. Teenage boxers who are just beginning will try to be very brave and aggressive in their style. They haven't got the experience for that. If people get to know Mario is the son of the country's first Olympic gold medal winner there will be a lot of added pressure. He will feel responsible for living up to the family reputation, just as others will try to knock down that reputation. It will create a dangerous situation. I know from my own experience. He could very easily get into the ring with a boxer of much greater experience and get injured."

So, young Behrendt went to Leipzig as just another Behrendt, a fairly common name in the GDR. He even wound up reaching the semifinals in his weight class, a development Klaus Huhn tried to keep in mind when he made out his daily schedule of Sports Festival photo assignments. He knew that, no matter what the assignment, when it was time for Mario to fight, Wolfgang would sneak in the back door of the boxing hall, and lean against the rear wall trying not to let anyone notice his rapt attention on the ring. Then, fight over, he would sneak back out again and go back to work without saying a word to anyone so as not to arouse any suspicion. On the side he even did a little coaching.

"The youngster who was the toughest puncher in the division drew Mario in an early fight," says Wolfgang. "This boy could really hit, and at one point his trainer came to me to warn me of it. He didn't want to see Mario get hurt either, and he suggested if Mario got hit hard he should go down and stay down. This worried me a little, so I went out to watch the other boy in an earlier fight and saw an immediate flaw in his style. Then I went to Mario and told him to forget any strategy he had planned and just throw nothing but very quick left hooks right from the opening bell."

Mario Behrendt won that fight with a first-round technical knockout. And then went on to finish third overall. In October of 1978 he won his first international, representing his country in a junior dual meet with Great Britain. A couple of days after that fight, Wolfgang told me he might soon let everyone else in the country know who Mario really is.

Behrendt's concern comes from the fact he knows what's involved in elite international sport. His feelings are much the same as Margitta Gummel's, who really wanted to get to the bottom of things as they really are in her sociological study of the effect of the special sports schools on family life. The GDR is fortunate to have so many former champions working within the coaching system at the high-performance level.

They also seem to be fortunate to have a society that believes in close personal relationships between athletes and coaches. Everywhere one went in the Spartakiad, the coaches appeared to have close, trusting relationships with their athletes. In the gymnastics finals, most of the young, teenaged boys were having all kinds of trouble on the parallel bars, trying their best to control their bodies with arm and chest muscles that in many cases had not quite developed enough strength as yet. Whenever an effort ended in failure, there would often be total disappointment and tears, but invariably the coach would be there with a smile and a big hug rather than a remonstrance.

This business of touching carries through to the officials of the various sports as well. In the ski jumping, I watched an official at the start line placing his hand on top of the hand of the athlete while checking for the signal for all-clear. The signal to start came when he took his hand away. A Spartakiad diver who did a belly-flop and was wiped out of the medals contention was greeted by a nearby swim official who had a big towel and yet another hug. Seldom if ever did you see a coach losing his temper and berating an athlete in front of everyone else.

If you want to see that in North American society, all you have to do is go to almost any Little League baseball game, preteen football game, or kid's hockey match. There you'll see coaches getting on their kids, and parents getting on coaches, officials, their kids, and even each other. All in the hallowed name of winning. The amazing thing I have noticed here, from personal experience, is that most of these North American parents feel they would never want their children involved in an East European sports development program. They say they want sport to be fun.

In Leipzig in the summer of '77, it was fun. You could see it in the faces of the kids, in spite of the fact they were being run through events almost on a production-line system since they were trying to get the whole Olympic program in all three age groups over and done with in just one week. The day Innes Schimmel ran her semifinal in the 800 meters, the DTSB officials were running a race every two minutes and thirty seconds, making it often a case of "forget the niceties of starting blocks, just get to the line and get going."

When a race would finish, the officials in charge of results would have just a couple of minutes to race around like a squad of Keystone Cops getting the information into the proper order. At night, somehow, it would all come together in voluminous results tabulations; just as efficiently as at the Olympic Games. Through it all, very little escapes the eyes of the national team coaches as the week progresses. What's more, the national team athletes have a support role to play, too, coming to the Festival to have sessions with the young Spartakiad performers after the competitions.

The Festival is for everyone, which is why, in spite of the eventual Olympic successes, a lot of top GDR athletes have their fondest memories related to their first Spartakiads. Innes Schimmel, no matter what level she eventually reaches as a competitor, will no doubt always remember that day in Leipzig when the foreign journalists picked her out of a crowd and asked so many strange questions. How was she, at fourteen, to know that what the journalists were attempting to describe is considered to be some sort of sports miracle by the rest of the world?

Every country, after all, has hundreds of Innes Schimmels— youngsters who get out and run on their own, who have a natural talent for sport and the love of it. But most never get the opportunity to get discovered in the first place, or then get the top-flight coaching that is required to get them to the top in the second place. In the United States we depend on the luck of an Arthur Ashe in stumbling into a situation that gave him access to a tennis program that 99 out of 100 black athletes could never afford. We depend on the luck of a Marty Liquori enrolling in a high school with an interested track coach who spotted his talents immediately and encouraged them. The United States still does well in international amateur sports, of course, but only through sheer force of numbers and a very high level of general affluence throughout the country. And the potential elite talent lost along the way is beyond measure.

In some areas things are certainly improving. In 1970, before the days of Olga Korbut, the United States had around 5,000 active gymnasts in serious training. Now, just nine years later that figure has topped 500,000, more than any other country in the world. The United States will soon have twice as many gymnasts as the GDR, which is the traditional home of gymnastics. However, on a per-capita basis the United States will not have really "caught up" until it has approximately fifteen times as many gymnasts, somewhere close to the 4.8 million mark. That would take approximately a tenfold increase in coaches, facilities, judges, and officials. It sounds impossible, but then again in 1970 everyone would have said 500,000 gymnasts was impossible. They would have said that gymnastics was simply not an

American sport. Olga, Nadia, and network television have proven that position wrong. Without Olga, Nadia, and television, gymnastics would still not be an American sport. With them it has now become one.

Television today plays a much bigger role than even many people in that medium realize, especially since the Olympic Games have now become the world's top-rated television show when it comes around every fourth year. In just a few months' time the cameras will be trained on Lake Placid, New York. For the first time Americans will see the sport of luge conducted on an American course. A ski jumping competition with a possible American challenger. An expected American domination of speed skating with Eric and Beth Heiden. American figure skating favorites in three divisions, with Charles Tickner, Linda Fratianne, and the pair of Randy Gardner and Tai Babilonia having won World championships in the last two years.

The GDR will be competitive in every event listed above. And that will be thanks to their Spartakiad, their 8,000 Leipzig coaching graduates, their sports medical specialists and researchers and the government emphasis on *Citius, Altius, Fortius*.

The final day of the 1977 Leipzig Festival was a day for doing things. The Spartakiad finals were over, and so were the competitions involving Workers Sports Clubs and invited internationals. The streets were being swept clean from Friday night's parade through the center of town. But still there was activity. Some 23,000 runners headed for Clara Zeitkin Park to run a final Festival Mile and win a final Festival sports badge.

And then it was on to the Stadium for the closing ceremonies. The afternoon Sportshow had involved every facet of the GDR mass sport program, but the closing ceremonies would be turned over to the elite. National team gymnasts, looking incredibly tiny as they performed solo in front of 100,000 spectators, had the center stage. Dancers from the special schools for ballet performed to the music of the students from the special schools for music. Massed bands put on a dazzling show as the entire infield filled with all the participants from the Sportshow. Then, with the lights suddenly dimmed, the 10,000 Spartakiad athletes came running through the tunnel to encircle the track and then flow upwards into every aisle. They received a tremendous ovation, which immediately turned to a hush as the lighting dropped completely. Then the Spartakiad athletes ignited the torches—plastic hooded flashlights really—to create a new lighting system. Now it was almost the equivalent of a candlelight ceremony.

Waldemar Cierpinski came out to the edge of the track and said a few words, on behalf of, and to, all the assembled athletes.

The entire Festival was supposed to end at 11 P.M. At 10:58 the spotlights focused on the flag while the military band played the national anthem one final time. At 10:59 the bell in the Werner Seelenbinder tower began to peal through the night while the spotlights flashed to the tower and the flame that had burned continuously throughout the week. As the bell tolled the flame grew smaller and smaller, and finally, just as the bell silenced and the clock hit 11:00 on the nose, it was extinguished.

And then the massed bands played Beethoven's *Ode to Joy*.

The sensation was awesome.

The twenty-minute fireworks display that followed was almost a necessity, just to help the tension subside.

Epilogue

In preparing this book, I spent a lot more time talking than writing. It all started with presentations to university physical-education classes in Canada to test public reaction to the subject. Beyond that, there were countless discussions with leading athletes, coaches, officials, and people on the periphery of sport from all over the world—literally from Australia and Japan through the Third World and on to Scandinavia, West Germany, England, and the Soviet Union. Almost no one crossed my path between 1974 and 1979 without getting involved.

Virtually without fail, however, all discussions finally boiled down to one question: "How does all this apply to the democratic West?" The answer, I have finally concluded, after wavering at times from one side of the question to the other, depends almost entirely on attitudes.

If you believe that the excellence in the Communist system comes from that society's ability to coerce its citizens, then you'll probably see few applications to the West. Some still believe that the threat of a stick, or a gun, or a gulag, can create a sullen East-bloc Olympic champion out of a youngster who had no other choice. This idea has not been without its media promoters through the Cold War years and beyond. It rather overlooks the fact that most youngsters everywhere in the world who have a natural talent for sport are willing to spend incredible amounts of time and effort developing it as much as possible.

Americans, I am constantly being reminded, will never get involved in mass-participation sport in a big way. The life-style is against it. They have too much money and too many interesting things to spend it on. The government doesn't care. As a people we are very suspicious of mass organization. Sport should be an individual thing, just a hobby.

I used to believe a lot of that myself. But those who still believe it today are simply not paying that much attention to what's going on in the West, particularly in the last three years with the jogging boom. In the mid-Seventies the New York marathon was nothing more than a club run through the parks. In October of 1978 it attracted more than 11,000 runners, more than 85 percent with college degrees, more than 50 percent with postgraduate degrees: 767 lawyers, 547 doctors, and 977 teachers. There were ninety-eight company presidents at the starting line! All of them intent, not just on a Sunday jog through Central Park, but on actually running 26 miles, 385 yards through all five boroughs of New York. That is an even more amazing fact than the GDR's second-place finish in the Montreal Olympics. Just think of the buying power of that marathon field in New York—and the immense promotional possibilities of the whole fitness craze in the United States.

And yet, the undeniable fact is, it's still largely unorganized at the top. Sport really is getting strong mass participation, but it is not politicized. It does not fight for its interests in the way, for example, that the National Rifle Association fights gun control on behalf of everyone interested in guns.

Could there be an NRA for amateur sport? Why not? At the moment there are perhaps twenty million Americans who are members of some form of sports organization that requires payment of a fee. What if they couldn't join any of them unless they also belonged to a National Sports Association, an umbrella organization representing everything in U.S. sport, and had to pay a 10-dollar fee to belong to it. The NSA would then have a budget of 200 million dollars, none of which would have come from government funding— money enough to put out a monthly newsletter to all twenty million members keeping everyone informed of all the political issues of sport.

It could operate at the national level, the state level, and the community level.

At first suggestion many would wonder how to get twenty million Americans to join such a group. One way would be to legislate it, but perhaps a better way might be to make sure members got a 10 percent discount on sporting goods purchases. That way anyone who spent more than 100 dollars a year on equipment would be dollars ahead with a membership card. It becomes a better buy than a lottery ticket. Would the retailers go along? Some would, and if by doing so they got all the business from twenty million Americans, everyone else in the field would soon be out of business. The sporting goods industry, then, would be indirectly subsidizing the National Sports Association. And why not? Who has profited more over the last few years from the boom in amateur sports? And who figures to profit even more if it continues?

What the U.S. would indirectly be creating is an organization pretty much along the lines of Manfred Ewald's DTSB in Berlin. Don't forget he didn't get that system functioning as he really wanted it to function until he was able to break it away from direct government control and make it as autonomous as any agency can ever be in an East European situation. A National Sports Association, in any country, cannot be very effective if it is faced with policies constantly changing on governmental whim.

If the DTSB can raise seven million dollars in one day by having its membership work one day overtime and have the money funneled into the National Sports Festival, imagine what could be done by ten times that membership in the United States at U.S. salary scales. Think of the 1978 New York marathon. Think of a day's pay from 767 lawyers, 547 doctors, 977 teachers, and 98 company presidents, and then multiply that by a complete national factor. Would you believe at least eight hundred million dollars? The active sportsmen of America, then, could pay for the 1984 Los Angeles Olympic Games with one day of overtime without dipping into a single penny of government funding. But it wouldn't happen that way at all. If sport was ever that totally organized in the United States, then the pressure on all levels of government for increased spending, particularly on facilities, educational programming, and coaching needs would be tremendous.

Heady stuff, isn't it? Even if it is about as substantive as a mountain of cotton candy. The organizational problems would be immense. Who, for instance, would head up such an organization? I can think of a lot of candidates from the ranks of the NCAA, the AAU, the U.S. Olympic Committee, and the other groups who have squabbled over U.S. sport jurisdiction throughout this century. Would all of those organizations be willing to come under the influence of such an umbrella? Could a man be found to run it with the integrity Pete Rozelle brought to the National Football League in the 1960s and 1970s? Or is all of this just so much wishful thinking?

I used to think it was, but now I am not so sure. An awful lot has quietly been going on without much public notice in the last two years. The West has been stung by the Olympic success of the East in Munich and Sapporo, Montreal and Innsbruck. I will admit that the depression of Montreal is starting to ease with the good news from the American girls on the swimming front. Eric and Beth Heiden have developed into the talk of winter sport's speed skating. Renaldo Nehemiah is suddenly, at a tender nineteen, the greatest hurdler the world has yet seen. Our figure skaters are winning World championships again. And yet, the United States today is still developing only one Olympic medalist for every dozen developed in the GDR on a per capita basis. Are they ahead? Yes. Do our kids have the necessary tools to compete in the Olympics? No. Can we get them those tools within the context of our system? We can if we want to.

In Canada the problem is hockey and how to regain the top position in the world from the Soviet Union. Since the best professionals in the National Hockey League were tried and found wanting in New York in February of 1979, a lot of thought is now going into the creation of a national team concept for the future that will allow young players to stay in school, complete their education, and play the European international style of game rather than the North American professional game.

Alan Eagleson, President of the NHL Players Association, and agent for Bobby Orr, perhaps the greatest talent ever to play the game, was working on the problem during the World championships in Moscow in April of 1979.

"Bobby Orr turned pro with Boston when he was eighteen," says Eagleson, "and we had a national team in those days, too. We looked into it at the time, and if there had been any way that I could have got him 30,000 dollars a year to stay 'amateur' I think we'd have done it.

Let him play for Canada and finish up his school and turn pro much later. Back in the Sixties there just wasn't any way to do that. If we want to start that program again today, the only way it will work is if we can make it financially feasible."

Government inquiries into hockey have been held in Canada in 1977 and 1978 and all have been surprised at the degree of parental concern with the problem of education. The idea of special sports schools for hockey players is now being investigated. Coaching certification programs are now being developed for each governing body in Canada concerned with a nationally developed sport. Soon the uncertified Canadian volunteer coach will be a thing of the past.

Does this mean that we in Canada are simply copying the Communists? That we are becoming obsessed with prospects of international success and are turning the amateur pursuit of sport into an unhealthfully obsessive vocation? Or are we simply finding our own practical solutions to problems every country faces in elite sport development? I think the answer to that depends largely on your own attitude toward obsessions.

In the States, you can take the case of Al Oerter, perhaps the greatest U.S. Olympic champion of them all, with gold medals in the discus from four successive sets of Games between Melbourne in 1956 and Mexico in 1968. Now, after some ten years in retirement, he's trying to make a comeback in hopes of doing it again in Moscow at the age of forty-three. Already, a year and a half before the Games, he has thrown farther than any of his previous gold medal performances. It's already an incredible success story even if his obsessive dedication doesn't result in a place on 1980's U.S. Olympic team. In New York, Bud Greenspan's Cappy Productions is making a documentary about it. It should be one of the best Bud's ever made.

He's also making one about the GDR Olympic story. In pursuit of that in November of 1978, he and I were sitting on the banks of the Elbe River with Frank Ruhle, a member of the Dresden Four, which was perhaps the greatest rowing unit in Olympic history, undefeated internationally from 1966 to retirement in 1972. Ruhle is a coach at the Einheit Dresden Club today, a job that allows him to train a little on the side now and again. Once a month he gets together with the other three to row the old training course just for old times' sake. No feeling of obsession, just an awful lot of satisfaction. I asked him if he missed the world-class competition. "No," he said with a thoughtful smile, "when we retired it was a good time for us to step aside and make way for the others. We could have gone on but if we had we'd have been discouraging the development of young oarsmen rather than encouraging it."

Frank Ruhle, despite his country's national preoccupation, has made his peace with international sport. Perhaps more so than Al Oerter.

Questions of attitude aside, what then can we in the West gain from a practical understanding of sport in the GDR? What can we apply?

Almost anything we want—if we let ourselves.

Afterword
by Gail Gilbert

On Monday, July 9, 1979, while in San Juan, Puerto
Rico, covering the Pan American Games for The Edmonton Sun, Doug Gilbert was struck by a car and died a few
hours later. The tragic loss was felt by his professional
colleagues in Canada, the United States, and abroad,
who hastened to offer their assistance to Mrs. Gilbert in
seeing this book to publication. The publisher and Mrs.
Gilbert are grateful for this assistance. To this acknowl-
edgment, Mrs. Gilbert adds this personal Afterword.

This is my husband's book—the product of his curiosity about
people, events, and places and his consuming interest in "the story
behind the stories." It is the result of years of research involving weeks
of travel and countless hours of conversation with people all over the
world. That he ever finished it is a miracle in itself. He was never able
to set aside his regular jobs in media, so work on this book had to be
crammed into weekends, late evenings and early mornings, and a
couple of occasions when our two children and I left for a few days to
visit family so he could have uninterrupted time to devote entirely to
it.

Doug didn't live to see the book in print. He was struck by a car
while covering the Pan American Games in San Juan, Puerto Rico,

and died on July 9, 1979. Only a few days earlier he had completed the corrections on the galleys.

Doug won't now have the experiences that authors could expect to have upon publication of their first book. And yet we have reason to be thankful, for this book was an instrument of something of everlasting significance in Doug's own life. Briefly, this is Doug's own "story behind the stories."

The year 1976 had been one of change in our lives, a time of drawing together in a united purpose. Doug's had been a bustling world of activity, excitement, new people and adventures, and mine a whirl of children and household responsibilities. The change began when God drew me to a personal commitment to Jesus Christ as Savior and Lord and revealed His love for me and His purpose for our lives. Now He was drawing Doug.

During the latter months of 1976, after permission to do the research and interviews in East Germany had been obtained and a publisher had been found through the efforts of our lawyer in New York, it became necessary, for tax purposes, for us to form a corporation. When preparing a list of possible names for our corporation to submit to the federal government with the charter application, Doug gave me an opportunity to suggest a "churchy" one. It will be no surprise to those who have walked with the Lord to learn that that was the name the Government chose!

In one of the chapters of this book, Doug relates a time spent in hospitals in Dresden and East Berlin because of severe abdominal pains that struck him in both cities. Neither was coincidental.

In that hospital in Dresden, away from distractions, Our Heavenly Father got Doug's full attention. For the first time in his life, Doug had no one to talk to, and nothing to read but East German publications and two Christian books that I had smuggled into his suitcase! In one of these—Harold Hill's *From Goo to You by Way of the Zoo* (now published under the title *How It All Began*)—Doug signed his name to a prayer of commitment inviting Jesus Christ to come into his life as Savior and Lord and to take charge of it. And, during Doug's hospitalization in East Berlin, doors were miraculously opened into areas of research that had eluded him up to that point.

This book will mean different things to different people. For me, it will always stand as a reminder of the faithfulness of our God, Who desires that all should have eternal life in Him. Jon and Jennifer and I choose to confess God's goodness in this time of personal loss and sadness.

That Doug had an impact on the lives of people he met is evidenced in the mail that is flowing in to us now, and by the expressions of loss that have circulated through the various media. His death would seem meaningless if viewed with eyes focused only on earthly accomplishments. But Doug had exchanged his rights in this earthly life for rights to life in the only Kingdom that will stand forever; and though one who was precious to us has been taken away, life's purpose for our family has not been altered by his death.

To those whose hearts are sorrowing I would like to repeat the message of our pastor, Don Rousu, of Bethlehem Lutheran Church in Edmonton, who said at a memorial service of praise and thanksgiving on July 12, 1979:

"Don't cry for Doug. He's with the King. And when we sign on in the Kingdom of God, we will join him and be with Jesus for ever and ever."

INDEX

W = Winter

S = Summer